REPRODUCTIONS OF REPRODUCTION

Routledge
New York and London

REPRODUCTIONS OF REPRODUCTION

Imaging Symbolic Change

Judith Roof

Published in 1996
by Routledge
29 West 35th Street
New York, NY 10001

Published in
Great Britain by
Routledge
11 New Fetter Lane
London EC4P 4EE

Copyright © 1996 by
Routledge
Printed in the
United States of America
on acid-free paper.
Book design:
Jeff Hoffman

Portions of chapter 3 have appeared
in a different form in *Hypatia* 7:2
(Spring 1992); and *Lacan and the
Politics of Aesthetics*,
ed. Richard Feldstein and Willie Apollon
(Albany: SUNY Press, 1995).

Library of Congress Cataloging-in-Publication-Data

Roof, Judith
  Reproductions of reproduction: imaging
    symbolic change / Judith Roof
  p. cm.
  Includes bibliographical references and index.
  ISBN 0-41591242-3. — ISBN 0-415-91243-1
  1. Social change—United States.
  2. Human reproduction—Social aspects—United States.
  3. Patriarchy—United States.
  4. Symbolism.
  5. Postmodernism—United States.
  I. Title.
HN59.2.R66 1996   95-43749
303.4'0973—dc20   CIP

ACKNOWLEDGMENTS

This book is for Kellie, Moonyoung, Michael, Paula Jayne,
Beth, Frank, Kathrine, Bill, and Catherine
in the hope that some of your generosity is returned.

PRODUCING THIS book was a lengthy endeavor, spanning years of conference papers and few essays that somehow inevitably worked towards a thesis I arrived at only more recently. For this reason I owe thanks to all who invited, heard, or commented upon the papers that eventually became this book. I particularly thank its more enthusiastic supporters, most recent readers, and those who helped with research and suggestions: Dale M. Bauer, Tom Byers, Rick L. Cook, Richard Feldstein, Eric John "The Prince" Martin, Patrick O'Donnell, Michele Shauf, Frank Smigiel, Paula Jayne White, Cary Wolfe, Lynda Zwinger, Eva Cherniavsky, Tom Foster, Robyn Wiegman, and Andrea Newlyn, especially the last four who put up with a very intense summer.

CONTENTS

PROLOGUE

Significant Trends

"PAY NO ATTENTION TO THAT MAN BEHIND THE CURTAIN"

The munchkin denizens of Oz, that fantasmatic terrain where the cyclone dumps Dorothy, have an immediate answer to her alienation. After ascertaining that she believes she is no witch, they advise her to "follow the yellow brick road" that will lead her to "the great and powerful Wizard of Oz." The Wizard of Oz, they croon, is a wizard because he does wonderful things. Seeking this powerful paternal doer, Dorothy, her dog Toto, and the three figuratively castrated companions she accumulates on the road brave the threats of the Wicked Witch of the West to get to Emerald City, the home of the wizard extraordinaire whom they plan to petition to rectify their separations or supply their lost parts (brain, heart, courage).[1]

The Wizard, however, is not as forthcoming as a beneficent Papa should be, and he denies the foursome their favors until they rid him of the pesky and (we find out later) much more powerful Wicked Witch of the West. This Witch challenges his rule by writing in the sky with a smoldering broom, casting spells (swaying consciousness), and provoking visions of "other scenes" in a crystal ball (enlisting the unconscious). A spunky gal, Dorothy sets out to purge this threat to the West and accidentally succeeds in doing so with a bucket of water; a "mechanics of fluids," water fittingly melts the witch into a steaming pool.[2] Triumphant, Dorothy returns to Oz to collect the reward she has now earned only to discover, through the agency of the always intrepid Toto, that the Wizard's pyrotechnical facade of billowing flames and booming voice is just a simulation of power wielded by a little, very human, "humbug" man behind a curtain.

His real stature revealed, the little man (who, it turns out, is an estranged carnival showman accidentally transported to Oz in a hot-air balloon) isn't completely bogus. Although he seems to have trouble operating the mechanism of his wizard simulation and the balloon, he understands enough about desire to demand payment in advance and enough about castration to know that symbolic objects will suffice to cure Dorothy's companions' feelings of incompleteness. Hence a degree for the brainless Scarecrow, a ticking heart-shaped watch for the Tin Woodman, and a medal of valor for the Cowardly Lion are enough to compensate. But the beset Dorothy, whose trip to Oz separated her from the avuncular bliss she had enjoyed before the evil Miss Gulch tried to confiscate her Toto, sees through the Wizard's guise of power and discerns that he is in the same boat as she.

When the Wizard resorts to the literal and decides to reinflate the carnival balloon to try to transport Dorothy, Toto, and himself back to Kansas, he accidentally takes off without Dorothy. But all is not lost. The good Witch of the North who advised Dorothy to seek the Wizard in the first place now informs her that she has always had the ability to go home if only she had sufficient desire. Telling her to click her heels together three times and incant, "There's no place like home," the Good Witch enables Dorothy to regain domestic bliss and heal oedipal trauma through the repetition of the word—not the Name-of-the-Father, but the literal signifier of domestic space.

Victor Fleming's 1939 adaptation of L. Frank Baum's turn-of-the-century children's tale cannily sets out not only crises in incipient consumerism, timely allegories of totalitarian threat, and endorsements of secular humanism, but also the spectacle of the Father's unveiling and his reduction to the literal and impotent.[3] No match for machines, the Wizard, who has masterfully manipulated a commodity system (or because he has mastered the commodity system), sacrifices his reign in a vain attempt to help Dorothy. The apparatus of his powerful persona collapsed, he replaces himself with the now-brainy Scarecrow, a weightless collection of detachable parts. In his absence, the figurative daughter's Symbolic, reduced to the vague myth of familial domain, becomes instantly accessible in a pedestrian version of the Internet.

A DEAL YOU CAN'T REFUSE

It is a legend that a Don cannot deny the request of a supplicant who comes to him on the day of his daughter's wedding. The opening scene of *The Godfather* (book and film) depicts the undertaker Bonasera's desperate request that Don Vito Corleone avenge the beating of his daughter.[4] Having gone first to the police and then through the American justice system, which gave the perpetrators only a suspended sentence, Bonasera belatedly seeks the Don's help, asking him for "justice." But Corleone coldly makes clear the terms of his largess: Bonasera must become his "friend," must become indebted to the Godfather for a justice clearly understood not as retributive murder, but as the disbursement of equal suffering. "Some day," Don Corleone says, "and that day may never come, I will call upon you to do me a service in return. Until that day, consider this justice a gift from my wife, your daughter's godmother" (33). The lesson to the undertaker is clear: eschew the false and impotent law of culture and believe wholeheartedly in the power of the Godfather; sustain yourself with a system composed of symbolic family ties instead of appealing to an impotent nest of opportunistic lawyers, corrupt judges, and usurious bankers in an order that has already failed.

SPERM TALES

3

As visual technologies improve and smaller and smaller vistas can be distinctly displayed, the narrative of human reproduction shifts from its macroscopic frame of romance and avian/apiarian fable to an increasingly microscopic, epic narrative of travel and penetration. As the frame of reference shrinks, the scale of seminal accomplishment expands and the sperm's figuration shifts from the metaphorical (little critter, for example) to the synecdochically paternal (the father's genetic material). Reproduction's courtship narrative—an egg and a sperm blissfully uniting—imagines a coming together of tiny elements that simply substitute for human players in an invisible imaginary field. The more "scientific" narrative enabled by electron photoscopy and videography images sperm as little wriggling, directed beings with heads and tails who take a really long and well-planned trip through a hostile terrain crowded with barriers they must heroically penetrate. Synecdoches of their penile delivery system, the sperm continue as little penetrators until their message is delivered and production begins.

Heroic mites, sperm have become the overly literalized vestiges of paternity and Beowulf. Initially gathered in the epididymis in response to nerve stimuli, the sperm become the payload in a complex system that "must function perfectly." Leaving the epididymis, the sperm are joined by fructose (supplies) from the seminal vesicles and a fluid medium (a vehicle) from the prostate gland and are propelled through the penis by involuntary muscular contractions (an engine). Once through the seemingly endless twelve inches of the male system, the sperm encounter the "dangerously inhospitable" environment of the female vagina where one fourth of the sperm force dies immediately. A large contingent of defective sperm malfunctions. Foreign cells in the woman's body, some healthy sperm are attacked by antibodies. Other deeply anxious sperm hit prematurely on incorrect cells. The remainder swims mightily against contrary currents, "programmed" as they are to "seek the egg."

If they are lucky enough to find the mucin strands provided by the cervix during ovulation, the sperms can swim in gangs into the uterus, an outer layer of sperm protecting an inner layer against the female body's various dangers. When the gang gets to the uterus, some stay in the cervix, perhaps to provide "backup." In the uterus, the sperm encounter a binary dilemma, the choice of two tubes: one with an egg, the other without, on/off, a primal, genital computer. Half of the group chooses the wrong tube; the other half contends with fallopian cilia, which create a gentle downward current against which the still-determined sperm must swim. Some sperm get stuck in the cells lining the fallopian tube; others lose their sense of direction. By the time they reach the egg, only fifty sperm out of two hundred million are left. These fifty must race to digest the two layers of nutritive cells that encase the egg. Only one will win through to the final penetration that echoes the original, displaced from its primal scene twelve to fourteen inches.

The sperms' series of travails resembles allegorical epic or romance. But while the allegory's protagonist labors in one cosmos that clearly refers to another more spiritual locus, sperm protagonists struggle synecdochically in a too literal, too fleshly scene.[5] While the allegorical protagonist proves the truth of a conceptual system, sperm reiterate the already literal. Impersonating the microscopic specifics of a BOATS (Based on a True Life Story) film, the story of reproduction assures us that what we see on the surface is really what happens down the line, inner equaling outer, the whole process reifying sexual difference and biology on the cellular level (and beyond, if we can image it). Scratch an allegorical protagonist and you find God; scratch a sperm and you find patriarchy's chemically encoded genetic message.

This rendering of the sperm's story comes from *The Miracle of Life*, presented on Nova in the 1980s.[6] Envisioning reproduction's constantly opening frames requires technology; one penetration simply compels another in a constant search for the moment when all comes together, when the sperm looses its genetic payload and somehow the coded strands of DNA intermingle and reorder their sequential code into a new message. A metonymic voyage, the sperm's microid tale transforms the metaphor of condensational oneness into a series of repetitive stages, each characterized by a penetration and loss and each linked to the next by physical contiguity. The sperm have become a cyborg community, organized into self-sacrifice, programmed to a goal, dispensable in large numbers, highly inefficient but successful carriers of information. Paternity is an all too literal endeavor.

MARIO BROTHERS

In the late 1980s Nintendo introduced Mario Brothers, a video system that enabled a more complex prolonged narrative game than Ping Pong, Tennis, or Space Invaders.[7] Metonymical epics, Mario Brothers (and its sequels) take a cartoon protagonist controlled by the game's player(s) through succeeding levels of difficulty, each crowded with increasingly complex hurdles and requiring better hand-eye coordination. Peopled by various threatening denizens, each level has a specific theme and environment; within each level are various windows that open as the protagonist penetrates into various apertures (magic doors, large standing pots) to gain valuable advantages. The exits and entrances from level to level are contiguous; each opens into the next in a series of unfolding panoramas.

The prototype for many video games, Mario Brothers' sequential narrative depicts conflict as epic; that is, where the protagonist is "superior in degree to other men (sic), but not to his environment."[8] Mario Brothers 2 situates the entire process within an overtly romanticized narrative of a Princess's rescue, located in a reified subconscious terrain. The protagonist Mario has a dream in which he is asked to defeat the enemy Wart, who has put the land of "Subcon" under a spell and "return Subcon to its natural state" (3). When awake, Mario and his friends go on a picnic only to discover the very same world featured in Mario's dream in a small cave. But this is a dream world of repetition and displacement cast in the almost meaningless discourse of good and evil personified by various versions of animated mobile masks.

The games are captivating; like programmed pieces we are pulled from level to level through the illusion of our prowess, but also (and more significantly) by the lure of extra lives, new vistas, and the sense that if we could try one more time we would penetrate further. And we are also lured by the fact that within each level's rolling sequence are shortcuts that "warp" players from level to level in a macro progress far more empowering than laborious engagement with a series of annoying obstacles. At the end of each level is a big enemy who spits and throws things—in some cases a male enemy "who thinks he is a girl and . . . spits eggs from his mouth" (27). Overcoming these enemies is rewarded with uplifting martial music and the chance to win extra lives.

The "natural state" of Subcon is a state renaturalized by a metonymical logic of sequence and progression. Not the subconscious (or the unconscious) but rather a cultural unconscious whose good/evil dichotomies become ever more like cartoons, ever more like a programmed venture into a seven-world, twenty-level cosmos with an already camily familiar mechanistic epistemology.

THE SON OF TIME

In the late 1960s, digital technology in the form of hand-held calculators and digital watches first became widely available in America. Calculators' binary proficiency rapidly replaced the slide rule's analogue virtuosity. The timepiece's representational shift from the analogue clock's ever-changing tableau to the instantaneous conclusions of digital's incremental leaps made graphically visible a cultural shift from the precedence of metaphor—or figuring by analogy—to an increased emphasis on metonymy, whose discontinuous, nonspatial, divisible, sparse economy of specific serial digits cuts up time's erstwhile luscious flow.

Just as its instantaneous displays are metonymical, digital representations are themselves the visual conclusions to an adjacent metonymical process. Sustained by a hidden logic of micro-circuit contiguity, the digital depends upon the binary operation of computer chips that make calculations through a series of on/off electronic switches. While the metaphoricity of analogue time emphasizes the relation of earth to sun, hand to hand, time to space, and process to product, digital's metonymy emphasizes product (a number) over its elided process, appearing to provide the authority of discrete numerical signifiers, but also leaving temporal gaps between process and product, between one answer (one minute) and the next. (What time is it when the number is changing?) Digital's metonymic gaps produce an anxiety whose symptoms and defenses are a persistence of image (single numbers remain long past their time) and the insertion of the image of analogue timepieces—the tiny clock or minute hourglass—in the more protracted temporal gap at the moment of computer processing. This vestigial metaphor spatially occupies the duration of calculation that would otherwise appear to be empty, fulfilling a nostalgia for metaphor's dubious plenitude.

QVC

Home-shopping channels, where electronic media meet consumer culture, reveal commodity culture's departure from any exchange among people to people's exchanges of objects.[9] Item after featured item, an endless array of commodity alternatives appears, each equivalent to the next, each posed as fulfilling some desire, but each equally capable of fulfilling that desire. Referring to no real need, these commodities comprise a system in which commodity trades with commodity in an endless chain.

"The substance of life, unified in this universal digest," this mediatized shopping spree, "can," Jean Baudrillard exclaims, "no longer have any *meaning*: that which produced the dream work, the poetic work, the work of meaning, that is the grand schemas of displacement and condensation, the great figures of metaphor and contradiction, which are founded on the lived articulation of distinct elements, is no longer possible" (35). Only perpetual displacement and deferral remain, "the eternal substitution of homogeneous elements"—QVC, shopping malls, catalogues, billboards, commercials—an endless, chained display of syntagmatic objects that finally stand only for objecthood and the consumable, and consumption itself as the only meaningful activity in an order that is losing its metaphoric underpinning.

ELEMENTARY, MY DEAR OEDIPUS

In 1900, Karl Landsteiner discovered human blood groups. A tool for the identification of criminals and fathers, blood groups enabled the elimination rather than positive identification of suspects.[10] The first paternity tests based on red-cell blood types "excluded only 15 to 19 percent of alleged fathers." Refined over the years, hematology and serology yielded ever-more specific markers; red-cell antigens "identified 75 percent of 'non-fathers,'" and by 1981, a new test based on Human Leukocyte Antigens yielded 99 percent accuracy.[11] The even greater identificatory potential of DNA testing, developed in the early 1980s and made prominent in the O. J. Simpson case, feeds the hope of positive identification of individuals rather than the elimination of suspects.[12]

Oedipus didn't recognize his own father; like the deductive Sherlock Holmes, he had to infer from circumstances, belatedly establishing his filiation from witness testimony and cultural law. As the medico-pharmaceutical establishment delves inward, paternity becomes less and less the guess of prophecy, Tiresias's testimony, or clever deduction and more a matter of discerning patterns in the nearly infinite combinations of chemical codes. Imagining DNA testing as a highly reliable identificatory procedure that replaces the masterful Holmes's deduction skills, science writers signal the revolution in method by the repetition of Holmes's name in the titles of their columns: "Leaving Holmes in the Dust" (*Newsweek* 1987); "Not So Elementary, My Dear Holmes" (*The Economist* 1989). Paternity has been a mystery to be solved; the titles' hint that science has finally exceeded Holmes's skills suggests that someone has finally solved the paternal mystery. The appeal of a test that renders human identity in a form like a "bar code" is finally the certainty of paternity itself; "'this type of test will take us closer to the time when there need no longer be disputes concerning paternity, because test results will be so accurate that true fathers will be more likely to settle out of court than fight a losing battle'" (*Science News* 1981, 317). Science thinks it has replaced the Name-of-the-Father.

Whether or not father can ever be identified with complete certainty, Landsteiner's turn-of-the-century discovery unveiled, at least in the imagination, the mystery of the man behind the curtain.

INTRODUCTION

THIS PROJECT concentrates on several manifestations of reproductive anxiety (the bodybuilder/superhero, law, the pregnant father, the vampire, the shift from analogue to digital) in western and primarily American culture. These examples of anxiety are symptoms of a more profound Symbolic change that begins to show as western culture shifts from an analogue to a digitally based order. Because reproduction embodies the terms of Symbolic Law (or Symbolic Law models itself after the elements of reproduction), representations of reproduction often reveal anxieties about Symbolic change as well as providing compensations for it. Focusing primarily on post–World War II phenomena, this study presents the idea of a change in the Symbolic itself as part of the broader sweep of cultural and epistemological transition that has been occurring for at least the past two-hundred years. Understanding these changes as also occurring in the Symbolic means possibly seeing how such change might be directed so as not to reiterate the gender inequities linked to the Symbolic relation between the paternal and Law.

This project began as several disjointed attempts to explain the recurrence of certain images and patterns in American popular culture—for example, the fact that vampire motifs show up in *Aliens*. Circling around not only reproduction (the alien's) but also the clash of reproductive systems (alien v. human), such combinations suggest some threat to the system or order reproduction represents. But as these patterns are located in a larger historical context, it soon became apparent that there was a larger story here, a trajectory that arced from Mary Shelley's *Frankenstein* (1818) to Kenneth Branagh's *Mary Shelley's Frankenstein* (1994), from *The Vampyre* (1819) to Francis Ford Coppola's *Bram Stoker's Dracula* (1994) and through such disparate phenomena as Dada, Pop art, superhero narratives, and television baseball.

Slim as the thread might seem, vampires, aliens, and feminist heroics, all represent anxieties about an unauthorized reproduction that challenges proper (i.e., paternal) reproductive order and human aegis. Frankenstein, bodybuilders, Pop art, and male pregnancy compensate for reproductive anxieties by multiplying and extending creative paternal power. Taken together, these disparate instances express a pattern of threat and restitution around paternity and patriarchy that has occurred in various forms since at least the inception of a mechanized industrial culture. The pattern of challenge/compensation reflects insecurities about Symbolic order that appear in the guise of issues about paternity, human authority and creativity, and/or technological threat.

By the Symbolic, I mean the sets of rules and language that comprise the sociocultural order in its largest sense. This means not only language and laws, but the principles of substitution and displacement through which language and Law work. Inextricably interwound with the Imaginary (the dimension of conscious and unconscious images) and the Real (objects and experiences), the Symbolic order's substitutive process contributes to the psychic development of individuals and grounds the organization of societies. While the Imaginary "infuses the unconscious into consciousness to create discontinuities, inconsistencies, and irruptions," the Symbolic "connects, labels, and orients Imaginary incidents, so giving import, perpetuity, and reality to otherwise solipsistic perception."[1] The Imaginary enables identification, desire, representation, while the Symbolic stabilizes, "gives form to and 'translate[s]' the Imaginary" (Ragland-Sullivan 156).

It is possible for the Symbolic to change and, in so doing, manifest its transformation through symptoms that appear in the representations that constitute a cultural Imaginary. Analogous to and an extension of the intra–psychic imaginary order, this cultural Imaginary, comprised of images, relationships, and identifications, works on the level of the social and cultural systems of image, narrative, and fantasy. And the Symbolic is changing, showing signs of slow transformation. Jacques Lacan suggests that "the oedipus complex cannot run indefinitely in forms of society that are more and more losing the sense of tragedy."[2] I would suggest that tragedy can no longer exist in forms of society that are increasingly employing a digital rather than an analogue (or metaphorical) form of organizing, storing, or even conceiving of information and relations. Radical effects of Symbolic transformation appear in everything from the recent recognition of multicultural diversity to the breakdown of the nuclear family to commodity culture's simulations.

Although the Symbolic works through principles of both substitution and displacement, substitution pulls together the linguistic and larger social rules of culture. "The paradox and tragedy of being human," comments Ellie Ragland-Sullivan, "stems from the fact that, by accepting language as a substitute for an impossible union [between mother and child], language itself as a symbol builds absence—Castration—into the structure of the subject and ensures that the human condition will be marked by eternal wanting" (172). Substituting a symbol for something else means that the symbol, while importing meaning, also refers to an absence. This mode of substitution also characterizes systems of rules and law that organize and regulate human interactions by prohibiting some relations (incest) and fabricating others (property, contract, paternity). Rules of order on all levels share the same substitutive structure as language, a substitution linked primarily to metaphor as the figuration of substitution as well as to metonymy as the mechanism of displacement. Although the Symbolic does not consist solely of metaphor and metonymy, the two processes characterize the mechanisms by which Symbolization occurs and the Symbolic operates.

My emphasis on the paternal comes from the way the paternal works as the emblematic metaphor of the Symbolic not only in lacanian psychoanalytic theory, but in the more overt power structures of modern western culture. This emphasis is both on paternity's literal gendered form and on how patriarchal tradition imbues western conceptions of reproduction, continuity, law, and order. Organized around a series of prohibitions and exchanges, patriarchal order deploys the father's name, concepts of generation, real property, legacy, and tradition to maintain the illusion of continuity, rightly directed productivity, and meaning in its reproductive organizations. Linked to bourgeois familial ideologies and particular conceptions of regulation rather than to the necessities of nature or technological capability, literal patriarchal formations such as nuclear families and male-centered hierarchies jealously protect the realm of metaphorical figuration by which order is understood.

THE IMPETUS TO CHANGE

What stimulates the emergence of symptoms linked to instabilities in the Symbolic? Do changes in the Symbolic lead to changes on the level of representations? Or is it changes in the Real—the realm of objects and experiences—that force a resymbolization? Apart from natural phenomena (earthquakes, meteors hitting earth), what object or experience isn't already, in some way, produced through the Symbolic and the Imaginary? If I want to link Symbolic change to technological change, for example, what stimulates technological change in the first place? How is it that we can imagine technological advances before we can accomplish them? Rather than representing some sudden integration of an alien mode of organizing or the discovery of a completely new world, the transformation I'm suggesting is a possibility already contained within the system. Any shift is a shift in emphasis.

The transformation of the Symbolic has multiple causes and effects whose circular interrelation confuses any linear sense of evolution or sustained and organized transformation. The invention and increasing use of mechanical forms of production both incite the beginnings of a change in the way humans perceive their relation to the world and are continually produced by an imagination already capable of envisioning the mainly metonymical workings of machinery. Scientific advancement increases the ability to particularize, to forge increasingly complex and minute cause-effect relations that gradually transform metaphorical scientific accounts of phenomena into the imagined potential for a completed chain of causal links. For example, Freud's metaphorical accounts of psychic operation characterize processes he imagines as finally biochemical, if only the biochemistry could be adequately particularized.[3] The father, who was for so long proved by the name, becomes a spermatic activity discernible through enhanced microscopic tracking and organized genetic markers. The desire for such complete and microscopic—such gapless—explanation is, in turn, stimulated by an already burgeoning mechanistic culture, an imagination already inflected by metonymy's alternate power—the power to fill in the links that metaphor elides or substitutes for. But even the imaginary plenitude of metonymic facts leaves gaps, tiny fissures from cause to effect that excite the reassertion of metaphor.

The project of this book is not to detail the eighteenth- and nineteenth-century causes for this Symbolic shift, but rather to trace some of the twentieth-century cultural resistances to and compensations for it as those appear in popular cultural representation. The configurations I have selected all manifest some anxiety about reproduction that repeats in their reappearances in the nineteenth and twentieth centuries and is, in all cases, linked in some way to mechanical reproduction. Linking them to trends in technology and historical repetitions provides a larger scope of examination that ultimately suggests that our Symbolic is not a newly contrived result of recent technological revolutions, but has been in the process of changing at least since the introduction of a machine-based industrial culture. Seeing these representations as evidence of Symbolic change adds another rationale to their already complex functioning.

For example, the vampire's association with death seems a sufficient menace to human existence to explain its recurrence. Although vampires' practices might represent everything from fantasies of oral sex, lesbianism, male homosexuality, or even rape to delusions of allomorphic potency, vampires also represent an anxiety about the continuity of order and proper kinship. Infiltrating patriarchy, seizing the virgins human males have (traditionally) reserved for themselves, vampires spawn vampires, twisting the rules of exogamy and limit into the beguiling prospect of interminable sanguinary feasting. If we connect this vampiric anxiety about human continuity and order to the behavior of Ridley Scott's aliens, their point of common threat, apart from the iconic similarity of their skeletal figures and hypertrophied teeth, is their usurpation of human order through unauthorized and extra-patriarchal reproductions. The figures that overcome the vampires' threats to patriarchal reproduction—strong fathers (Van Helsing) or heroic mothers (Ripley)—reassuringly reassert and supplement tradition or die in the attempt. Like bodybuilding and superheroics, the emphatic reassertion of the masculine, the familial, or the human attempts to counter instabilities in patriarchal tradition and order.

Appearing in the early nineteenth century, again in the 1890s, and re-emerging as a major figure in the flurry of vampire films of the 1950s and 1970s, the vampire's mainstream textual representations coincide with industrialization, the invention of cinema, and the invention of the digital computer.[4] But if this play of recurrent cultural images has any relation to more concrete cultural change, what besides mechanical reproduction might threaten patriarchal order as that functions as a symptom of Symbolic transformation? Let me make it clear at this point that there are probably numerous causes for the kind of drama I have begun to sketch. Much of the rapid complex social and technological change of the last two hundred years, for example, produces anxiety in western cultures as does the invention of the nuclear bomb, the cold war, a loss of American national prestige, and the rise of a less-centralized world marketplace. This book will follow only one—the drama of threat and compensation to literal and metaphorical reproductive orders salvaged by various refigurations of a much enhanced, specifically (re)productive father or his figurations. Although reproduction in its various biological and technological meanings is only one of a number of possible loci where the trajectory of cultural anxiety might register (others might be nationalism, racism, sexism, isolationism), the father's alignment of reproduction with conceptions of continuity represents a particularly suspicious, Symbolic instance of overcompensation for an order that is giving way.

Other texts and events seem to ratify this hypothesis, providing examples of the anxious alliance of the mechanical and the reproductive (the invention of photography and cinema, computers), paternal unveiling (the strategically timed *The Wizard of Oz*, for example), or symbolic compensation (the mechanisms of Pop art or television's fifty-year preoccupation with law and order). Taking texts and movements together writes one strand of a process of cultural change where cultural texts suggest a reading of the effects of technology's history and a history of technology suggests a particular relation among cultural texts. If texts anxious about reproduction dramatize tensions about changes in the Symbolic, then the centrality of the paternal is no accident, but is itself a symptom of the kind of Symbolic under seige.

Since I read these sites as running texts within a broadly historical context, they have enough recurring elements and a sufficiently stable structure to enable a psychoanalytically informed reading of their symptoms and some of the cultural work they do. It may well be that psychoanalysis is what leads to explications of these instances as versions of paternal malaise, but I also interpret the paternal as a Symbolic rather than literal function except where culture seems to have already supplanted the Symbolic father with the literal. In a way, psychoanalysis' own predilection for the father is evidence of psychoanalysis' incipient examination of the foundations of order at the point in time where that order has begun to fall apart. In this context, psychoanalysis itself becomes a way simultaneously to acknowledge the fragility of the father and to reassert a fail-safe Symbolic, which, in manipulating the terms of order on the level of analysis, becomes itself coterminous with the Symbolic it defines.

But even if this project is some psychoanalytic solipsism, psychoanalysis is a symptom of the same instability/compensation structure I identify in more popular terrain. In the same way that psychoanalysis is preeminently a European-American phenomenon, so the pattern of Symbolic shift and compensation I discuss is western and modern. The context of the symptoms I have selected is "western culture," which for the purposes of this book means primarily American culture with western-European influences. Although some phenomena—Frankenstein, vampires, and the photographic prehistory—I discuss are predominantly European, I am particularly interested in how these appear and function in American culture from the 1950s on.

Because the premises of this argument derive from specialized psychoanalytic and linguistic concepts, it is necessary to define the terms of this project—the Law-of-the-Name-of-the-Father, metaphor, metonymy, the digital. These concepts, though taken from psychoanalysis and technology, characterize a certain relation between representation and social law. The context of their definition is always already the context of their change; we catch them in flux, exposing their mechanisms as products of an intellectual trajectory that is itself part of a more sweeping symbolic change. So Freud and Roman Jakobson, who in their various ways define metaphor and metonymy as the basic poles of human symbolization, can identify them because the system is already in flux; so, too, can Lacan identify the paternal function as central because it is in the process of failing. I define these terms, then, as symbolic decay exposes the terms of its own sustenance, as they no longer quite work and yet work quite well to refigure themselves.

THE LAW OF THE NAME

Like Michel Foucault, we can certainly attribute grand shifts in culture and society to changes in deployments of power and sweeping transformations in societal organization; however, the seemingly coincidental literalization of the father may not be so coincidental if the paternal metaphor that emblemizes the Symbolic has, in fact, already become literal on some level.[5] If Lacan's characterization of the Law as paternal is correct, at least insofar as the paternal grounds a traditional Rule of order, property, and propriety, then a change in the status of the father's symbolization would affect the entire system and vice versa. This would happen regardless of the way the system works—even if that system actually worked the other way around, even if the father empowers the Symbolic rather than the Symbolic empowering the father.

This book's argument depends upon reading Lacan's notion of the Law-of-the-Name-of-the-Father with suspicion. Itself a metaphor, the Law-of-the-Name-of-the-Father centers symbolization as a delusively patriarchal and highly metaphorical formation; the Symbolic's "differential logic" makes sexual difference its terrain and the dramatic environment of human reproduction and the family its setting. As the figure of the Law, the father's prohibitive function is linked to a lack of provable relation in concrete terms; the "something" of the father's name stands in to cover both the lack associated with the literal father's failure or absence (with the idea that the real father doesn't necessarily wield the father's power) and the lack of provable connection between father and child. The Name also prohibits the child's over-realized relation with the mother. Within this familial model, the Law-of-the-Name-of-the-Father becomes the metaphor of the cultural tendency towards metaphor as a principle of order and limit challenged by mechanical reproduction, digital technologies, and paternal certainty.

But the terms provided by Lacan's paternal metaphor are themselves the symptoms of a compensation in the field of reproduction, as reproduction provides the model for social order (the family, kinship, legacy, property) and as the paternal metaphor represents the figure whose absence founds the metaphor that characterizes order itself. Reproduction in its various mechanical, artistic, and biological guises becomes the terrain for the Symbolic's renegotiation, again through the beset figure of the paternal metaphor. Its various ancillary features—gender, the name, prohibition, lack—become the players in a field of shifting systems as the mechanical is superceded by the digital, as visual metonymies become the invisible operations that install fundamental changes in the relation between reproduction, time, and a decreasingly visible mechanics.

15

I take the association between the paternal and metaphor not as the truth of Law, but as the identification of a governing representational fiction in western culture. In so far as the psyche is interwound with cultural/familial signifiers, the father's identification with the law comes from the father's conflation with the prohibitive figure interrupting preoedipal bliss. "The father is a function and refers to a law, the place outside the imaginary dyad and against which it breaks. To make of him a referent is to fall into an ideological trap: the 'prejudice which falsifies the conception of the oedipus complex from the start, by making it define as natural, rather than normative, the predominance of the paternal figure.'"[6]

This paternal Law is not the literal father, but rather the father's function as performed by the father's name. According to Lacan,

> To speak of the Name of the Father is by no means the same thing as invoking paternal deficiency (which is often done). We know today that an Oedipus complex can be constituted perfectly well even if the father is not there, while originally it was the excessive presence of the father which was held responsible for all dramas. But it is not in an environmental perspective that the answer to these questions can be found. So as to make the link between the Name of the Father, in so far as he can at times be missing, and the father whose effective presence is not always necessary for him not to be missing, I will introduce the expression *paternal metaphor*.[7]

The function of the father becomes the function of the Name-of-the-Father, but what we are dealing with here, is, most simply, two paradoxes. The first is that the father's function can be filled without a literal father while the presence of a literal father does not guarantee that the paternal function is filled. The Name, then, stands for the paternal function fulfilled both in the father's presence and absence.

The second paradox is linked to the Symbolic orders of kinship and legacy. Historically, we have never been able to tell with complete certainty who the father of a child is. That niggling doubt generates a symbolic apparatus that seals that gap in knowledge by substituting a name for what is not known. This substitution—this name in the place of no knowledge—is the progenitive metaphor of Law. The Name-of-the-Father, coming from outside the mother–child duo, not only pretends to seal the relation between father and child, it also works as a term of symbolic separation, becoming the Law that says that the child and mother must separate, that the mother's desire is forever fixed elsewhere. The father's name also locates the child within the larger social symbolic, the system of names and generations by which we discern familial relations, determine the devolution of property, and define the right of identity.

There are three crucial features to this Name-of-the-Father: (1) it operates as a *Name*; (2) the Name functions as metaphor; (3) the Name metaphor moors the Symbolic system. As Jacqueline Rose explains,

> Lacan uses the term 'paternal metaphor', metaphor having a very specific meaning here. First, as a reference to the act of substitution (substitution is the very law of metaphoric operation), whereby the prohibition of the father takes up the place originally figured by the absence of the mother. Secondly, as a reference to the status of paternity itself which can only ever logically be inferred. And thirdly, as part of an insistence that the father stands for a place and a function which is not reducible to the presence or absence of the real father as such.[8]

As François Regnault comments, "it is of the nature of a name to be substituted: it is substitution itself."[9] And Lacan says, "The Father has so very many [Names] that there is no one which suits him, except the name of the Name of the Name" (Regnault 73). "The Name-of-the-Father is another name for the symbolic as such . . ." (Regnault 73).

The paternal metaphor—the Name-of-the-Father standing in relation to the Law—represents the principle by which the individual relates to the social order: the name of the father that determines the child's lineage and place in society. "The paternal metaphor," Catherine Clément explains, "establishes the correlation between the family name—necessarily the father's name—and the subject coming into the world."[10] Thus, the paternal metaphor is also metaphorically connected to the social ordering principles of patriarchy, effecting not just a law of division, but also a law of connection to the larger sweep of the social rules of kinship exchange. "The primordial Law," according to Lacan, "is therefore that which in regulating marriage ties superimposes the kingdom of culture on that of a nature abandoned to the law of mating. . . . This Law, then, is revealed clearly enough as identical with an order of language. For without kinship nominations, no power is capable of instituting the order of preferences and taboos that bind and weave the yarn of lineage through succeeding generations" (*Ecrits* 66).

Locating this function in the metaphor of the Father's Name would seem merely to describe or reify a patriarchal ideology, but that is precisely the point. Just as the paternal metaphor sutures and cements the lie of the Father, it sustains the falsehood of patriarchy itself. Patriarchy is preserved by the Name—not just the Father's name, but the name itself as the epitome of substitution. Naming is a power, offering the illusion of designation and control bolstered in the end by the fact that until recently, "the attribution of procreation to the father can only be the effect of a pure signifier—the effect of recognition, not of a real father, but of what religion has taught us to refer to as the Name-of-the-Father" (*Ecrits* 199).

This metaphorical Name, then, defines psychic and cultural signification as always acts of substitution. In "The Position of the Unconscious," Lacan locates this paternal metaphor on the side of the Other—on the side of Desire and Law:

> On the side of the Other, the locus in which speech is verified as it encounters the exchange of signifiers, the ideals they prop up, the elementary structures of kinship, the paternal metaphor considered *qua* principle of separation, and the ever reopened division in the subject owing to his primal alienation—on this side alone and by the pathways I have just enumerated, order and norms must be instituted which tell the subject what a man or woman must do.[11]

This Symbolic order, finally, "is synonymous with difference and the escape from Loss and identified with order (over chaos and confusion) and law (in the father's name)" (Ragland-Sullivan 293).

In this sense, literal fathers are only metonymically related to the divisive function represented by the figurative connection between Law and a Symbolic absent Father. In a discussion of Freud's *Totem and Taboo*, Lacan links the absent Father to the murdered father of Freud's tribal myth: "If this murder is the fruitful moment of debt through which the subject binds himself for life to the Law, the symbolic Father is, in so far as he signifies this Law, the dead Father" (*Ecrits* 199). The Symbolic dead Father holds sway not through presence, but rather through the debt of guilt and sin provoked by the reason for his absence. The debt of guilt metonymically attaches to the Name-of-the-Father, the signifier that represents not the father, but the power of the Law transgressed. The Name-of-the-Father according to Lacan, "sustains the structure of desire with the structure of the law—but the inheritance of the father is that which Kierkegaard designates for us, namely, his sin."[12] Thus, a broken law—the murder of the father—generates the Law sustained by the debt incurred in this originary transgression. Law always operates at a deficit, yet was already there to be transgressed. The Law is also linked to death, the Law that cannot be transgressed.

Even if Lacan's focus on the paternal is itself a symptom of an overgrown patriarchy, for that reason alone it is logical that the symbolic operation of the paternal signifier encapsulates—works as a premier metaphor of—signifying systems and their transformation. The father's literalization through proofs of increasingly microscopic reality may not so much signal the final reality of the father as the demise of a cultural imaginary that has confused the literal father with metaphor (law and order meets the nuclear family). While the paternal metaphor may sustain Law, the cultural drive to discern the father and to see the father as the answer to problems of cultural disorder already signals a shift in the status of Law, a transformation that tracks the gradual transition from metaphor as the primary rule of Law to metonymy as its over-particularized substitute.

Law, then, is not law as we know it, but rather the principle by which law operates. The Name-of-the-Father as metaphor that moors the Symbolic constitutes Law as a substitutive process. "It is in the Name-of-the Father that we must recognize the support of the symbolic function which, from the dawn of history, has identified his person clearly with the figure of the law," says Lacan (*Ecrits* 67). The Name-of-the-Father's particular substitution of something for nothing defines the character of this law. Law is that which produces a relation where none exists. Laws as specific and literal manifestations of Law delineate systems of duties, obligations, and prohibitions; these outline and assume a relation that is not necessarily there, creating, for example, an entity called the "state," delineating its relation to its citizens, or devising concepts like contract or property that create and distribute duties and privileges, or even underwriting the functions of a language system where the relations between signifier and signified are metaphorical as well as metonymical. To understand Law only as prohibition is to take one piece—the necessary separation of mother and child—of its complex generational metaphor and make it stand for the whole. Law as prohibition is a synecdoche of the larger, more metaphorical Law.

It is important to understand this Law as the quintessence of metaphor where something comes to stand in for nothing and where nothing but a signifier—a name—comes to stand in between the something of mother and child and to stand for the mother's absence. This metaphorical something is more than just a creditor figure organizing familial relations; it is a figuration of cultural order organized through paradigms and systemic substitutions. Governments and churches and business hierarchies are likened to families; professional relations are governed by privilege and an incest taboo. Domestic ideology swells the airwaves; international relations look like sibling rivalries.

RIVAL FIGURES

Both metaphor and metonymy are figures of classical rhetoric, ways of fixing the relations between terms. Metaphor, for Aristotle, "consists in giving the thing a name that belongs to something else, the transference being either from genus to species, or from species to genus, or from species to species, or on grounds of analogy."[13] The application of a "name" that "belongs to something else," metaphor is the appropriation of a signifier from one order to another. The Wizard of Oz is metaphor since various guises belonging to the genus of power—a large head, a booming voice, a ball of fire—transfer to the diminutive person of the Wizard, who, in reality, has very little power. The Wizard's use of metaphorical self-representation endows the Wizard with power he doesn't have.

Metaphor "makes the link between the Name of the Father, in so far as he can at times be missing, and the father whose effective presence is not always necessary for him not to be missing."[14] The father's name, a patronymic from the order of kinship relations, is taken from its function in the environment where the father is missing to the realm where the quality of the father's presence is such that he doesn't need to be missing for the name to be necessary. Or, more simply, the father's name stands for "a place and function which is not reducible to the presence or absence of the real father" (Rose 62).

The father's name also creates a metaphor when the name stands not only for the relation of the father to his own kinship, but for the child's relation to his putative father. The name refers "to the status of paternity itself which can ever only be logically inferred" (Rose 62). The paternal metaphor in this guise is more than an observation of similarity; as philosophers have commented, metaphor *produces* thought as much as it reflects or expresses it.[15] The father's name produces a relation between the child and culture displaced from the name's original locus in the father to the child.

This appropriation, however, is not unmotivated. As Jacques Derrida points out, Aristotle discusses metaphor in the *Poetics* which begins as a "study of *mimesis*."[16] The property of likeness or analogy, an explicit part of Aristotle's definition, also provides metaphor's impetus. Thinking similarity begets substitution. The father's name as a metaphor both assumes a similarity in the father's and child's position in the social milieu, and also creates that similarity through the operation of the name.

But if thinking similarity produces a metaphor through the substitution of a name, similarity also depends upon difference—the difference in order (genus, species) to which the names belong. Metaphor, according to Paul Ricoeur, "proceeds from the encounter between the thing to be named and that foreign entity from which the name is borrowed."[17] The two things coexist, their difference melded by the commonality of a shared name; metaphor continues the tension between the two to produce meaning. Thinking relation begets a relation; metaphor brings the terms together and in Lacan's paternal scheme, substitutes for something that is missing.

The concept of metaphor as a basic operation is linked to linguistic rather than philosophical conceptions of metaphor. While philosophy rightly worries about the productive propensities of metaphorical thinking, structural linguistics is concerned with metaphor's status and operation as a basic linguistic operation. As Jonathan Culler summarizes, "the *via philosophica* ... locates metaphor in the gap between sense and reference; the *via rhetorica* ... situates metaphor in the space between one meaning and another."[18] The paternal

20

metaphor is somewhere in between the "gap" and the "space," referring more to what Culler identifies as philosophy's rendering of metaphor as "a necessary and pervasive feature of all language" than to rhetoric's worry about "'proper' verbal expression" (219).

The concept of language as intrinsically metaphorical depends upon the idea that language substitutes for something somewhere else. In other words, as a system of signifiers, language stands in for phenomena—objects, actions, relations, sense impressions—that are themselves nonlinguistic. This idea of language as intrinsically substitutive is connected to Lacan's notion of language as filling in some lack in being, as substituting signifiers for what is missing in subjective structuration. This substitution links language as a cultural system to language as a system of functions that resonate with unconscious processes. Following from Saussure, this conception of metaphor depends upon understanding metaphor as more a structural than a semantic process. Discerning, through his study of aphasia, two "gravitational poles" in language—metaphor and metonymy—Jakobson sees metaphor linked to "the faculty for selection and substitution," or similarity and metonymy as "combination and contexture" or contiguity.[19] "The difference between metaphor and metonymy," Russell Grigg explains, "is thus a difference between *semantic* similarity and *semantic* contiguity."[20] "So," he continues, "since both metaphor and metonymy rely upon positional similarity, they would both appear to be rhetorical devices that preserve syntactic structure while modulating the paradigmatic axis of selection and substitution" (60).

Although both metaphor and metonymy coexist in linguistic operations, the predominance of one or the other helps define not only an individual's stylistic "predilections and preferences," but also characterizes the defining qualities of various literary styles. "The primacy of the metaphoric process in the literary schools of romanticism and symbolism," Jakobson notes, "has been repeatedly acknowledged, but it is still insufficiently realized that it is the predominance of metonymy which underlies and actually predetermines the so-called 'realistic' trend, which belongs to an intermediary stage between the decline of romanticism and the rise of symbolism and is opposed to both" (77–78). And, I might add, belongs to the rise of 1980s and 1990s hyperrealism as well as metonymy's habit of elaborating facts and details.

Jakobson links these two "gravitational poles" to Freud's dream structures, appending contiguity to Freud's "metonymic 'displacement' and synecdochic 'condensation'" and similarity to "Freud's 'identification and symbolism'" (81). While we may shift this correlation slightly (as Lacan does), the point is that, whatever one calls these poles, they are intricated and interdependent, representing directional tendencies in organizational emphasis. Briefly tracing conceptualizations of this binary, for example, Roland Barthes denominates "syntagm" and "association," planes roughly aligned with metonymy and metaphor. "Syntagm is a combination of signs, which has space as a support. In the articulated language, this space is linear and irreversible."[21] "Association" is where "the units which have something in common are associated in memory and thus form groups within which various relationships can be found" (58). A far cry from the classical definitions of metonymy and metaphor, Barthes's conceptualizations distill their functional and structural characteristics. Tsvetan Todorov, another structuralist, provides a slightly different view of metaphor and metonymy's organizational trends. In his exploration of the mechanisms of linguistic symbolism as the combinative interplay of word and proposition, Todorov sees metaphor as a lexical equivalence that produces a propositional transduction resulting mainly in example. In this scheme, metonymy represents lexical coexistence, producing implication and allusion.[22]

The point is that (1) metaphor and metonymy are interrelated and to a large degree interdependent; (2) they refer to modes of relating and organizing both on linguistic and psychic levels; (3) metaphor involves similarity and substitution; (4) metonymy is aligned with contiguity and sequence; (5) metaphor is paradigmatic; metonymy syntagmatic; (6) metaphor permits (requires) absence and loss; metonymy allows coexistence; (7) metaphor enables transduction and the ordering of systems; metonymy orders a sequence; (8) both tend to preserve structure despite their different modalities.

Lacan picks up the metaphor/metonymy binary as a model for the processes of subjective structuration, keeping their tense relation of inseparability and polarity, but following Jakobson's lead, continuing and expanding their link to mental operations. "In the unconscious," Lacan pronounces, "is the whole structure of language," though, as Lacan makes clear, linguistic structuration is not the same as the various "psychical and somatic functions that serve it in the speaking subject," since "language and its structure exist prior to the moment at which each subject . . . makes his entry into it"(Ecrits 148). Language in a sense comprises the Symbolic, since linguistic structures order "the elementary structures of culture" (following Claude Lévi-Strauss) that follow the logic of the signifier (Ecrits 148).

The field of the signifier, according to Lacan, is comprised of two "sides," metaphor, whose "formula" is "one word for another," and metonymy, which is based in "the word to word connexion" (Ecrits 156–57). "Metaphor," he says, "occurs at the precise point at which sense emerges from non-sense" (Ecrits 158). And "so, it is between the signifier in the form of the proper name of a man and the signifier that metaphorically abolishes him that the poetic spark is produced, and it is in this case all the more effective in realizing the signification of paternity in that it reproduces the mythical event in terms of which Freud reconstructed the progress, in the unconscious of all men, of the paternal mystery" (Ecrits 158). The Name-of-the-Father represents and makes visible the mysterious debt to the father upon which cultural relations are premised.

Lacan's reading of metaphor/metonymy picks up resonances from Freud's use of condensation and displacement, but shifts Jakobson's reading slightly, by aligning metaphor with condensation and metonymy with displacement. "'Condensation', is the structure of the superimposition of the signifiers, which metaphor takes as its field," while "'displacement', … is closer to the idea of that veering off of signification that we see in metonymy, and which from its first appearance in Freud is represented as the most appropriate means used by the unconscious to foil censorship" (*Ecrits* 160). While metaphor is "the very mechanism by which the symptom … is determined," metonymy is "eternally stretching forth towards the *desire for something else*" (*Ecrits* 166–67). "The symptom *is* a metaphor …, desire *is* a metonymy," metaphor linked "to the question of being" and metonymy "to its lack" (*Ecrits* 175).

Transforming rhetoric into a lexically based structure connected to being and lack, Lacan outlines a dynamic significatory structure appended both to the Symbolic of culture and the structures of the unconscious. These structures embody the play of meaning and order; "differences are *not* found within sign systems as metaphoric/metonymic ruptures, they arise from the analogous energetic functioning of metaphor (in making meaning) and metonymy (in repressing meaning)" (Ragland-Sullivan 88). Being and lack, meaning and its repression, metaphor and metonymy emerge as much more than either rhetorical or philosophical forms, but as the defining components of ontological order and signification itself. Moving from the word to order, Lacan connects being to the word and Symbolic order to words' ordering. Thus, what we have are not mere rhetorical ploys, but intricated proclivities related not by opposition, but by their cooperation in the production of meaning and desire both for the subject and in culture.

Lacan takes language to the level of a Symbolic that works on the level of the cultural; for him, language infiltrates the cultural imaginary, ordering signifiers that bear the impression of meaning, fullness, order, and continuity *in relation to* the lack and desire linked to the metonym's syntagm, which, in relation to metaphor's metaorder, seems nothing more than a chained sequence of particulars. Just as Jakobson can hypothesize that artistic movements are characterized by the prevalence in them of one trope or the other, so we might enlarge the recognition of the prevalence of metaphor or metonymy in cultural forms themselves. On this level, literalizing the Law-of-the-Name-of-the-Father means that the concatenation of metaphors the father's name represents ceases to function so powerfully as the order of meaning, when the name and the figure whose absence (or puissance) the name represents are identified as the same. This is not so much a matter of the identification of specific fathers, but of a change in the status of the paternal from the unidentifi-

23

able to the certifiable—the shift from symptom to a desire linked to the knowledge and cause and effect that reproduce the paternal on the level of science. With the collapse of the paternal metaphor, metonymy, whose "subjacent chain," according to Umberto Eco, "constitute[s] the framework of the code and upon which is based the constitution of any semantic field," takes over, filling in with the license endowed by the paternal metaphor's transformation to something more like metonymy.[23]

If metonymy substitutes for metaphor, isn't metonymy a metaphor of metaphor, and doesn't the Symbolic remain a substitutive order? It is, perhaps in the sense that substituting a primarily metonymical order for a metaphorical one seems to keep the Symbolic intact in terms of its own rules. But the substitution of metonymy is the last act of a metaphorical Symbolic, since metonymy's ordering principle is ultimately different, constantly displacing and deferring instead of substituting, inclining towards desire and deference rather than being.

This doesn't mean the paternal metaphor is dead, but that it is changing its character. This transition, however, is fitful, partial; neither metaphor nor metonymy, oscillating between orders, the paternal's crisis stimulates and is stimulated by cultural rifts that metonymy increasingly fills. The genotype of the father will never be the same as the Name-of-the-Father, but it might constitute a Symbolic that would work as well.

METONYMY TIME

An hourglass represents time as the passage of tiny grains from one compartment to a contiguous one. Sand substitutes matter for time; the two chambers enact the relative fullness of future and past. The present is a conduit. The hourglass is a metaphor of the experience of time, which cannot be conceived of except in metaphor.

A sundial registers the movement of the sun through a shadow cast by a fixed point aligned with the North. Imitating cosmic relations, it gauges time by reproducing on its face the rotation of the earth. A healthy series of metaphors, the sundial is the quintessence of analogical thinking.

A clock face transmutes the analogies of the sundial into the movement through space of the previously fixed point. Another analogy, the twelve-point circular clock provides a two-dimensional imitation of the earth's three-dimensional movement. Analogue time is unbroken in its seeping, sweeping continuity. It is full; it bears meaning; it signals being.

A digital clock presents a successive sequence of discrete numerical signifiers. It does not portray a metaphor of time's passing, but, instead, presents the signifiers of a measured time, a time whose "flow" is accomplished through counting. This time is separable and countable; numbers are like the tiny grains of hourglass sand—caught, individualized, accounted for.

The first three mechanisms are metaphorical, computing, as Anthony Wilden notes, "by means of an analog between real, physical, CONTINUOUS quantities and some other set of variables."[24] The last is metonymical, computing via "DISCRETE elements and discontinuous scales" (Wilden 156). Clearly, each of the two mechanisms employ both metaphor and metonymy, the analogue devices privileging metaphor as a mode of signification, the digital clock rendering numbers (metaphors in the very basic sense that language always stands for the nonlinguistic) as the final product of its binary computer intelligence.

Digital clocks are a prosaic example of the digital, which, though it has existed since the abacus, has become the primary mode of computation, information storage, and electronic technology only since the 1960s. "Computing," Nicholas Negroponte says, "is not about computers anymore. It is about living."[25] And the living it is about is a full-scale shift from analogical media to images and information produced by or reconstituted through a transposition into the electronic binary of off/on. Traced through pathways whose structure resembles the sequence of metonymy rather than the similarity of metaphor, digital systems have already transformed our notions of time and production, and our understandings of the interrelations of knowledges, textuality, language, and reproduction. Digital copies, for example, are perfect; if a copy is identical to or better than the original, is it a copy any longer? Can we retain that sense of an original, an originator, or, for that matter, an author or a procreator? Is there any longer such as thing as reproduction?

25

The intrusion of digital technologies is not the cause of a gravitational slide towards metonymy, but the effect of such a shift. The fact that computers have been imagined throughout the twentieth century suggests the gradual nature of such a shift. Since technology follows imagination as much as it stimulates it, metonymy has already infiltrated the ways we think. Take, for example, the simple case of cable television. While cable appears to offer multiple equivalent options that would enable us pleasurably to select something we wish to watch (it seems to fulfill a commodity dream of metaphorical substitution), cable viewing consists of metonymical permutations of program switching, channel surfing, and cut-and-splice viewing that reorganize the integrity of programming and interrupt the sustained psychology of commercials. This would seem to be a somewhat radical practice in relation to an old idea of media consumption premised on what seemed to be the desire for sustained attention to metaphorical narrative units—desire signaled by ratings, award shows, and narrative integrity itself. Instead, the metonymical viewing practices of jumping and switching pick up the already metonymical organization of television, making it signify through a different system and in a different way, but viewing phenomena already metonymically organized. MTV, for example, with its short segments and constant changes, seems to be a more metonymically arranged form, but the more symptomatic sign of metonymical presence occurs in the smaller, oft-repeated "bites" that commercials have begun to employ. No longer developing any intricate narrative, some commercials have resorted to condensed, graphically attractive ten-second messages that repeat more often. Channel surfers catch the short spots in transit, getting the message anyway. This is also true of embedded commercials, where more than one product is hawked in a single frame. No one may watch the whole commercial, but a fleeting glimpse will provide multiple endorsements.

Metonymy also governs certain viewing predilections linked not so much to sustained narrative but to the desire to fill in gaps, to provide complete chains of information. Metonymical ordering is linked not only to contiguity, but to the illusion of connection. The market for facts and information as fact responds to a chaining impulse that provides an illusion of fullness. This sense that enough facts can produce whole knowledge has existed at least since the enlightenment, but its current prominence comes from the simultaneous technologies of visibility, which give us the illusion of seeing biochemical cause and effect, and computers, which organize the chaining of multiple facts into a logic that makes it work and makes facts easily available.

But metonymy's gaps are never quite closed. More facts, yes, will seem to fill them, but like the action of a digital clock, there is always a minute pause between one number and the next, a small seam that defines the chain as a chain and not as a whole, integral field. These gaps seem to stimulate some compensation, some covering with something else. For example, during the period it takes for a computer to process in Windows programs the image of a clock or an hourglass appears. The image of analogue time stands in for time's passage, the gap between computer command and response or question and answer. This image of a metaphorical function covers over a discomfort caused by an expectation of metonymical instantaneity. If the gap is too long, something must fill in so we no longer notice the gap at all. The appearance of digitally simulated analogue images (which aren't really working) is not the nostalgic return of tradition but the simulation of tradition's return as a way of diverting our attention from the gap the timepiece image represents. These digital images are almost like fetishes, covering over what we wish not to see, representing that which seems not missing, but all too present—time.

Metonymy's gaps make us nervous, not because we are still deeply aligned with metaphor, but because metonymy instills a desire for a fullness comprised of facts and connections that constantly defer to another and, finally, leave no fact unturned, no moment unfilled. If metaphor makes us seek facts, then facts make us seek metaphor, a metaphor refigured as simulation or metonymy. The metaphorical father becomes the metonymical mother. Proliferations produce the sense of fullness, not in substitutive variety, but in multiplied simultaneity—Windows programs in computers and televisions, cable or satellite-dish television, QVC, multiple, myriad news stations, America On-Line. Displacements respond to a different logic of separability and simultaneity where physical fitness, for example, is detached from work, information becomes entertainment, restaurants advertise movies, presidents make commercials and commercials make presidents, wars become video games, and video games promise the simulated transport to days of yore. Where before metaphor ordered a system in which commodities were metonymies, now metonymy orders a system in which simulated metaphors are commodities. Finally, a return to realism in BOATS films, pseudo-documentary television shows, the expert improvement of movie special effects, and virtual-reality mechanisms reflects the same kind of metonymical prominence that Jakobson sees in the nineteenth century's literary realism. This realism is not only allied to the sense of fact that has become metonymy's trademark, it responds to the need to fill in gaps—the gap between life and image.

So far this analysis has aligned certain concepts in what may appear to be a face-off. Metaphor, the father, analogue, and human craft stand against metonymy, reproductive technology, digital, and mechanical reproduction. The tendency to affiliate these terms in a binary opposition is not quite an accurate picture of the process I am delineating. Although there are links between the metaphorical and the paternal, metaphor and analogue, analogue and human craft, these terms are not synonymous. While metonymy is linked to the digital as well as to mechanical reproduction, none of these terms is entirely opposed to those associated with metaphor; the systems are interwound, cooperative, and alternative rather than oppositional, which is what makes symptoms of Symbolic change so complex and contradictory.

AN ALLEGORY OF SYMBOLIC TRANSFORMATION

The Wizard of Oz occupies a curious position among the texts ranging from the 1818 *Frankenstein* to 1994's *Junior*. Written in 1900, the same year as Landsteiner's discovery of blood groups, Baum's novel dramatizes not only the unveiling of the metaphorical father, but also the contrasting promise of an organizing, but already coexistent, metonymy. A journey epic like Nintendo and 1980s' renditions of human reproduction, *The Wizard of Oz* might also be read as a moral lesson for feminism. While this reading does not bear out the probable investments of the tale's two historical contexts, gender politics becomes more conspicuously applicable after 1956, the year the film version began its celebrated annual return to television.

The novel and film's discouragingly antifeminist (or really anti-alternative order) narrative centered on Dorothy reinforces the importance of the paternal and the familial, and situates gender as the vexed symptom of cultural change. After all, the film presents the tale of a girl who disobeys the law in Kansas, is whirled away by a storm, and is asked to kill any powerful countercultural female presence in a foreign land. She kindly helps three castrated men regain the illusion of wholeness, but when it comes to getting help herself, patriarchy fails her and she must get back to the prairie by herself. The role of the female protagonist in *The Wizard of Oz* is clearly to help others, suppress any powerful castrating females (like the doubled Witches and Miss Gulch), and return home. Her incidental threat to order is the consequence of the winds of change. Although Dorothy had the ability to transport herself all along, she could only use it when Oz's order had already transformed itself, when the Wizard had departed, the Scarecrow was in control, and the human girl was distinctly out of place.

The novel's connection between the girl and a dormant, but threatening "other" order becomes apparent if we look at one small, significant feature: the ruby slippers.[26] The shoes, an obvious locus of some power, originally belonged to the Wicked Witch of the East, whom Dorothy's house kills on its descent into Oz. The Good Witch of the North (Glinda) gives the shoes to Dorothy in defiance of the Wicked Witch of the West's dramatic claim that they belong to her. Wearing the shoes throughout novel and film, Dorothy never knows their power until the end, until all the others' problems are solved and she is the only one who remains unsatisfied. In the film Glinda explains the delay as a period that enables Dorothy to garner enough desire to really appreciate home. The novel doesn't explain it at all.

But why wait until the end to reveal the shoes' power? Certainly, if Dorothy had known their power from the beginning, there would be no story, but why must the story derive from the girl's ignorance of her own capabilities? And why is her power—a power to self-transport—vested in shoes? What desire must she cultivate through continual bravado and self-sacrifice? If the shoes are a fetish (they seem a stereotypical fetish object made of precious materials, are overvalued by the Wicked Witch, and seen as significant by the Wizard), they would be used by others to disavow Dorothy's lack (or recognize her lack of castration). The girl herself seems unable to employ their power until their fetish magic is exhausted (all the story's males are reconstituted as whole). But the shoes are more than just a fetish; they enable Dorothy's potent mobility, substituting for her transporting house. In a narrative about journeys, transportation is power. If the shoes are in some way a house substitute—she gets them as a result of her house's action, she finally employs them to return home—then what kind of power do the shoes really represent?

Home for Dorothy is a plain house on a sterile Kansas prairie, peopled by Auntie Em and Uncle Henry, instead of the more traditional nuclear family of mother, father, and child. In the film the integrity of home is imperiled by the evil Miss Gulch, who wants the Sheriff to impound Toto for having bitten her. Driven away from home by the threatened confiscation of her dog, Dorothy is unable to rejoin the family group in the storm cellar and is, instead, forced into the house to ride out the approaching tornado. We might, then, read Dorothy's desire for home as a desire to return to the innocence and safety that preceded her fall from grace (in the film she literally falls into the pigsty), but in the film, her preoedipal innocence has already been interrupted by Miss Gulch's attempt to separate her from Toto. In other words, even if this were an oedipal myth and Dorothy wanted to return to some preoedipal haven, the film has already removed any pre-oedipal possibility there might be. Home, in fact, seems to represent more than anything a desired *place*—like "over the rainbow"—rather than a primal scene or a utopian nest. This sense of place, which has played throughout the film's spatial dislocations, is a synecdoche not for the nuclear family (which is already absent and/or metonymized into Aunts, Uncles, and hired hands), but for what Glinda calls "a civilized country," a place devoid of witches (12).

If place—Oz, Kansas—is the operative figure and shoes are its most appropriate metonymy, then Dorothy's desire is a metonymical one—that is, one characterized both by its spatial objective and its sliding fixation controlled by a deliberately imposed ignorance. Dorothy's desire must be manipulated by forcing her to travel, by constantly displacing her from the meaning she already bears in herself. And Dorothy and the witches are the only ones who can travel throughout Oz; the normal denizens are limited to their respective borders. Dorothy's travel is necessary not out of (or only out of) some misogynist cruelty or paternal misdirection, but because the metonymy of her desire is the narrative's engine—her desire to go over the rainbow and return when she's had enough.

In crucial contrast to Dorothy's metonymy is the Wizard's metaphor. The "great and powerful" Wizard resides in Emerald City in the exact center of Oz. He is, the Witch of the North assures us, "a good wizard" who will help Dorothy. But instead of helping her, he has her help him in exchange for a promise he can't keep (just like a father, just like a Phallus). After Dorothy and her companions destroy the Witch and return to claim their favors, the Wizard's disembodied voice again puts off their request. Their rage at him instigates Toto to knock down a little screen at the side of the throne room, revealing a "little old man," who, it turns out, is the "humbug" wizard (134). The Wizard's various incarnations or manifestations (a big head for Dorothy, a lovely Lady for the Scarecrow, a terrible beast for the Tin Woodman, and a ball of fire for the Lion) have always been the deliberate production of metaphor. Speaking as the Symbol driving the system, the Wizard has always known that only metaphor will do. "I have fooled everyone so long," he explains, "I thought I should never be found out" (136). The Wizard's unveiling (or de-screening) reveals the mechanical ploys—wires, threads, costumes, illusions—by which his metaphor has been sustained. The Name-of-the-Wizard, the power of the Voice, are only carnival tricks used to maintain The

Wizard's Rule, managing to preserve Rule through the Name-of-the-Wizard his tricks represent.

In relation to Dorothy's metonymical desire (a desire originally organized around the symbolic centrality of the Wizard), the unveiling of the charlatan simultaneously plays out a twentieth century drama of the literalization of metaphor vested in a paternal figure and the gradual replacement of metaphor with the metonymies of the mechanical. Representing a larger transformation that has characterized twentieth-century American culture, *The Wizard of Oz*'s longevity comes from its haunting prediction, rehearsal, and reaffirmation of the gradual, insistent ascendancy of Dorothy's metonymy over the metaphor the Wizard—and culture—tries to sustain. *The Wizard of Oz* replays the literalization of Law and the Father as he is replaced by the power of shoes, by a metonymical desire signified by Dorothy's triumphant *glissement* through Oz. But this threat is quelled and the patriarchal is reformed as Dorothy willingly returns to the homey and familiar with only a lesson about misplaced desire. So Oz, too, is the drama of renegotiation, of how the Wizard wields power, when he has none, over Dorothy's powerlessness, when she has some, of home as preferable after all, of an order that outlasts even the Wizard's unveiling. The fathers are all dead, but the uncles and charlatan Wizards still prevail.

A SYMBOLIC DISRUPTION

The drama of Oz, which has, since 1956, been a regular part of American cultural consciousness, arranges its players in an allegory of the kind of symbolic shift that haunts symptomatic representations of reproductive anxiety. Father/metaphor, daughter/metonymy traces the dethronement of the former, the enfranchisement of the latter, and the reassertion of the former in some new form. Oz delineates a narrative of transition from metaphor as the grounding process of symbolic systems and western epistemologies to metonymy as metaphor's increasingly pervasive replacement.

Accompanying the introduction of machine culture and the harnessing of electricity, the increase in urbanization, improved communications' technologies, rapid colonization, leaps in scientific knowledge, and, more recently, failures in nationalism, the rise in feminism, and the transition to commodity culture, a transformation of the Symbolic anticipates, accompanies, and dramatizes the gradual loss of the paternal metaphor as the father becomes completely literal, traceable, and scientifically certifiable. Metaphor's loss of dominance manifests itself in versions of cultural disorder ranging from lawlessness to single-parent families, but also enables the expansion and recognition of more cultural positions and categories, the destabilization of reproduction (both mechanical and human), and a coincident focus (fixation) on sexuality, sexual variety, and diversity. This is not to say that these various expressions of a more metonymical order are inherently disorderly or decadent, but that their emergence as social categories reflects another kind of order.

While metaphor gradually relinquishes its ordering prominence to metonymy, a western cultural imaginary busily cultivates defensive formations in the form of simulated metaphors—the maternal father, the analogue interface to digital technology—that compensate in various ways for Symbolic loss. Another, perhaps more accurate, way to understand this change is to consider that, in the field of reproduction and especially around the figure of paternity, the gradual revelation of the lack that grounds Law—the unveiling of the father's nominal metaphor through the literalization of paternity—stimulates attempts to recoup the lost metaphorical relation between the paternal figure and cultural order.

TRACING THIS SYMBOLIC TRAJECTORY THROUGH SMALL BUT SIGNIFICANT SYMPTOMS

Taking all of these concepts together, the chapters that follow analyze knotted sites of Symbolic transition and renegotiation. In each, the Symbolic is challenged in a slightly different way; for each challenge there is a slightly different strategy for cultural reordering. These variations suggest that the phenomenon of Symbolic transformation is neither singular nor unified. Nor is its progress rapid and coordinated. For every ounce of change, there is a pound of Symbolic reinscription. When representations evoke an instability in order, other representations—or sometimes even another aspect of the same representation—which evoke a familiar and stable order step in to repair the rift. The agent of this repair work is the conservatism of the psychic structure, whether that structure operates as the individual expression of artists or the instinct of corporate manipulation or some larger cultural imaginary that compensates for loss at multiple sites. As I analyze these representations I also resymbolize them within a metaphorical Symbolic as the only way to make sense of them in the conventions of critical language. My attempts at a more metonymical organization (as in the prologues, for example) may produce more confusion than clarity.

The first three chapters, "Reproductive Prehistories," "The End of Pop," and "Law in the Age of Mechanical Reproduction" trace compensatory images around paternity as the literal paternal is confused with Symbolic order. "Reproductive Prehistories" tracks the emergence of mechanical reproduction in the realm of image production, suggesting that the increasing centrality of the mechanical gradually constitutes a threat to metaphorical systems of reproduction and authority. At the same time, human overreaching in the realm of reproduction, emblemized by *Frankenstein*, represents both systemic upheaval and a mode of compensation for a threatened Symbolic order. Pop artists replay this relation between mechanical reproduction and Frankensteinian compensation by appropriating the mechanical for the name of the creator. Chapter 2 treats how the phenomena of bodybuilding and superhero movies

31

provide compensatory images for a patriarchy confronted by feminism, a loss of American prestige, and the introduction of digital technologies. Finally, the family itself becomes the locus of paternal resymbolizations as the son becomes the father to culture in the *Terminator* series and as Arnold Schwarzenegger becomes a mother.

"Law in the Age of Mechanical Reproduction" investigates the proliferation of laws around reproductive issues, including abortion, paternity, and reproductive technology. If Symbolic Law is premised upon a metaphor and if that metaphor is lost or undermined, what happens is that laws fill in to produce the continued illusion of Law. This happens not only in the tomes of legislation produced from the early 1970s on, but also in proliferations of law television shows that work to resituate law as metaphor and provide the illusion of a stable Symbolic.

Chapter Four, "Going to Bat," considers the self-contained figuration of Symbolic threat and recuperation represented by the vampire, examining the figure of the vampire as it functions as a mode of unauthorized reproduction. Invading and transforming traditional patriarchal systems, the vampire poses a metonymical reproduction against the father's metaphorical aegis. At the same time, the vampire's uncanny menace is mastered through his destruction on the level of narrative. The relation between the uncanny and the assuagement of threat is replayed on the level of the vampire's image in vampire films.

The last chapter, "Digital Dad," discusses the context and possibility of interventions into the process of Symbolic change as it plays out in the transition from mechanical reproduction to digital technology. The entrenchment of preeminently metonymical orders such as computer technology may provide opportunities to effect cultural resymbolization. The point is to consider the Symbolic shifts as a significant site for intervention. Doing so demonstrates the very real connection between theory and praxis that effect our identification of appropriate points of intervention and our understanding of social action, suggesting the tactics we might use.

The purpose of organizing and analyzing these scattered, vaguely reproductive, vaguely paternal texts is not only to suggest that the Symbolic is shifting and to account for certain cultural formations as somehow responsive to that shift, but also to begin to suggest how we might best take advantage of such a shift to promote social and cultural change. If the metaphorical underpinnings of culture are necessarily linked to the patriarchal and if metonymical systems scramble to refind and reassert the patriarchal in its metaphorical place, this would seem to be the time to disturb that renormalization, to take advantage of metonymy to expose the conspiracy of gender, nature, order, ideology, and psyche that partly produces and perpetuates inequalities and oppressions. To do this, however, we must know where the weak points are, where the fleshly breaches have not been plasticized.

REPRODUCTIVE PREHISTORIES

Conceptions of Reproductive Impiety

chapter 1

PAPA'S BABY

In 1818, Mary Shelley wrote the story of Victor Frankenstein, who, having discovered "the cause of generation and life," "became," as he describes it, "myself capable of bestowing animation upon lifeless matter."[1] Victor exults, "A new species would bless me as creator and source; many happy and excellent natures would owe their being to me. No father could claim the gratitude of his child so completely as I should deserve their's" (49). Frankenstein fabricates a hyperbolic being from charnel-house gleanings, offsetting impossibly minute anatomical intricacies with its larger-than-life size. When complete, the being's animation fills his heart with a "breathless horror and disgust," sparking a delirium that lasts for months (53). The year 1818 is not ripe for such vivid incarnation; Frankenstein's error lies in his meticulous literalization of the figuratively deific: "In the beginning was the Word."

REPRODUCTIVE PREHISTORIES

THE END OF DADA

In 1903, Guillaume Apollinaire wrote *The Breasts of Tiresias,* a play in which a husband, weary of his wife's feminist protestations and worried about French underpopulation, decides to propagate children himself.[2] Succeeding in producing such an extraordinary quantity of offspring that only mass production could account for it ("40,050 children in a day"), the husband is rewarded by becoming a "millionaire ten times over," while the play's resident fortune-teller predicts that those "who don't make children . . . will die in the most abject poverty" (89). Linking reproduction to lucre, Apollinaire appears to mount an argument against France's reproductive laxity. But by making the father the mother and displacing the mother into the Army (at the end of the play she becomes the "head of the army in Room A at City Hall"), Apollinaire forges a direct link between father and children. Not only do we know who Daddy is, we no longer even need a Mommy. Daddy's singular fecundity, less arduous than Frankenstein's gross anatomy, is so much more efficient than the slow commerce of the sexes.

This 1903 play was not produced onstage until 1917, its symptomatic response to wartime population depletion anticipating the end rather than the beginning of a Dada that had just moved to Paris from Zurich. While Apollinaire's play and the productions of Dada were both challenges to institutionally sanctioned forms of reproduction and shared the same proto-Surreal quality, *The Breasts of Tiresias* cuts to the anxious paternal heart of the procreative matter, allaying, via a prodigious and certain procreation, anxieties about reproduction that haunted the more filial Dada. Continuing its confrontations with institutional art's commodified mimeticism, Dada survived Apollinaire's paternal short circuit to transform itself into Surrealism in the early 1920s, but, in its oedipal anti-art philosophy, highly planned appeals to chance, conscious play on art's commodification, and the plastic improvisation of its adversary events, it thrashed somewhat uselessly through a proliferated play of free-associated oneiric signifiers.[3]

POP'S PROGENITOR

Just as Dada's antagonistic performances heralded the beginning of "good for only one show" throwaway art, Dada's contemporary and associate, Marcel Duchamp, invented the "ready-made," the displaced utilitarian object whose signification worked primarily through recontextualization. While a Dada collage or play was still metaphorical, standing for something somewhere else even if that something was the process of artistic production itself, Duchamp's ready-mades were pure metonymy. If a urinal placed in an art exhibit and given the title *Fountain* becomes art, then art becomes a matter of strategic displacement and canny renaming.[4] Duchamp, we find out later, is the Dada of Pop.

JUNIOR

The pregnant father returns, in 1994, in Ivan Reitman's film *Junior*.[5] An "expecting" Arnold Schwarzenegger emblemizes one response to a trajectory of reproductive anxiety that began with the introduction of mechanical forms of reproduction in the industrial revolution. When human productivity is taken over by the machine and artistic realism bettered by the camera, the effect is registered in the realm of reproduction, and more specifically in permutations of paternity. As the most threatened and most overdetermined confluence of Law, biology, and social relations, human paternity, always insecure, must reassert itself to compensate for the multiple threats to its aegis and to order itself. Testimony to cultural inventiveness, paternal compensations take a wide variety of forms from Pop art to built bodies to pregnant men. And the sad fact is that no matter what the struggle in the paternal field, the father has always been beside the point, a figurehead whose age is fading. Large-scale cultural change, the kind that sweeps over centuries, is not about the father at all, who is only the symptom who steps in with his tiny hubris to defend what was his only in name.

MECHANICAL REPRODUCTIONS

The previous four examples, extending through nearly two centuries, accompany the shift from the industrial machine to the computer. The transition to steam-powered machinery altered the relation between human beings and the production of goods. The advent of the machine redistributed labor so that the relation between worker and product became less direct; production was increased at the same time it was alienated. The mechanical's incursion into production spurred anxieties not only about encroaching machinery and human rule, but also about artistic reproduction, as mechanical reproduction changed the ways art was reproduced and disseminated. These shifts represent an incipient disturbance in the Symbolic. One register in which anxieties about this disturbance appear in a Euro-American cultural imaginary is in representations of reproduction cast as reasoned attempts to grapple with the import of mechanical reproduction (Benjamin), symptomatic expressions of a paternal hypercreativity (Apollinaire), or attempts to recuperate mechanical reproduction for the human (Pop art).

The example of the introduction of photography and cinema illustrates one intersection of the mechanical and the reproductive that introduces a radical change in the assumptions and processes of image production. Photography's introjection of a more metonymical process of reproduction serves as an illustrative model for the process by which the reorderings of metonymy incite anxiety and signal shifts in order. The nineteenth century introduction of photography and the turn-of-the-century advent of cinema inaugurated representations reliant on metonymy rather than on the more

35

traditionally metaphorical painting and sculpture. Both photography and cinema optically displace images from one time and place to another through a technology that combines contiguous operations with analogue representations. Their technologies and our ability to imagine them (which of course preceded their invention) signal the gradually shifting relations of production and reproduction incident to the rise and waning of industrial capitalism and nationalistic imperialism. Mechanical reproduction signals an expanding culture that infiltrates and extends itself synchronically, careless of tradition and history.

The development of representational technologies such as photography and cinema enacts a gradual shift in emphasis from metaphor, relation, tradition, ritual, historical narrative, originality, and authenticity to metonymy, separability, and image proliferation. With the advent of mechanical forms of reproduction, plastic arts are relegated to an artisan culture that sequesters and conserves in a cause-effect narrative of tradition and historical influence. Focusing on the fertile felicities of the traditional relation between artist and creation emphasizes artistic authority, originality, and craftsmanship; photography and cinema's substitutions for and condensations of the plastic arts initiate a cultural wonder at the apparent disappearance of a distinction between image and original (hence the continued valuation of realism). Mechanization's series of distinct processes enables a growing esteem for the separable sites of production—artist, mechanical apparatus, image. Dispersing attention among mechanical reproduction's proliferated appendages intimates both the omnipresence of reproductive agents (artists, cameras) and infinite reproductive capacity (images produced everywhere by everyone).

Reproductive technologies in art emerged with ancient bronze casting, but became epistemologically influential with the printing press, whose combination of mechanical pressure and repeatability began the first full-scale deviation from the realm of the original to the domain of the reproduction. The press's extension into image reproduction through engraving and lithography enabled the mass reproduction of words and images.[6] The various modes of printing, however, still reproduced only other already reproduced images such as letters and drawings. As practiced up until the invention of photolithography, printing staged a lengthy, repetitive, and not untroubled transition from the metaphor of the letter to the metonym of its propagation.[7]

In contrast to printing technologies, photography embodies a significant and more metonymical departure from printing's mode of mass production; not only does photography appropriate and alter printing technology, it initiates a gradual shift from the word to the image as primary locus of cultural meaning. And it does this not by reproducing other images, but by preserving "real" scenes and by creating what appears to be an identity between original and reproduction.

As a technology, photography represents the recorded effect of the camera obscura's transposition of light rays.[8] A Renaissance perspective aid, the camera obscura was a tool in the creation of graphic art. The transpositive operations of the camera obscura's peephole box, which clearly delineated perspectival relations, were posed halfway between the analogue image produced by hand tracing the camera obscura's cast image and the metonymy of the photographic camera's contiguous mechanisms.[9] The nineteenth century invention of light-sensitive emulsions enabled the substitution of chemicals for the human hand; the "touch" of light initiates certain chemical changes that correspond to light waves emanating from the camera's field of vision. While lenses, developed through the sixteenth to seventeenth centuries, continue a more substitutive (and often literally condensing) metaphorical focusing process, the photographic product of the lens's intercession is subject to a series of contiguous chemical and mechanical operations.[10]

Evolving toward complete automation, photography increasingly concealed its operations. Throughout the nineteenth century, the duration of image production was gradually reduced as emulsions were developed to record light more quickly. The development of a negative-to-positive print technology allowed for multiple copies of the same image, permitting photographic mass production. When the flexible medium celluloid was introduced in the late nineteenth century, additional mechanisms were devised to advance and roll film inside the camera. Instantaneity and flexibility gradually cloaked the operations of photographic reproduction so that the camera became a seemingly automatic reproduction machine. As development techniques became more sophisticated, additional layers of contact (between negative and print) replicated an image through several literally contiguous stages. While film development is still a separate and mainly hidden process (for most of us, done in labs), the introduction of Polaroid's self-contained development mechanisms allowed the camera to literally spew forth reproductions or store them marsupially in a holding container.

But even more symptomatically metonymical than the apparatus of photographic technology are conceptions of the photograph's ontology. "The photographic image is the object itself, the object freed from the conditions of time and space that govern it."[11] André Bazin's 1945 declaration in "The Ontology of the Photographic Image" reflects a conceptual contiguity between image and reproduction. The identity between image and object is, according to Bazin, the product of mechanical reproduction's "objectivity"; "for the first time between the originating object and its reproduction there intervenes only the instrumentality of a non-living agent" (13). "Photography enjoys a certain advantage in virtue of this transference of reality from the thing to its reproduction" (14). "The photograph as such and the object in itself share a common being, after the fashion of a fingerprint" (15). Although we could just as easily understand photography as a somewhat metaphorical transposition because of the intervention of the lens (which despite Bazin's claims, is not "objective" at all), or because it is, in fact, an analogue of light's pattern, Bazin's ruminations on photographic ontology signal a credence (or the desire for one) in a distinctly metonymical reproductive capability linked to the contiguity of original and reproduction.

While cinema would seem to be simply an elaborated extension of photography, its apparatus follows its own history of mechanical reproductions that link its inception back to the era of Shelley's *Frankenstein*. Although the invention of cinema per se, meaning the introduction of a functioning apparatus to film and project moving (photographic) images, is most often located at the 1895 Lumière brothers' show in Paris, technological elements necessary to cinema's design—winding mechanisms, the maltese cross gear, flexible photographic media—were introduced gradually from the end of the eighteenth century.[12] Like photography, most of cinema's necessary operations—"the reproduction of motion by changing 'phase pictures,' the reproduction of constantly moving pictures by rapidly moving slots, intermittent motion of the phase pictures with approximate or complete periods of rest, optical compensation for the motion of the phase pictures by lens and mirror, long strips of pictures, and their projection"—are physical enactments of the processes of contiguity and displacement.[13]

The 1832 Phenakistoscope, for example, displays a series of only slightly changed images that are associated solely by contiguity, as is typical of early nineteenth-century novelties. Like classical film animation, these "phase pictures" create the illusion of movement when they flash by the eye quickly enough.[14] The Phenakistoscope's images were arranged around a flat circular disk, while those of the Zoetrope (invented in 1834, but not marketed until 1867) were printed around the inside circumference of a circular, rotating drum.[15] The Zoetrope's images were viewed from outside the moving drum through a series of slots contiguous to the images within. The 1866 Choreutoscope devised a mechanism by which a strip of phase pictures moved intermittently through a shutter device; a mechanized combination of shutter and movement was a first attempt to produce the intermittent motion necessary to prevent blurred images when the pictures moved.[16] Projection, a much older technology, was still accomplished by the more metaphorical operations of lenses, which generally enlarge the images they project or reconstitute anamorphic images (as in cinemascope).[17]

That these nineteenth century mechanical devices depend upon the contiguity of the chemical/mechanical components to reproduce images is not at all remarkable given the long tradition of printing technologies and the century's increased dependence upon mechanical production in industry. The technology enabling photography and cinema in the nineteenth century is the same employed in other winding, perforating, punching, and intermittent motion machines such as the sewing machine and the telegraph tape.[18] While probably the oldest technology contributing to cinema is the more metaphorical process of projection, most technological advances are distinctly metonymical, deriving from the necessary contiguities of mechanics rather than the artisan's transformative substitutions.[19] Although machines themselves often begin as analogies to human movement, to be efficient, they cease to operate by analogy and begin instead to produce analogies. The sewing machine no longer sews like a human since it has combined processes more efficiently; its product is like hand sewing only stronger. The photograph leaves the recording of an image up to a chemical process, but the result is still like a painting only more realistic. Removing the human from the reproductive equation, according to Bazin, results in a "psychological" dividend, "to wit, in completely satisfying our appetite for illusion by a mechanical reproduction in the making of which man plays no part. The solution [to the problem of realism in art] is not to be found in the result achieved but in the way of achieving it" (12).

Protocinematic ventures such as the Phenakistiscope and the Zoetrope relied upon the long-lived doctrine of a "stroboscopic effect" or a physiological "persistence of vision."[20] The observation that images may linger on the retina after the source of the image itself has disappeared was one way of accounting for the illusion of motion perceived in rapidly shifting images. While accounting for the illusion of movement, persistence of vision also sutures the metonymical gaps produced by the darkness between images, transforming the metonymical technology back into a fuller, more substitutive process located in the mind. More recently, a second, more "psychological" hypothesis, the "phi phenomenon," explains the illusion of movement as the result of a mental tendency to substitute knowledge of cause and effect or sequence for broken movement.[21] The brain sees what it thinks should be there. In both cases, the machine's metonymy is glossed by more metaphorical processes displaced from the work of art or its technology to the brain itself.[22] Although the photographic imagination, as evidenced by Bazin, may seem to marvel unduly at the mechanical wonders of technology, it finally equates the end with the means—the picture with the process—both technologically and psychologically.

While Bazin is entranced with human evacuation from the processes of image reproduction, the solution to art's problem with realism is not so much human absence, as ultimate human control of the process. The photographic/cinematic artist is no longer midwife, middleman, or the hubristic purveyor of errant visions or the "pseudo-realism" of "illusory appearances" (12). Instead, the artist becomes the proud initiator of a visionary activity that is no longer illusion, but a "true realism" that gives "significant expression to the

39

world both concretely and its essence" (12). As "liberation and a fulfillment," photography is the conclusion of an age-long trajectory towards the reproduction of the real (16). Arriving at the "real" real, Bazin privileges an end significant because of the objective nature of its means. Photography's realization might free painting from the slavish depiction of reality, but photography's realist apotheosis also situates it as the *sine qua non* of a representation that becomes increasingly synonymous with reproduction.

Bazin's proclamations of photography's "objectivities," however, necessarily position photography as more than mere reproduction. Photography's technical means might be primarily metonymical, but photographic art is still the product of a creative will. Photography is simultaneously more natural—and more like the thing itself, with less human intervention—and a truer vision of the world inscribed by the visionary photographer. By locating photography as an art with such winsome fidelity that nature "imitates the artist" (15), cinema as a photographic art can only be an even better art. Capitalizing on its metonymical faithfulness, photography captures the best of both nature and human creativity.

Products of industrial culture, photography and cinema not only complete the evolution of realist art (or at least they appeared to until the invention of digital representations), they accompany the precipitation of the more traditional components of artistic production (artist, medium, creation) into separable, disarticulated elements. This separation, the consequence of rifts produced by the clash of traditional plastic arts and mass-production technologies, is also partly the effect of an end or product orientation created by the machine's effacement of its own processes. Unlike painting, whose technique is traditionally quite visible—even evidenced in the finished work—the mechanism of the photo/cinematic apparatus hides its processes as well as the ideologies that structure these machines in their particular viewer-centered, realist forms.[23] This obscuration effects a displacement from the marvel of humanly imprinted technique to the miracle of the reproduction represented by the image itself. The more spectacular the reproduction, the more emphatic the fix on it; hence, the ascendance of cinema over photography. This fascination with image retroactivates a captivation with the mechanical effects of the media, not as wielded by the artist or in necessary relation to the images they produce, but as an object of interest in themselves.[24] Television documentaries about filmmaking, for example, focus more on special effects than on specific filmmakers.

At the same time, if the end product of artistic production is detached from its creator or instigator by the intervention of a human-free machine, then the parts of the creative process no longer seem unified. Where a machine intervenes in some part of the process, the artist is necessarily divorced from art, since artists themselves no longer "touch" their reproductions. Their personal vision is extenuated since what they reproduce is superficially no longer the direct, unmediated product of their imaginative "vision," but a selected imprint of real time and space. Their mastery over the machine, however, ultimately begets an equal emphasis on the personae of photographers/filmmakers, who have become as famous as their images—Hitchcock, Warhol, Spielberg. The metonymical organization of the mechanical separates and links the discrete components of an artistic production that was once a series of overlapping substitutions.

Finally, the separation of mechanical reproduction's components occurs as an effect of technological reproduction's devaluation of originality. If there is no original with a history and aura to experience and venerate, the concatenation of artist, work, history, and tradition that combine to produce an original no longer necessarily coheres as a sensible unit. This devaluation of originality follows the general rise of a metonymical order in larger trends such as commodity culture. The narratives of capitalism and Lyotard's postenlightenment "legitimating metanarratives of knowledge" had focused on production sustained by elaborate metaphors ranging from Christianity's eternal reward to the myth of personal satisfaction.[25] Capitalism and its corollary narratives of science and social progress have been most insidiously sustained by their analogue, biological reproduction, whose felicitous, but not-so-coincidental paradigm of maternal medium and paternal investment provides the illusion of a natural backing. Investment stands in the same relation to labor as father to mother, neither investment nor paternity certain, their relation to product constantly produced by metaphor, their aegis generated and protected by the metaphorical operations of law.

In the face of these metaphorical elaborations, whose function is to suture both elitist ideologies and the causal gaps that fracture capitalism, technology's metonymy is necessarily threatening. Inextricable from industrialization, metonymy, nonetheless, disrupts the fine metaphorical closures presented by systems—capitalism, nationalism, imperialism, science—reliant upon constant circular substitution (labor/product/profit, personal interest/national interest, national interest/international interest, or method/knowledge). Its capacity to disintricate its parts suggests that systems that seem to be whole and inviolable are, in fact, disintegrable. For this reason, metonymy was, until the 1960s, displaced into and delimited as a technology that is controlled by law and ideology. If the metonymy of technology is "only" technology, then metonymy is evidently still controllable, even if the threat of a loss of human control over the mechanical is manifested in narratives from *Frankenstein* to science-fiction horror. Law as a kind of control, as I'll discuss later, works through a specific resistance to and compensation for metonymy; ideology remetaphorizes errant metonymy by superimposing sometimes ill-fitting compromise formations such as the American Dream or the recent "Contract with America."[26] But of all these cultural alibis and panaceas, human reproduction is the most resilient and ideologically efficacious appeal to continual metaphorical reorganization. And human reproduction is the metaphor most threatened by mechanical reproduction's metonymy.

The ideologically valent model of human reproduction and its not-so-coincident connection to other forms of property, production, and mechanical reproduction already represented a reproductive anxiety cued by the 1818 *Frankenstein* as well as by other early nineteenth-century narratives of unauthorized reproduction such as John Polidori's 1819 *The Vampyre* and, later, by Bram Stoker's *Dracula* (1897).[27] Linked to Frankenstein's hubristic assumption of generative prerogative, this reproductive anxiety seems to be about the loss of a proper authorial or paternal aegis as threatened by technological advance and the potential confusion between original and copy; it is an anxiety about reproduction cast in the register of representation not only in fictional narratives of reproductive usurpation such as *Frankenstein*, but also in the very mechanisms—photography, lithography—of art's transmission.

Tracing reproductive anxiety as it relates specifically to art, Walter Benjamin hypothesizes that the introduction of mechanical modes for the reproduction of art threatens art's aura of authenticity, its site of ritual, and its environment of tradition, producing a greater emphasis on exhibition (to the detriment of art's ritual value) and the increased participation of the masses in an art that becomes quantity instead of quality. Linking shifts in art's production and consumption to political and cultural change, Benjamin connects traditional art, with its emphasis on originality, authenticity, and aura, to ritual. Traditional works of art are distinctly metaphorical, signifying not only some representative object of veneration (the statue of a deity, for example), but an entire culture, whose tradition gives art meaning in the first place. While traditional works' originality and uniqueness physically limit their display, industrial culture's shift to mechanical reproduction removes art from its ritual context. Multiple copies make art available for wide exhibition. According to Benjamin, detaching art from ritual and enabling its wide dissemination makes art an ideal political vehicle for promoting the interests of a rising proletariat. Unless the political is itself aestheticized (made into ritual, as in Fascism), mechanically reproduced art and the art of mechanical reproduction catapult metaphorical art/ritual towards a more open culture.

Benjamin's prognosis for mechanical reproduction is generally optimistic. Tracing a trajectory from ritual to the political, from authenticity to reproduction, from original to endless multiples, he outlines a broad cultural shift effected by industrial capitalism that provides a cultural/political analysis of the effects of a shift from the primacy of metaphor to the growing domination of metonymy. But his analysis also reveals an anxiety about the loss of aura forced by mechanical reproduction that is connected to a loss of authority rather than

42

to a loss of ritual. Even though art's disimbrication from ritual is a positive step towards a political art (and political change), art will never be the same, will never again radiate the patina of accumulated history, tradition, singularity, and originality. And if we are not careful, art and its reproductions will wield only a negative influence.

One symptom of this anxiety about art's authority is Benjamin's concluding analysis of Fascism. The problem with Fascism (apart from the obvious) is the way it dangerously revivifies an improper and dangerous artistic authority. Revitalizing the idea of an art for art's sake, Fascism gives the masses the "right" to artistic expression while preserving traditional property relations (or enfranchizes the masses in order to preserve traditional property relations). While mechanical reproduction should break down property's elitist system, Fascism emphasizes expression over radical political reformation, making the illusion of self-expression the basis for a regressive and repressive politic. The effect of Fascism's mechanical reproductivity is to make humanity its own artistic object; when humanity becomes the object of its own contemplation, "its self-alienation has reached such a degree that it can experience its own destruction as an aesthetic pleasure of the first order" (242). Perverting the ritualized reproductive metaphor of artist and creation, culture becomes its own object; it endlessly reproduces itself in a destructive, narcissistic stasis (a danger of mechanical reproduction's endless proliferations). The problem with self-reproduction is not so much alienation, but the evacuation of any creative, heterologous reproductive principle. Self-creativity becomes destructive instead of procreatively spawning the political change mechanical reproduction's refreshing difference should initiate. The political becomes the aesthetic instead of the aesthetic becoming the political.

Although Benjamin's fears appear to focus on Fascism's perversion of the relation between culture, art, and technology, his analysis of mechanical reproduction's effects also bespeaks an anxiety about the relation between artist and creation, a relation solipsistically distorted by Fascism, but one that is also imperiled by mechanical reproduction's expansive capabilities. What Benjamin describes as Fascism's preservation of property is really its preservation of metaphor, of an enlarged metaphor of originary purity and self-sameness that functions as a compensatory, conservative maneuver against the radical changes mechanical reproduction's metonymical alterity threatens. Benjamin's constant attention to distance—between artist and art, between art and consumer—makes distance the register through which anxieties about artistic authority come into play. "The distinction," he says, "between author and public is about to lose its basic character. The difference becomes merely functional; ... at any moment the reader is ready to turn into a writer" (232). While the loss of distance might be seen as positive, and Benjamin seems to take it as such, his reiteration of this loss is also a nervous worry about some of mechan-

43

ical reproduction's other effects such as its replacing "the shriveling of the aura with an artificial build-up of the 'personality' outside the studio" (231). As in the example of Fascism, mechanical reproduction has the potential to go the wrong way, representing not the radical interests of the masses, but the limited interests of propertied capitalism.

While the metaphor of ritual seems conservative, the metonymy of mechanical reproduction is perhaps no less dangerously so, as it alters the relation between artist and work and between art and the world. Where metaphor's mooring in law provided the illusion of a governing system, metonymy's free-floating access, its detachment from tradition, and its illusory objectivity make it dangerously available to any interest. The transition from art's traditional, authentic, singular, and totalized picture into film's pervasive reassembled fragmentation is not necessarily a transition from property relations to popular enfranchisement, as the example of Fascism demonstrates. Instead, as Bazin and Benjamin suspect, while mechanical apparatus may provide an objectivity (or the illusion thereof), the apparatus does not disappear and leave only unmediated reality. Instead, its immense residue is the necessary commodity market, whose focus on the intrinsic spectacle of mechanical reproduction itself both magnifies and elides not the machine, but the potentially reformative power of artistic authority.

The problem with mechanical reproduction, finally, is the loss of rule, in whose absence the proper political direction cannot be guaranteed. How do we make mechanical reproductions properly serve the political needs of the proletariat instead of reasserting the interests of the dominant order? Benjamin manifests this anxiety about authority and control in comments about the increased distance between artist and creation (as opposed to worries about the over-proximity of art and consumer). Stretching the distance between artist and work too far causes the mystical and highly metaphorical ritual insight of a cultural shaman or political seer to shrivel to the trashily metonymic, mass-produced commodity production of a capitalist manufacturer or Fascist magnate. If there is no authority left in either the artist or art, if the artist's relation to his/her work is not still somehow grounded in metaphor—in the mystique of art or the artist's larger-than-life legend—the crude metonymy of mechanical proliferation renders both art and the artist shams, political whores, or at best mere templates for reproductions instead of crucibles of creativity or posts for political action. Even if art is in the hands of the proletariat, how can one insure that the proletariat will exercise the proper control, especially since mechanical reproduction seemingly operates all too easily within capitalist relations? In this sense, Benjamin's generally positive ruminations on the effects of mechanical reproduction represent a distrust of the potential uses of an emerging metonymy that becomes the increasingly visible register of both the mechanical and the reproductive.

POP THOU ART

Benjamin centers his discussion of mechanical reproduction around film; "to an ever greater degree," he says, "the work of art reproduced becomes the work of art designed for reproducibility" (224). While this is clearly the case for photography and cinema, it is not until the more "traditional" art—painting—also begins to manifest a metonymical cast that reproductive anxiety, lurking within more obvious worries about the mechanical, mass culture, and regressive aestheticization surfaces with the appearance of Pop art, the mid-1950s artistic movement coincident with the mainstream imaginings of a digital technology. If we understand digitality to be a manifestation of a representational shift to metonymy and Pop to be about the displacement of obsessive reproductions from one context to another—another metonymy—then the coincident appearance of the digital and Pop represents a 1960s recognition of the increasing prominence of metonymy, which looks like a progressive economy of reproductive mastery but which masks a continuing anxiety about reproduction (mechanical or not) gone somewhat awry. This anxiety is the symptom of the more profound Symbolic transition that Pop art negotiates.

By the mid-1950s, at least according to contemporaneous American art histories, American art had reached its apex in Abstract Expressionism, whose nonfigurative representations might represent the flip side of Benjamin's worries about mechanical reproduction. Personalized, interiorized, almost rarified paintings, they embodied an art meant neither for mechanical reproduction nor the proletariat. But even this last great bastion of an artistic tradition that increasingly centered in the sensibilities of seer/artists would give way suddenly not to the pressure of proletarian evolution, but to the crisis represented by mechanical reproduction's more pervasive metonymies. The ensuing art would be a celebration neither of political enfranchisement nor mechanical reproduction for its own sake, but, rather, would represent a clever moment of mass compensation.

While painting had traditionally been both metaphorical and metonymical, its virtue resided primarily in its metaphorical quality—in its ability to substitute a produced image as a version of and commentary upon another scene, whether that was the real world or a subjective state. Abstract Expressionism might be seen as preeminently metaphorical, rendering feelings and ideas via abstract images. Abstract Expressionist's heroic painters had broken the domination of European art, establishing the first truly influential American movement. But the insurrection mounted by such painters as Jackson Pollock and Frank Stella was, in some ways, less an artistic revolution than a long-awaited affirmation of America's place in tradition. Believing that "only the act of painting itself could reveal value, individuality, and genius," Abstract Expressionists embraced rather than challenged what Benjamin might call the "aura" of a tradition that had begun to pass with Dadaism.[28]

45

Although Pop's contemporary critics tended to oppose Pop to Abstract Expressionism, vilifying it with suggestions of homosexuality and drug addiction, Pop was more a collection of canny cultural readings that understood, perhaps as well as Benjamin, the very commercial ideological stakes of western culture's movement away from metaphor.[29] While Pop's twentieth-century precursor, Dada, attacked the institution of art itself, Pop, employing some of Dada's styles and techniques—collage, found objects, ready-mades, improvisational display—appropriated the commercial in such a way as to show it up as commercial. At the same time, Pop's many vestiges embodied art's deritualized metonymical cast, making metonymy itself art's subject as well as its technique.

Credited with shedding history and tradition, Pop art is nonetheless perceived by contemporaneous critics as a historical development that arrives at its appointed time in the juncture between technology and consumer culture. Even at the time, it seems, Pop understood its mission. In 1965, critic John Rublowsky observes that "the pop esthetic is neither a primitive offshoot nor a maverick development. It is a natural extension of a line of artistic development that could have come to fruition only in this particular time and place. The leaders of the pop movement gave formal reality to an esthetic truth that was already in the air."[30] While Pop art occurs at the right moment in the narrative of art history, it also "derives its unique vision and inspiration from the mythogenic forces generated by a new social and economic reality" (7). Pop art is, therefore, also a product of the culture it embodies. Thus, in Rublowsky's account, Pop represents the conjunction of two histories—the history of traditional art and the history of capitalist culture. Coming together in Pop, these two trajectories seem to wed and reproduce an art all about reproductions. As artist Jim Dine declares, "I don't believe there was a sharp break and this [Pop] is replacing Abstract Expressionism. I believe this is the natural course of things. . . . I tie myself to Abstract Expressionism like fathers and sons" (Amaya 45).

The timely collusion of art and capitalism in Pop, however, is more a collision than a family narrative. Most understandings of Pop's inception and historical place express a shift from the filiation and tradition typical of art's history to the contiguity and spontaneity Benjamin associates with mechanical reproduction. The "natural" child of the commercial instead of the legitimate son of tradition, Pop's embrace of the mechanical opposed it to one convention (the artistic), while it allied it to another (the commercial). Although Pop's turn away from aestheticism might write another oedipal chapter in the history of artistic countermovements (one Robert Indiana fashions when he envisions Pop springing "newborn out of boredom with the finality and oversaturation of Abstract Expressionism"), Pop becomes a bastard instead of an heir, the scion of a different art culture instead of tradition's dutiful son (Amaya

45). And this does not occur because of any raging, principled rebellion, but rather because Pop's genesis seems to belong to a different logic—the same metonymical logic its art embodied. Seen as historically contingent, Pop is a product of cultural contiguity rather than tradition. An offshoot of consumer culture, Pop is "an expression of our industrialized, mass-production society," rather than the logical end to a narrative trajectory through Abstract Expressionism (Rublowsky 7).

The contradictory understandings of the relation between history and culture in contemporaneous accounts of Pop's genesis reflect the character of Pop's intervention. The confusion between filiation and a kind of cultural parthenogenesis displays exactly the problem of reproduction that Pop ultimately mediates. If, as Indiana suggests, filiation is "over-saturated," the only place to go is "back to some less exalted things like Coca Cola, ice cream sodas, big hamburgers, super markets and "Eat" signs. They are eye hungry; they are pop. . . "(Amaya 45). "Eye" hunger begets a different economy from the more traditional notion of art as soulful self-expression; eye hunger initiates a prolific horizontal scansion, an inclusive repertory of barely touched images, or images reproduced so as to look barely mediated. Reference and allusion are immediate and multiple instead of layered with historical legacy. But as Benjamin's example of Fascist art suggests, this visual abundance and technological generation betray an anxiety about control, an anxiety Pop artists and their critics resolve by reinscribing the gloss of a more traditional relation between artist and art.

47

Pop's litany of influences and characteristics are, not surprisingly, environmental rather than traditional or intellectual. Citing advertising, science fiction, consumer culture, television, and technology, contemporaneous critics explain Pop art as essentially already culturally metonymical—as a sensibility that borrows and rearranges existing elements.[31] Pop's appropriation of the subjects and styles of what had previously been seen as "commercial" art blurred the lines between art, product, and reproduction as well as categorical imperatives about artistically appropriate subject matter. Pop, for example, seemed obsessed with images of commercialized food (i.e., diner food, fast food, processed food) that matched its "eye hunger." On the level of what it imaged, Pop thus accomplished what Benjamin had predicted: it moved art from the realm of ritual to the practiced reproduction of culturally pervasive, debased little "rituals" and commercial signifiers.

But in an American (and European) culture already completely overtaken by commercial images, Pop's choice might just as easily have been to ritualize art even more than it already was by removing it completely from the realm of the everyday. In a sense this is what Abstract Expressionism did; the coexistence of the two, in the 1950s, suggests the kind of artistic reproductive dilemma a larger cultural shift to metonymy occasioned in a technological commercial culture. In a culture where art is increasingly produced for its reproducibility, Pop cleverly reproduces reproducibility itself in such a way as to emphasize mechanical reproduction's deliquescent pervasiveness. Embodying the attributes of an "art designed for reproducibility," Pop stressed its own and commodity culture's mechanical reproductive quality, imaging not only the Ben Day dot signifiers of mechanical transfer, but enacting mass culture's proliferations, commerciality, object orientation, image fixation, and bastardizations in images taken from advertising, comic strips, road signs, celebrity photographs, or food. Appropriating, proliferating, literalizing, displacing, Pop artists, like their precursor, Duchamp, produced an art that called attention not to the mastery, aura, or ritual of its own creation (though that would come through the "star" status of artists such as Warhol), but to art's context and to the continuities and discontinuities among image, context, and meaning in consumer culture.

Consumer culture also provided the context and model for Pop art's consumption. As Reyner Banham observes, "The aesthetics of Pop depend on a massive initial impact and small sustaining power, and are therefore at their poppiest in products whose sole object is to be consumed, that *must* be consumed, whether physically, like soft serve ices, or symbolically, like daily papers that can only last twenty-four hours by definition" (96). Noting that Pop "comes to you," Banham characterizes it as the plenary illusion of "goodies" packaged for the consumer (95). The significance of this fullness is its expendability, for Pop, unlike traditional ritualized representations is itself empty; only the experience of consumption is full. "In fact," as Banham goes on to say, "physical and symbolic consumption are equal in Pop culture, equal in status and meaning" (96). Metonymical yet again, Pop art's meaning is in the necessarily contiguous act of consumption.

Pop art, thus, was not so much an effete cultural commentary or a popularization of art for the masses. Rather, it was seen as a celebration of the culture (and its consumption). Referencing camp sensibility ("a love of things being what they are not"), Rublowsky describes Pop as "a slavish desire to reproduce objects almost exactly as they are found, with the least possible amount of art intervention" (20). Pop is a "quotation" without "feelings," a "visual fact without any additions or subtractions" (20). Rublowsky's mid-1960s description of an art without intervention echoes Bazin's claims for photography, repositioning photography's highly metonymical technology as the desirable apparatus for art itself, an apparatus that is sought, employed, and finally depicted as part of Pop's subject matter. According to Mario Amaya, Pop artists "welcome the photograph as another visual source of found images, in an age of mass printing and reproduction. They see it, like television and the movies, as a visual stimulus which has sunk so deeply into our consciousness that we take it for granted; they feel it must be redefined for and by itself as both object and mechanical describer" (22).

But what does it mean that Pop art's critics and some Pop artists valorize the delusively objective capabilities of mechanical reproduction, as Bazin did in his excursus on photography? What is the relation between the continued celebration of the machine and the specific representational anxiety Pop itself represents? Pop certainly allied itself with the photographic and the mechanical, but while Bazin employed objectivity as a way of arguing for the aesthetic advance of cinema, Pop actually imitates the camera on the two levels Amaya describes. On the level of creativity, Pop deploys the metonymical action of photography by displacing images in space and time. Pop's various forms of object and image displacement—Roy Lichtenstein's enlarged comic cells, Warhol's multiple Marilyns, Claes Oldenburg's ghost toasters—emphasize metonymy over metaphor, featuring the products and conditions of mass production, removed from their context by their very reclassification as art, as Pop's subjects. While Duchamp's ready-made snow shovels, bottle driers, and urinals were displayed to challenge "pre-conceived notions as to what a work of art should be" (Amaya 57), Pop's various objects pointed to the way objects and their representations already dominated the American imagination.

On the level of production, some Pop artists tried to imitate the camera's metonymical mechanisms, employing transfer techniques, such as silk screening, episcopy, and photography, that tended to erase the subjective hand of the artist. Rublowsky claims that Oldenburg tries to purge "himself of everything extraneous to the visual experience," developing "the rare ability to perceive the essence of an object with a minimum of social and psychological distortion" (5). Pop artists enact Bazin's claims for the camera. Warhol, Rublowsky says, is "the most daring. By using mechanical techniques, he has attempted to obliterate all personality and sensibility in his art. The artist, in Warhol's view, becomes a machine—a sensitive device for recording and transmitting the new realities as they are generated by the world" (5). Like Bazin, Pop artists celebrate the machinelike objectivity of the artistic apparatus, but the important difference is that Bazin was talking about a machine. Pop artists, perhaps, betray an anxiety about the machine on the level of production as they try to replace the machine with themselves.

Pop's images were, in fact, highly processed to look like processed images, but they didn't have the objectivity of a photograph. Lichtenstein redesigned and rescaled his comic blocks. Oldenburg's giant food items were remarkable in their cloth interpretation. Warhol labored over mechanical transfer. The point was not that these were found objects like Duchamp's, but rather that artists produced artifacts that looked like found objects. The hand of the artist supplanted the machine's inscription, doing the machine one better, taking the machine's threatening objectivity and turning it back into human expression. Pop is not only the celebration of mechanical reproduction, but the act of wresting reproduction back from the machine.

49

Pop's valorization of a machine sensibility is both a product of consumer culture and, as it was for Benjamin and Bazin, the symptom of an anxiety about authority and creativity. It is also the expression of the uneasy transition from a metaphorical system based on narrative expectation to a metonymical one that defies goal orientation in favor of ontology itself. In 1963, Leonard Meyer hypothesized that Pop art was non-narrative: it "arouses no expectations, except presumably that it will stop. It is neither surprising, nor once you get used to it . . . is it particularly startling. It is simply *there*" (Rublowsky 29). The lack of narrative or goal, according to Meyer, signals acceptance rather than expectation, and objectivity instead of personal vision: "The artist should accept the unanticipated results without seeking to impose his personal will on the materials or making them conform to some syntactical preconception of what ought to take place" (Rublowsky 29).

Meyer's description seems to endorse a loss of control on the part of both artist and art consumer; no expectation, no traditional shape, no goal leads to an ontology beyond even the "art for art's sake" that Benjamin found so dangerous. Contemplating the thing itself, the thing which is already not itself, but a consumer-culture simulation, does not mean a loss of narrative, but rather signals a shift from a narrative that works via metaphorical understandings of cause/effect and time to a metonymical logic that works via a chain of associations that link images to contexts through their consumption. But Pop art controls this process by revisioning it. "Is 'Pop' really with it, then?" Banham asks. "He is too much with it! Far from being a normal consumer of expendable goods he knows about origins and sources" (96). Pop is a pop when pop seems to be dying, when narrative, history, and tradition no longer seem to function as the time-honored guarantee of originality and artistic aura. By representing the manifestations and potentials of mechanical reproduction, Pop seems to control them, heartily and almost vengefully reestablishing the relation between the work of art and the now reproductively savvy artist, who, like the most successful of all Pop artists, Andy Warhol, becomes the Pop icon of Pop, not only in image, but most importantly, in name.

For Warhol, art is finally about becoming the machine, about mechanically reproducing a purely mechanical reproduction. Like his contemporaries, we can understand his oeuvre as a clever vision of mass production and an insightful critique of commodity culture. Rublowsky analyzes the Marilyn Monroe prints as

> the story of a human being transformed, of a woman changed into a commercial property . . . carefully manufactured, packaged, and sold like a can of soup. Her painted mask is reproduced endlessly until it is no longer possible to say where the mask ends and the woman begins. Illusion and reality become confused. The tragic transformation is complete. A nov-

elist might tell her story in a hundred-thousand words; a playwright, in
three hours behind the proscenium arch. Andy Warhol has told it in a small
painting, a silk-screened image daubed with garish colors (110).

Or we might also understand its overdetermined mechanical nature, its market control, and its manipulations as a response to the same Symbolic crisis that
appeared in *Frankenstein*, was elaborated by Apollinaire, and was emerging in
the 1960s discernable shift toward metonymy. Warhol's self-effacement, manifested in everything from the mechanical nature of his reproductions to his
various anecdotes about the accidental and cooperative quality of his work, is
really a displacement that relocates control even more resoundingly in the
name/image nexus of the Warhol persona.

Warhol not only puts himself in the place of the machine, he locates himself in the place of that which controls the machine. The cultural anxiety about
mechanical reproduction expressed in various ways by Benjamin and Bazin is
manifested again by Warhol, whose almost obsessive occupation of loci of control while appearing to perform its disavowal, is a sign of the same anxiety.
Painting to rock-and-roll music that would "clear my head out and left me
working on instinct alone," Warhol "wasn't sure if you could completely
remove all the hand gesture from art and become noncommittal, anonymous'
(*Popism* 7). Removing "the commentary of the gestures" from image production locates even more control in the artist, who is able to supercede the
machine that has superceded him. As Warhol comments, the ideas are what
count.

51

While the anxiety about control appears to have everything to do with the
problems of mechanical reproduction—the failure of originality and authenticity, mass-cultural meaninglessness, instant commodification—it also
bespeaks an anxiety in the more literal reproductive locus. Putting oneself in
the place of the machine repositions the artist again as creator and enables
control over reproduction; despite its clever play on and critique of commodity culture, becoming the machine is a compensatory maneuver that resituates
the artist as father in the old defensive reproductive metaphor—in name. As
Warhol himself says, "The moment you label something, you take a step—I
mean you can never go back to seeing it unlabeled" (40). While Warhol is talking about labeling movements (such as Pop), the same principle applies to
artistic production itself. The point is understanding that the name—the
label—is what effects the transformation, locates the control, defines the
artistry. When Warhol reproduces the image of a can of soup, his name substitutes for the source of the image; he, thereby, creates it anew. The image of
Campbell's Soup, which is really already the image of an image, is
Frankenstein's monster, if image, like being, can be usurped and reappropriated by nothing more substantive than the addition of a name.

In a culture obsessed with image, image is subordinated to name. Warhol's Marilyns or Elizabeth Taylors are just that: *Warhol's* Marilyns and Lizs. Their images, already culturally pervasive, become creative observations and artistic artifacts through a complex and effaced process of mechanical transfer that picks up on the metonymy by which the images already circulate. But this metonymical process is capped by the addition of the name, which functions as a completely compensatory, vengefully metaphorical, correction in mechanical reproduction's malaise. Pop's spectacular metonymies may obscure the metaphorical process of renaming by which artists attempt to regain control of cultural production, but the connection of name and image is, finally, what remains. A defense to the anxieties created by technology, mass culture, and the loss of "aura" as well as those represented by Apollinaire's symptomatic paternal overcompensation, the name cures a disturbance in the symbolic realm, in the ways we comprehend order, and in the locus of the paternal in its function as metaphor (as a name), as symbolic signifier, and as an all-too-literal fact.

Pop renames reproductive disquiet with the name most singularly, most brashly, most accidentally appropriate: Pop. While Pop might render the commodity art, Pop art is not a commodity without the artist's name. Pop's apparent transience, its very acclimation to (even invention of) commercial environments and simulation culture seemingly acquiesce to and facilitate a different order. But as Warhol observes, labeling changes; Pop's label makes a complex inventive, but compensatory, practice into a manageable stage in artistic/technological evolution, rendering technology and commercial art as art, redrawing the parameters of artistic authority, and reasserting, once again, the paternal metaphor of creativity in a mess of multiple origins.

THE ART OF MECHANICAL REPRODUCTION

Pop art's serendipitous appellation points to what seems to be the symptom of a long-standing cultural malaise—the fear of a loss of human authority in the face of a burgeoning machine culture. In 1936, Benjamin takes a fairly optimistic view of the incursion of mechanical reproduction despite the Nazis' use of it or the regressive potential for self-involved expression. But Benjamin's socio-historical analysis of the potentials of mass art is a way of allaying the fear instigated by the spiraling dominance of the machine in industrial culture. "The Machines are gaining ground upon us," Samuel Butler wrote in 1863. "Day by day we are becoming more subservient to them; more men are daily bound down as slaves to tend them; more men are daily devoting the energies of their whole lives to the development of the mechanical life."[32]

Men are displaced; human rule is threatened, but only if machines are anthropomorphized. Butler's queasiness is not about the increase in machine production, but about humanity's place in relation to the machine, not so much literally (though for the working classes that is also the case) as figuratively, in the machines', effects on the order of things. That order is what Benjamin calls the order of ritual and tradition linked to the legacy and debt characteristic of property relations. But where Benjamin welcomes the potential to disrupt property systems, Butler fears competition with machines. Characterized as an apposite force, the "machines gain ground"; they threaten to make men property instead of being the property of men. In the twentieth century, Benjamin projects an optimistic reading of mechanical reproduction's political utility; in the nineteenth century the fear of a loss of authority is much more openly expressed.

The rather lengthy moment of Apollinaire's *Breasts of Tiresias* (written 1903, staged 1917) which comes between Butler and Benjamin, is thus not simply the whimsical raving of incipient Surrealism; it represents a compromise formation between Butler's fears and Benjamin's hopes. Suspended between two key moments of mechanical promise/menace—the late nineteenth-century introduction of cinema and World War I—Apollinaire's reproductive fantasy stages the productive amalgamation of man and machine in the register of literal reproduction. While many twentieth-century artists and philosophers located (or dislocated) anxiety about the machine in the realm of artistic production (which itself provides a useful metaphor for human reproduction), only Apollinaire cast the problem of the machine versus art in reproductive instead of artistic terms, exposing the bare stake of the paternal metaphor as the scion of the order threatened not by the machine per se, but by the atraditional, proliferating, objectivist order the machine represents.[33]

53

Many of Apollinaire's contemporaries attempted to govern the machine's threat to art either by making the machine art (the Futurists, Fernand Léger) or by problematizing mechanical reproduction in art (Cocteau's 1922 *Wedding on the Eiffel Tower*). But Apollinaire situated this anxiety at the point of stress itself: in its threat to the father's symbolic function. He quells the anxiety created by the machine's systemic metonymy by simply appropriating the machine's prolific function for the body and the name of the father. By literalizing the paternal and making it solely and prolifically reproductive, Apollinaire resignifies the paternal function as the nostalgic, but still-governing, metaphor in a civilization caving in to the dispersed automatism of machine culture. Functioning like a machine, the father becomes absurdly, but handsomely, procreative, compensating (and compensated) richly for all threats against paternal aegis beginning with the mother's feminism and ending with culture's reproductive refusal.

Apollinaire's paternal excess reveals both what machine culture threatens and a cultural mode of compensation for that threat. But is the machine's system the proximate cause of the threat to the symbolic, paternal, metaphorical order of property and tradition, or is the machine a symptom of another more focused threat to the paternal itself? In so far as the paternal already works as a metaphor for a larger system of relations, it would make sense that if the system of metaphor, tradition, and property is threatened, the paternal is threatened. And if the paternal metaphor is, as Lacan suggests, the support of an entire metaphorical system, then any threat to metaphor would register in the realm of the paternal as that operates both as a metaphor and as a more literal function. In this logic it would also make sense to employ the paternal as a way to recoup the threatened system. But what is the nature of this threat? What do the machine and its metonymy really represent?

THE END OF POP

Andy Warhol Meets Arnold Schwarzenegger

chapter 2

THE PREGNANT PA'S

What reproductive anxieties reflect in the realm of artistic production, they
also express in the sphere of human reproduction. Whereas Benjamin considers the loss of aura, more contemporary popular cultural representations
reflect an anxiety about a loss of authority, prestige, and order via investment
in a father figure who will return cultural health. What Pop art accomplished
by appropriating the methods and images of mechanical reproduction and
reasserting the name, popular culture accomplishes by combining the
mechanical with the human, creating a muscular machine that becomes both
productive and reproductive. Both Pop art and the art of Pop negotiate a
paternal refiguration as a compensation for the threat of Symbolic change.
Popular cultural representations of muscle-studded heroes proliferate as the
father becomes more biologically certain.

Frankenstein, Apollinaire, Dada, Pop, digital technology, metonymy: all add up to 1994's pregnant Arnold Schwarzenegger, who, fertilizing a stolen egg and having it transplanted into his own peritoneum by Danny DeVito, spectacularly lives out the fantasy of paternal maternity—the pregnant Pa—in the Ivan Reitman film, *Junior*. But there are crucial differences between Apollinaire's fantasy and a 1994 film. In 1903 or 1917 we still cannot determine with any certainty who the father of a child is; *The Breasts of Tiresias* actually duplicates that uncertainty since we never see the father pregnant and we have only the father's word for his solo fecundity. Until the late 1980s, the father's (or really the mother's) word was all we had until refinements in DNA technology enabled us finally to discern with some certainty (except in the case of identical twin claimants) who Dad is.

Junior's graphic rendition of paternal certainty is accomplished by modeling the father after the mother, transforming the father's metaphorical relation to the mother's metonymical one. Like Apollinaire's play, *Junior* situates the father as the agent of a cultural cure; an attempted adjustment to change, making the father the mother enables paternity to occupy the encroaching system of metonymy without losing any paternal prerogative. But does the metonym's prominence, growing since the late eighteenth century, lead to the conflation of father with mother or does the increased likelihood of a biomedical certainty of paternity anticipate the literalization of the paternal metaphor that finally forces this particular compromise formation? What happens when that which has always been figurative—the operation of the father's name—becomes grossly literal and perhaps even unnecessary?

This may be, in fact, what *Junior* best illustrates: how those indiscernible reproductive relations are still guaranteed by the name. The metaphorical name is set loose by the real Frankenstein of the narrative, the presumably sterile fertility specialist DeVito, who steals the frozen egg specimen, labeled "Junior," which just so happens to be the research scientist's own contribution. When asked by the female scientist what he would name his child, Schwarzenegger, knowing nothing of the egg's origins, replies, "Junior." "What a coincidence," she muses, "that's what I named my egg." Although Arnold has become mother and his relation to the child has become metonymical, his pregnancy represents a cultural strangeness restored to the familiar by the matching coincidence of the name, Junior, circulating among the biological parents and the child. In itself, "Junior" refers to the father in a particularly derivative manner; typically, the addition of Jr. is an extra compensation, a nominal overkill that once again guarantees the father's name. Without the rest of the father's names, Junior itself is a synecdoche of the child's nominal relation to the father, here a joke, since his relation is so certain to begin with.

Having thus already been applied to Mom's donation, Jr., the traditional diminutive synecdoche of the name of the father comes full circle, becoming the name the mother contributes in a futile and superficial gesture towards reestablishing the now-maternal metaphor from the other side. But the mother actually donates the name of the father in the guise of the name of the egg. In a circular metonymy, the name of the gamete substitutes for the Name-of-the-Father in a scenario where the father has become quite certain and where he is redoubled by the child's name, which refers most unctuously, most lavishly, most redundantly back to the father Junior is junior to. And mother, who if there were any symmetry to this fantasy, should now have an uncertain nominal relation to the child, is already certified by the coincidence of the germ cell's tongue-in-cheek moniker, which ironically remetaphorizes the Frankensteinian certainties of a science whose opportune literalism shakes the system.

If we finally know with certainty who the father is, should there be any more reproductive anxiety? Are Frankenstein and Apollinaire and Pop really about some insistent paternal uncertainty, some failure of human rule over machines, or do they manifest the anxieties of too much knowledge, an excess that plays out emblematically in Frankenstein's monster's hyperbolic physique, in Apollinaire's bulging nursery, in the proliferations of mechanical reproduction, and in the hyperplenitude of mass culture and commodity economies? In so far as biological reproduction has never really been the issue in the functioning of the law, the literalization of the father would do little by itself to disrupt the Symbolic, but in so far as paternity has served as a paradigm—a metaphor—for Symbolic relations, knowing who father is on the literal level suspends or forecloses the imaginary operation of the prohibitions and authorizations that occur in his name and place. Literalizing the father's name defeats the metaphor of Law in the cultural imaginary, emptying the imaginary place of Law and provoking the erection of compensatory images in its place. So while talking about the literal father is a literalization, there is a way in which culture has already made that mistake and has been covering for it.

In this sense, Frankenstein and Warhol, working in and with the imaginary, suffer from an imaginary (rather than an actual) foreclosure of the law. This is the case whether the law was foreclosed before they began their creations or whether their accession to the place of the figurative father emptied the otherwise metaphorical site of the paternal function. This foreclosure creates a kind of imaginary psychosis signaled by Victor's delirium and Warhol's runaway proliferation of images. In Frankenstein's case, his own usurpation of procreative prerogative both literalized the paternal function and replaced it with the monstrous that embodied the character of his paternal usurpation. For Warhol, the paternal was already rapidly becoming literal, the threat to metaphor registered in the multiplied authorities of advertising culture. For both, creative control seems the answer to the crisis, their creations enacting the panicked need to fill in for the metaphor that is missing. But while Frankenstein creates a being he doesn't name, Warhol renames to create.

57

What happens to Frankenstein and Warhol also explains the frantic responses we see on a cultural level. If, in our cultural imaginary, the paternal metaphor is destroyed as metaphor, we scramble for alternate figures to continue the imaginary functioning of the law. We have seen that struggle on a daily basis since at least the advent of Pop. Seeking to reauthorize art and resituate both law and paternity (or law via paternity), we insist on the mythical nuclear family as cultural panacea. We celebrate larger-than-life substitutes for both law and paternity in the ascendancy of bodybuilders such as Schwarzenegger and Stallone, and proliferate paternally parented television households such as *My Two Dads* and *Full House.* We make the law itself a fantasy spectacle in programs ranging from *Perry Mason*, *LA Law*, and *Law and Order* to court television and the trials of the Menendez brothers, Heidi Fleiss, and O. J. Simpson, and we emphasize law and order in a cultural milieu where both have clearly gone awry. We obsessively figure what Pat O'Donnell calls a "cultural paranoia," a species of psychosis grown overwhelmingly pervasive. Finally, we devise highly metonymic technologies such as virtual reality that bypass and fill in for the metaphor missing from the scene/screen like the tiny clock face in a Windows program.[1]

One of the functions of *Junior* , as a film appearing in 1994, is actually to try to heal the reproductive anxiety that surfaces when the Law-of-the-Name-of-the-Father is confused with the literalized father, when metaphor as an order sustained by the father's name breaks down. Making the father like a mother in what is really a metaphor of certain paternal relations, *Junior* reinscribes the paternal as the figurative even if that figure is metonymy. Like the Pop artists who reappropriated a mechanical reproduction gone out of control by simply inscribing their names thereto, *Junior* literalizes the literal so as to try to return the function of the father to the metaphorical, so as to disentangle whatever deleterious confusions there might be between literal fathers and the figurative process of law. If Arnold, whose image has served since the 1970s to shore up the American cultural imaginary, performs the final metonymy of maternity, then the missing law is replaced with another figure, a metonymy that might sustain, on an imaginary level, the renewed operations of a law returned to the register of an imaginary Symbolic. And this is not the mother, but the newly metonymized father who physically fulfills the Tiresian occupation of genders he has been attempting throughout the twentieth century.

Tiresias Returns

It is no coincidence that Arnold Schwarzenegger is the actor who becomes the hypermuscled father/mother super symbol in all of this, for he is already an example of an opportune literalism that has worked since the 1970s to compensate for anxieties about authority. The Arnold figure's overcompensatory muscles are situated at the nexus of interlocking American anxieties about control (the illusion of being able to shape culture), potency, masculinity, and paternity threatened by female independence, reproductive freedom, overgrown technology, and a loss of world prestige. These anxieties are refocused specifically in issues of paternity, whose loss is seen as causing cultural decay and whose revivification is imagined to be cultural salvation in the late 1980s and 1990s. As machine productivity becomes less material (from steel to superconductors, for example), the Name-of-the-Father becomes increasingly literal, and the image of human power becomes increasingly physical.

Muscles and paternity follow Pop, their newly heroic visibility a symptom of a failing paternal order linked to a centuries' long shift in the Symbolic that, in the nineteenth century, began to take shape as a specifically reproductive anxiety. Commencing as an anxiety about mechanical reproduction, the literalization of the paternal function traces a growing focus on the function of the father, who becomes the answer for society's ills just when his too-literal presence declares him missing. In 1992, when Dan Quayle complained about the portrayal of Murphy's single motherhood on *Murphy Brown*, he manifested the symptom of the erroneously overliteral even while his prognostications about a fatherless America exposed the net of anxieties surrounding paternity, masculinity, authority, and political dominance prevalent in American culture since the early seventies. Couching his complaint in the rhetoric of family, Quayle seemed to criticize Murphy's "immoral" pregnancy, but he was really ruing the absence of a father—actually, the absence of any desire for there to be a father. Blaming America's problems on Murphy's Daddy-snubbing egalitarian attitude, Quayle linked the show's satirical disrespect and news-room exposures of public foibles to the disappearance of a coherent patriarchal family, seeing *Murphy Brown* not as a cause, but as a symptom of a cultural problem caused by paternal absence and healed by paternal return.

Although Quayle disavowed the more ideological aspects of his critique in favor of the singular truth of the paternalistic family, his reaction to the show's daring assertion of a late twentieth-century single-parent fact of American life reveals how the paternal itself has come to stand in the place of jeopardized cultural continuity. Synechdochical of respect for authority, economic health, and American world dominance, the patriarchal family is the imaginary model of order and stability in America.[2] But the political insistence on such a model already betrays the futility of its interposition. The nuclear family is an answer because it can never be an answer; it allays anxieties to the degree to which it is able to remain a myth or metaphor of a nostalgic order. And video/simulation culture provides the perfect medium for the nuclear family's reconstituted legend.[3]

The paternal panacea that to some, like Quayle, seems the answer to issues of authority, disorder, immorality, sexual irregularity—in fact, to all of the problems seemingly introduced by a more metonymical commercial culture—

59

is the metaphor that still organizes the series of figures installed, since the 1970s, to shore up a sense of human (and primarily American) strength, symbolic stability, patriotism, heterosexuality, capitalism, family, and the work ethic. This paternal figure, however, is no longer the symbolic father of *Totem and Taboo*, but a simulation Dad projected over the too-full site of paternal certainty. The figures called to represent this renewed paternal certitude manifest this too-fullness, this hyperbole. In an overcompensatory manifestation, various Godfathers—Capone and Corleone—emerge as romanticized hyperfathers of a nostalgic, vengefully traditional (or traditionally vengeful) paternal order, whose success against the decadence of the paternally impaired mainstream certifies their absolute (deific) potency even more. Ronald Reagan, pater Americanus, is a travesty facsimile of *Father Knows Best's* paternal, suburban-Don benevolence; Sylvester Stallone's *Rocky* replays in overtly physical terms the transparent fairy tale of a regressively raced and crudely nationalistic American dream; and Arnold, the Austrian import, synecdochizes not only the imagined human control over physique that produces the hyperbolic body, but demonstrates the will to power and business acumen that makes him more than a successful bodybuilder.[4] If there were not an Arnold, we would have invented one, needing his idiosyncratic configuration of musclebound, Republican, Kennedy-connected success to provide the perfect compensatory image for complaints like Quayle's that reverberate with the squeal of castration.

The Godfather and the bodybuilder are complementary tactics for supplanting and appearing to fill in the literalized emptiness of the paternal metaphor. Although Capone had always been a figure of fascination, the 1960s television revival of his escapades in *The Untouchables* provided what was, at first, a morality lesson aimed at securing the paternal powers-that-be through the patriarchal persona of Eliot Ness. By the 1969 publication of Mario Puzo's *The Godfather*, and the 1970s to 1980s string of Coppola films adapting the story, the figure of the Godfather, as pumped up paternally and metaphorically as bodybuilders are pumped physically, becomes one response to a loss of paternal aegis.[5] Representing atavistic tradition, immense power, benevolence, and wealth in a renegade organization ironically more ordered than the legal side of culture, the romanticized mafia, like Robin Hood in a fedora, represents purity, authority, tradition, ritual, masculine prerogative, and power. Its overt positioning as an alternate narrative is quite literal; the "wrong" side of the law is, nonetheless, the right law when that law has elsewhere begun to falter.

The Godfather tenders the image of a still-viable, highly successful paternal arrangement in overt contradistinction to the disfunction of a culture without tradition, rigid gender roles, strict loyalties, and handsome financial reward. Although the image of the Godfather became more "realistic" in such films as *Goodfellas* and the early 1990s film and television remakes of *The Untouchables*, the failure of Godfather sons in Coppola's sequels is no evidence that the Godfather himself is failing, but proof of the continuing potency of his myth.[6] The Godfather provides an imaginary vigorous father whose main attraction is his hypostatization of metaphor, for the Godfather is always more than he seems. Never literal, he makes you a deal you can't refuse.

The alternate paternity of the Godfather and the spectacle of Arnold and the superhero narratives in which he stars are some of the ways social anxieties about gender and power are both organized and assuaged in the 1970s and 1980s. While we might understand Arnold's superhero status as a necessary hyperbolic adjustment on the "right" side of the law and Arnold as just another in a long line of American heroes, Arnold's accompanying series of "family" films—films about reproductive permutation such as *Twins* (1988) and *Junior*—situate Arnold not only as strongman, but as the agent of familial repair. By linking issues of reproduction and family—and specifically issues of paternity—to nationalized heroics, the figure of Arnold exhibits the nature of the connection between patriarchy, patriotism, and paternity. By gendering images of otherwise "neuter" cultural phenomena such as technology, patriarchy, in turn, links fathers (and the masculine) to concepts of order, revivifying masculinity, as Susan Jeffords convincingly argues in her analysis of representations of the Viet Nam War.[7] Casting overdetermined, hypergendered protagonists as agents of benevolent patriarchy responds to the crisis of control that ranges more broadly than war, a crisis where the loss of a war is itself only another symptom.

61

Aligned with a struggling masculinity, this crisis of control crisis plays out the compensatory logic of the paternal metaphor in spheres much less traumatic than lost wars—in fact, may work itself out most effectively in the realm of the trivial precisely because the more inconsequential a representation may seem, the less likely we are to analyze, defend against, penetrate, and dismantle it. Quayle's knee-jerk denunciation of a television character is about as momentous as America's smug deputation of NBA stars to the 1992 Barcelona Olympic Games or Arnold Schwarzenegger's position as fitness Czar in the Bush administration; however, despite their aura of profound insignificance and cheap politics, all are phenomena that demonstrate how prestige and control interrelate and how, in the case of the NBA Olympic team and Schwarzenegger, the image of the body as a metaphorical spectacle of strength arrives as the avenging savior of a gendered national pride, the nuclear family, and masculine virtue.

As a suspiciously compensatory image, the overmuscled body provides the obvious spectacle of strength, but its operation as defensive image is far more complex than its oiled surface would suggest. Bodybuilding seems stubbornly ensconced in the more-or-less marginal world of sweaty gyms and muscle mags, but this marginality founds the muscled body's hyperbole, grounding its

image of excessiveness. The overdetermined muscle of overly determined athletes responds to marginality, or the threat thereof, with a spectacular physique
that demands center stage.[8] Muscle muscles to the center in a culture where
spectacle is a guarantee of (at least fleeting) significance. While the muscled
body seems immanently concrete enough to replace neurotic fantasies with
real action, its strategic force comes from its metaphorical suggestiveness—its
imaginary organization of the chaotic disassociation of traits claimed as masculine and patriarchal. Even the relation between muscular and masculine is
not an automatic association between the "truths" of anatomy and gender;
rather, the bodybuilder's apparent alliance of the two works representationally
because the two are mediated by and conjoin the absent signifiers, phallus and
father. Finally, because the male bodybuilder is preeminently metaphorical (of
strength, will, human power, masculinity itself), he assuages the anxieties produced by the apparent loss of human rule, recalling and seemingly reasserting
a dying metaphorical system.

MUSCULAR DEVELOPMENT

The social and narrative position of the bodybuilder has shifted in the last
twenty years. Bodybuilding as a spectacle, Michael Budd has pointed out, has
existed for at least one hundred years, emerging as part of the physical-health
culture of the latter part of the nineteenth century.[9] Until the seventies, however, it existed as an eccentric, almost exclusively male endeavor, peopling
sideshows, driving a small magazine market, funding comic-book advertisements aimed at ninety-pound weaklings, and providing models for adolescent
fantasy superhero comics. Like much of what has become mainstream media
spectacle, bodybuilding as a truly big business commenced with the explosive
expansion of cable and video. But where before it seemed to function mainly as a panacea for struggling masculine self-images, its more recent mainstream ideological work appears to center not so much on the art of bodybuilding per se (though that is itself a continuing phenomenon symptomatic
of individual control anxiety), but rather on the strategic appearance of built
bodies in narratives that respond in some way to anxieties about social control.[10]

By assuaging war wounds (*Rambo*), elevating the underdog (*Rocky*), replay-
ing the myth of paternal return (*Terminator*), and/or, most recently, directly
undertaking issues of reproduction (*Twins, Junior*), the image of the built body,
analogous to the Name's metaphorical role, functions as a figuration of the
masculine (read, paternal) prerogative, anxiously missed but all too present in
a metonymical rather than metaphorical form. Where the paternal metaphor
regulated the devolution of wealth, legacy, property, and law in an assumed but
fairly invisible masculine locus (God, for example, or laws), as an embodied
spectacle, masculinity is only difficulty allied with the paternal metaphor. Since

the paternal metaphor resists the visual and the literal, proliferated images of masculinity in the form of a hypertrophic male body image are contemporary symptoms of a lack of clear connection between the masculine and authority; the multiplication of masculine signifiers in contiguous relation to sites of power is a metonymy produced by machine culture's own proliferations. As a secondary attempt to claim (i.e., name) these sites, visual masculinity literally stands by the machine governing its operation, or wields the gun, or captains business. While we tend to understand these as sex-role stereotypes, they may just as well function as metonymical compensation for an overly literal metonymical proliferation just as the sites of power multiply the uncertain relation between humanity and authority.

Masculinity becomes the metonymy to the father's metaphor, a sad, but defensive filial substitute. Where the Law-of-the-Name-of-the-Father works through the name, organizing signifiers around prohibition and desire, masculinity works through the body. The Law-of-the-Name-of-the-Father constitutes patriarchy, a system that theoretically can empower a signifier of any gender (i.e., if mother takes a prohibitive form). Visual masculinity resutures the connection between patriarchy and men by association with—by being "next to" perceived loci of power—government, the military, business. The proliferation and hyperbolization of masculine images suggests that the traditional suture between patriarchy and the masculine is unraveling, caused perhaps by the father's overliteralization. Since the Father's metaphorical function secured the patriarchal for the father and, by extension, the masculine, revealing the father as a literal agent destroys the metaphor that has sustained masculine aegis. Filling in for metaphor, images of masculinity accrue, not only in bodybuilding, but in sports and in the number of media-honed, overly present fathers on sit coms and in commercials and advertisements.

Although we might ascribe this paternal renaissance to the threats (and/or revelations) of feminism, feminism's rise may also have benefited from the father's overliteralization. In other words, while versions of feminism had circulated for at least one-hundred years before the 1960s, it is only then that feminist ideas begin to capture their largest audience since suffrage. While feminism's ideas are compelling, they are equally threatening. We could understand the 1960s' growth of feminism as an effect not only of larger civil rights and peace movements that precede and accompany it, but also as having opportunely reemerged just as the patriarchal Symbolic was already struggling to renegotiate its lock on the imaginary. While feminism and civil rights may have rocked patriarchy, their threats to order become more successful (achieve equal-rights legislation) during a period of time when the patriarchal is scrambling to resymbolize itself.

At the moment of the 1960s' insurgence of a feminist "new wave," bodybuilding, as a competitive sport and media subject featuring visible, hyperbol-

63

ic masculinity, began to grow with the advent of Arnold and the furious activity of promoter Joe Weider. "Atavistic," as anthropologist Alan Klein observes, "bodybuilding, because it is so obvious in its use of symbols and historical traits, serves as a revealing example of sport as historical metaphor" (84). "Recalling a time when life was more simple, orderly, and just," "bodybuilding has political and social characteristics akin to feudalism and an ideology uncomfortably close to fascism" (84). Like the Godfather. While Klein analyzes this phenomenon as the product of bodybuilding's relatively isolated social and economical system, the connection between bodybuilding's self-willed hyperbole and its *übermensch* idealizations is linked to regressive notions of individualism, an exalted work ethic ("no pain, no gain"), and credence in the significatory power of metaphor. Bodybuilding's appeal lies in its extension of the possibility of becoming metaphor—of literally controlling what one stands for. And this individual metaphor enables bodybuilding to rebind masculinity to metaphors of strength and power.

Bodybuilding's mechanics provide an illusion of power where there is none, or not as much as there might seem to be. Its metaphorical valence exists in its image of power rather than in substance or real strength. As Sam Fussell discloses in *Confessions of an Unlikely Bodybuilder,* bodybuilders focus on appearance instead of strength and are, in fact, not nearly as strong pound for pound as power lifters or other athletes. Bodybuilding's fixation on the appearance of power is perhaps most tellingly reflected in Schwarzenegger's own 1970s' ruminations; "I was always dreaming about very powerful people. Dictators and things like that. I was always impressed by people who could be remembered for hundreds of years. Even like Jesus, being remembered for thousands of years.[11] Or, "I wish I could experience the feeling President Kennedy had speaking to 50,000 people at one time and having them cheer and scream and be in agreement with whatever he said" (Butler 41). And perhaps most symptomatically, "My relationship to power and authority is that I'm all for it. People need somebody to watch over them and tell them what to do. Ninety-five percent of the people in the world need to be told what to do and how to behave" (Butler 34).

Expressing symptoms of mechanical reproduction's potential fascism, bodybuilding, too, preserves property relations and tradition. Concentrated in the physical persona of someone who performs self-aggrandizing work, bodybuilding's symbology is socially useful only as a sign of individual potential within the field of existing economic and social relations. For this reason, bodybuilding has had great appeal to some who desire class mobility, since it promises social advancement and wealth through the rigid individual adherence to a completely conservative, self-focused, Horatio Alger narrative of industry linked to consumer culture's fixation on image. Ultimately preservational and hugely consumerist, bodybuilding's own economy is conservative, but its focus on image makes it a ready-made cog in commodity culture. Not only do we purchase the body's image, the built body is the signifier of immense consumption in the form of food, time, and self-indulgence.[12] The hyperbolic body, thus, becomes the perfect vehicle through which patriarchal capitalist order might resymbolize the literally masculine into a more metaphorical control. This resignification occurs not in the more superficial and somewhat questionable domain of preening, posturing bodybuilding competitions, but in narratives about salvaging order.

Film narratives featuring muscular protagonists began to appear in their grand media-hyped scale in the later seventies, not only after the Viet Nam War, but also after the early seventies period of social rebellion, the resignation of a President, and the 1973 Supreme Court decision in *Roe v. Wade,* all of which signify some loss of a metaphorically paternal control. The 1976 *Rocky* combines a boxing narrative with a class war dramatized as an individual battle for achievement against the corrupt interests of organized crime and corporate media. Thinly masked as a boxer, Stallone is a bodybuilder (and the film is about building his body to inspiring music) whose personal battle gains greater metaphorical significance with its reverberations of social struggle; the boxing ring becomes the location of a contest between Rocky's hard work and truth and his African-American opponent's enmeshment in powers of manipulative simulation. The virtues of the work ethic become the territory of he who trains against the greatest odds even though Rocky doesn't win the fight. His blue-collar triumph is not really the glorification of working-class virtue though, but a celebration of the builder for the sake of his building, congratulations for the physique labor on which the film excessively focuses. *Rocky* is a kudo for the primitive man, endowed only with a natural manliness, who triumphs in spirit over all the commercial perversions—everything from his grasping future brother-in-law Pauly to the sports industry—that have divorced masculinity from its real natural power.

While the coalition of spectacular muscularity and superheroics in the persona of the cartoonlike protagonist continues the convention of the comic-book morality play (a larger-than-life "remade" character battles and triumphs over forces of evil and corruption), a character like Stallone's *Rambo* also cleverly reappropriates all challenges to conservative patriarchal centrality. Douglas Kellner observes how Rambo is able to transform countercultural images into their opposite; physical transformation becomes cultural transformation.[13] In the context of the much more specific, feminized chaos seemingly created by the confused (and confusing) amalgamation of a failure in leadership, a lost war, a loss of prestige, and feminism (including continued pressures and advances in the realm of reproductive technologies and rights), muscular superheroes like Rocky and Rambo operate as delusively simple appeals to patriarchal tradition as Susan Jeffords points out in *Hard Bodies*. They battle complex, feminized, corrupt, unnatural antagonists with old-fashioned manly attributes of strength and wiliness; their purity of spirit wins out over their compromised nemeses, who have always settled for less while trying to get more. But since some of the superheroes' enemies are also such patriarchal delegates as the police, capitalist business, and the military, Stallone's bulgingly virtuous heroes' motives and positions are muddier and less direct as they battle a decadent patriarchy infected by creeping consumerism, effeminized by its acquiescence to machine convenience, and weakened by a loss of tradition.

Even as it fights a contaminated patriarchy, the muscular form is never divorced from the operation of gender and control ideologies, but rather, hypermuscularity's ideological determination and functions are multiplied as the muscle man is gradually displaced from the gym to the realm of social disease. This displacement is really more of an amplification that follows and enlarges the mechanisms that already govern the bodybuilder's social valence and ideological operation. The fact that bodybuilding requires control and discipline, results in great strength, hyperbolizes a phallic muscularity, and is made public through ritualized display are the same qualities that enable the muscled figure to occupy the position of narrative protagonist, who through control and discipline acquires and wields great strength in spectacular situations that reprove the worth of America, manhood, humanity (as opposed to technology), and, in a more complicated operation, paternity and legitimacy. These last categories reveal the absolute complexity and degree of mediation attending the image of the muscled body.

66

ARNOLD ENTRAT

Arnold Schwarzenegger was a central figure in the sport of bodybuilding when it began to garner mainstream attention during the 1970s. Schwarzenegger's apparent control of the sport (he was Mr. Olympia seven times, Mr. Universe five times, and Mr. Europe) and fledgling strongman film career made it seem that the self-confident, personable Arnold was, in fact, responsible for bodybuilding's rise in popularity and visibility.[14] Already, however, Schwarzenegger was performing his function as the synechdochical amalgamation of masculinity and muscularity that represented and linked bodybuilding to the virtues of control, masculinity, strength, and patriotism. What made this combination work and what enabled his self-representation to avoid the obnoxious simplicity of a one-on-one equation between masculine and muscular was Schwarzenegger's self-conscious, ironic acknowledgment of precisely the mechanisms at play in his media image. Split off from the equally visible Lou Ferrigno who took on the large beast aspect of hulking masculinity, Schwarzenegger personified a sport cleverly aware of its own narcissism, myths of compensatory masculinity, and extremism.[15] For example, in 1977's *Pumping Iron*, the celebratory pseudo-documentary showcase of Arnold's

seemingly trouble-free domination of bodybuilding, Schwarzenegger grin-
ningly boasts that his body is "perfect"—perfectly proportioned, perfectly big.
He humorously equates pumping iron and displaying muscle to sexual
orgasm, quipping that bodybuilding is great because he gets to "come all the
time." And in a later interview, he jokingly dispels myths of bodybuilders'
penile insufficiency by claiming that he had to gain muscle in order to make
his physique match the size of his endowment.[16]

In the seventies, Arnold's comic cleansing of the muscle-man image served
to bolster the position of the bodybuilder, shifting it from what was seen as
the aberrant world of suspected phallic compensation and narcissistic homosexuality to the respectable world of sport and personal achievement.[17] In film
narrative, the positive coalition of muscles, phallic presence, and sexual prowess
articulated by Schwarzenegger aligned with comic superhero virtues of
strength and dedication on a more personal plane than Stallone's (albeit simplistic) social context. Schwarzenegger's earlier films—*Hercules Goes to New
York* (1970), *Stay Hungry* (1976), *Pumping Iron*, and *Conan the Barbarian*
(1982)—narratively confirm the healthy image of the muscular superhero
where Arnold plays a role—Hercules or Conan—defined by a kind of naive
muscular chivalry, or where Arnold plays himself—the winning athlete in a
competition narrative. And where, as George Butler proclaims, Arnold, like the
character Santo in *Stay Hungry*, "crossed social lines and did everything well,
including fiddling in a country band. Upon getting to know Arnold, we were
struck by the curious similarities between him and the fictional character he
was to play in the movie. It was almost as if Charles Gaines had created an
Arnold in fiction before we met him in fact" (55).

Schwarzenegger's self-conscious awareness of bodybuilding's associations,
however, complicates its representation and his representation of it in a basic
version of the mechanism by which built bodies come to stand as champions
of paternity and patriarchy and as enemies of mechanical reproduction. The
complexity of the built body's intervention into mechanical reproduction's
threat is most symptomatically revealed when the body becomes art. In 1976,
Arnold participated in a "live bodybuilding exhibition at the Whitney
Museum" (Butler 39). Seeing his body as a piece of sculpture, Arnold transformed hyperbolic masculinity's metaphorical strength into an art that could be
anything but mechanically reproduced. Titled "Articulate Muscle—The Body
as Art," the Whitney's performance drew 3,000 people, the "largest single event
in the history of the museum" (Butler 76). The show's popularity, however, may
say more about Benjamin's concern about self-involved art than it provides any
resounding response to mechanical reproduction. Instead of seeing the "art"
body as a facet of the traditional relationship between artist and work, the
Whitney exhibit's appeal was focused on the Arnold persona—on precisely the
commodity metaphor/metonymy that compensates for the loss of tradition.

67

"Souped up bodies may propel us into a future new golden age with sins so original they aren't even a gleam in their father's eyes," commented art critic Colin Eisler (Butler 79). Eisler is probably correct in one point: built bodies' functions are no gleam in the paternal peepers. Rather muscle's "original sin" is to regenerate an overly masculinized posthumous son.

Schwarzenegger's ironic self-consciousness situates a masculine and loudly proclaimed heterosexual persona in apparent control of his own representation, not only in terms of the body image he produces and projects, but also in his disparaging consciousness of the very myths of compensation that might otherwise undermine his image. Masculinity and brawn ally here not because of anatomy, though the body is the visible site of their joinder, but in Arnold's masterful performance and control of a version of masculinity he carefully restructures into a voraciously heterosexual, well-endowed, man-among-men category. The "masculine" that Arnold constructs is a masculine posed both as nature's fulfillment—the bringing to perfection of male anatomical potential—and as man's power over nature manifested through his ability to wrench the show of strength from a recalcitrant physique. This image of the masculine seems almost simplistically biological, but it is a biology employed to demonstrate the bodybuilder's ability to amplify and control nature.

The engagement of muscularity and masculinity, though carefully linked by Arnold's manipulation of personae, is also coupled through the phallic term represented by the muscled body's hard hyperbole. Arnold's joke about correcting proportion plays with the phallic politics displayed in the body's penile echo. The muscular swelling of the bodybuilder's physique reiterates the image of a potent, swelling phallic "muscle," connecting the culturally masculine, the biological male, and physical power. This spectacular connection certifies the much less certain association between masculinity and phallus on the one hand, and the paternal metaphor and the phallus, on the other. While the masculine is presumably grounded in and founded upon penile presence, it is, of course, a performance that only refers to the penis, understood often as compensating for some missing penile dimension, and designed around imagined penile attributes of hardness, forcefulness, domination, productivity.[18] The built body also negotiates the difference between the phallus and the paternal metaphor, a difference between a (or The) symbolic object of desire and the Law-of-the-Name-of-the-Father that governs symbolic relations. This is the difference between an imagined object that moves metonymically through a chain of desire and the metaphorical rule that organizes that chain in the first place.

Both metonymy and metaphor, the built body stands visibly for that which lays veiled but suggested by the single item of clothing bodybuilders wear to perform. In a representational loop the body and the imagined phallus figure one another's power through the image of big muscles. This relation of amplification, of harmonic proportion between the penis, the body, and the imaginary phallus, enacts an economy of being *and* having the phallus, where the body represents a spectacular phallus, transferring by association the built body's hard virtue to the hidden penis. This confusion between penis and phallus, between physical organ (or its embodiment) and the Symbolic signifier of desire (of what one cannot have), is profitably sustained in the bodybuilder's metaphorical embodiment of an appearance of power, an appearance of penile sufficiency, *and* in being the literal object of desire in an increasingly literalized field of symbolic relations.

In his insightful analysis of Arnold's physical/narrative trajectory, Jonathan Goldberg sees the muscle pump (the working of a muscle to draw blood to a muscle site and expand its size) as locating "an inadequacy within the Symbolic, a lack at the very site of the realization of the equation of penis and phallus, for, as excessive coming, the pump disconnects phallus and penis" (176). Since penis and phallus are not equated, but rather *confused* through the built body's hyperbolic self-reference, the issue is never really one of the Symbolic, but rather of an oscillation among having a penis, being a phallus, and being *and* having an object of desire in the Imaginary. This economy belongs to the Imaginary, not as a flexible system of compensations for the imagined insufficiencies of a real penis, but as an adjustable term in a cleverly restructured chain of phallic objects designed so that the bodybuilder is always the object of desire on some level. The built body, thus, appears to overcome desire itself by posing as the acquisition of that phallus which can never be had but only desired.

To begin any connection to what even the phallus cannot compensate for, the built body must be narrativized. Self-creation is no substitute for procreation. The phallus, while a part of the Symbolic, is not the Law-of-the-Name-of-the-Father. The Law, the foundation of a signifying chain, is metaphor; the phallus, enticing the chain in the realm of desire, is metonymy.[19] This is the relation between the phallus and the paternal metaphor: while the signification of the phallus might be evoked by the paternal metaphor, the phallus is neither the Name-of-the-Father nor the grounding metaphor of the system. Even so, "the main signifier to be substituted [for the Name of the Father] is the phallus, which represents something missing, the signification of the phallus, such that, as Lacan says, for the subject's imaginary, is evoked by the paternal metaphor."[20] "The phallic signifier," according to Ragland-Sullivan, "links the Imaginary to the Symbolic via intentionality: an unconscious stance toward Desire, taken in the Name-of-the-Father" (155). As she further elaborates

> Lacan suggested early on that the historical privilege given to the phallus lay mainly in its double nature as penian part-object and as differential trait in the father's ushering in of the post-mirror stage. The separation trauma is linked to the Name-of-the-Father at an abstract level, and the

> meaning evoked in the Imaginary becomes the paternal metaphor. The
> phallic signifier is therefore inscribed at the origin of the unconscious
> meaning system where Law, Desire, language, separation, and gender
> merge in a drama subsequently repressed (287).

The phallus, itself a signifier, becomes the first in a series of substitutes for the
law according to the Law.

The difference, then, between the phallus and the Name-of-the-Father has
to do with the difference (and connection) between an intricated
Imaginary/Symbolic, between a phallic signifier that erroneously seems to have
a referent and a metaphorical function that mediates the contradiction between
being and having the mother (and hence between being the object of the
mother's desire and having the object of the mother's desire). "The phallus
introduces the alienating effect of difference into the pleasurable and natural
mother-infant dad, and this Oedipalizing, dividing effect gradually becomes
substantivized around the name-of-the-father" (Ragland-Sullivan 290). The
phallus, thus, refers not to the Name-of-the-Father, or to the actual prohibition
that that Name (*nom* or *non*) represents, but to the principle of differentiation
the name inaugurates, as difference simultaneously presents the illusion of a
possible wholeness. The phallus stands as the wholeness that is desired but (and
because) no longer possible.

In presenting the appearance of being and having the phallus—what
Goldberg calls a "totality"—bodybuilders persist on an Imaginary slope in relation to the Law. By narratively conflating the phallus with an imaginary law
(rather than the symbolic Law) such as Right, Justice, and the American Way,
heroic narratives starring bodybuilders appear to seal an identity between phallus and Law. And while Goldberg argues that the pump might expose the
"lack" in that suture, the constant attempt to constitute a connection between
phallus and paternal metaphor in the cultural imaginary also bespeaks a lack in
the Symbolic itself, a lack to be propped up by a hyperbolized phallus/father.

Thus, being and having the phallus, which seems like overkill to cultural
sensibilities trained in psychoanalytical notions of overcompensation, allows
the illusion of a resymbolization that works through the self-cycling self-ref-
erentiality of the builder's body as it is narrativized as a cultural savior.
Appearing to provide a signifier in a patriarchal context, the body references
itself, small to large, penis to phallus, phallus to penis. Situated in narratives
about the salvation of order, this self-referential phallus appears to moor failing law on the level of the imaginary, which, in turn, seems bound up with an
always and ever whole Symbolic. The bodybuilder thus seems like a *return* to
a Law that never ceased to operate; hence, the feeling of both anachronism and
nostalgia around bodybuilder narratives. When the built body becomes a player in more overtly reproductive narratives, it becomes the metonymical stand-

in for the fading paternal metaphor, an operation made easy by the phallus's already metonymical part in the drama of desire.

Arnold's overt recognition of the body's compensatory mechanisms, however, disenables their operation on a literal level, displacing penile compensation to a more metaphorical social locus and paving the way for a "both/and" phallic economy that, crucially, permits pleasure in looking at the muscled male. But this recognition of compensation also aligns the phallus with the paternal by linking a consciousness of the body's metaphor with both potency and a return to tradition. In this way, Arnold's built body conjoins metaphor and metonymy, penis and phallus, phallus and the Law-of-the-Name-of-the-Father in a single, hyperbolically compensatory figure that functions not only because it is muscular, but also because Arnold knows muscle's meaning. This is like the James Bond phenomenon; while James Bond's popularity is rightly linked to cold war fears, Bond's movie success and longevity, with its compensatory assertion of power in accord with Law, is made as much through Bond's physical prowess or intelligence, as through his consciousness of the function of the figure he cuts.[21] While he holds it "up" for Britain, he telegraphs exactly what is at stake in his various run-ins with countercultural megalomaniacs, whose sins, like Frankenstein's, have to do with taking the Law (in this case the prerogatives of hugely paternalistic sovereign nations) into their own hands.

The psychoanalytical logic of the phallic superhero is close to the terms in which this cultural drama is taking place. Bodybuilders are phallic; Daddy is at issue (and at a loss). In a sense, the 1980s and 1990s witness the literalization of psychoanalysis itself as the very (sometimes disputed) terms of its analysis become the literal players in an anxious cure. The seemingly indisputable phallic spectacle of the built body also (in the same psychoanalytical logic) belongs to the logic of the fetish, as the phallus itself can never escape the specter of castration. While the threat of castration is not coterminous with a loss of the symbolic or a literalization of metaphor, it easily becomes the threatening term in the literalized dramas of potency that characterize the failures and recuperations of masculinity in the 1970s and 1980s. If the anxiety is paternal, if the form it takes phallic and the field it occupies is the visual, then it would be more than logical for initial responses to these threats to be the disavowal related to the fetish. And what more perfectly symptomatic fetish than the built body's displacement of the whole operation of disavowal from its feminine ground to a reputedly masculine totality?

WHAT YOU SEE...

On one level, the bodybuilder clearly builds for display, a puffing exhibitionism gratifying to both muscle man and audience, a muscular fetish in his spectacle of fullness that comforts the eye (and maybe the psyche). But the muscle man and his self-consciousness of simulated wholeness are not quite the fetish Freud had in mind. The fetish, as Freud formulated it, is a visual defense mechanism against a fear of castration: "The fetish is a substitute for the woman's (the mother's) penis that the little boy once believed in and—for reasons familiar to us—does not want to give up."[22] Its duplicity—that the presence of the fetish signals both absence of phallus and the clever disavowal of that absence in the presence of a visual substitute—is linked to gender, and specifically, to anatomical sexual difference. Freud's fetish consists of only one layer, the image of a substitute phallus occulting the female's phallic deprivation, a phallic figure on a feminine ground. Defensive and reassuring, the fetish is a way of controlling difference and contradiction by asserting the visual and unifying primacy of the male anatomy.

The bodybuilder's spectacular, hyperbolic layering of muscle and phallus creates two fetish layers instead of Freud's one. The bodybuilder reveals the outline of a penis on a body that looks like a phallus. The phallus on the phallic body stands in for and disavows multiple fears of castration—castration on the literal level (no penis), castration in the Imaginary (being less than whole), castration in the symbolic (powerlessness, lawlessness). Magnifying and proliferating the illusion of phallic presence appears to guarantee that the phallus will always be there, has been there all along, is strong, hard, and in control—and, if threatened by the Law of prohibition and castration, always has a spare phallus to stand in. The multilayered fetish of the built body, thus, provides the illusion of immunity to the Law by appearing to embody law's imaginary fullness, which in the case of superhero narratives most often takes the form of the superhero's insusceptibility to death.

The built body is the compensatory incorporation of both masculine and feminine as phallus on phallus in an image of wholeness that defies difference while it personifies its very phallic term. Both figure and ground, the body's hyperphallic comfort fills in as the potent hero. Reinforcing film narrative with an overly compensatory fetish figure moves these defensive processes into a visual field already made redundant by its narrative context. The story of a strong figure overcoming the forces of disorder in a fantasy world is reduplicated in the built body's arrangement of hyperbolic strength on a masculine torso. As imagistic overcompensation in an already overcompensatory narrative, the built body points to the gap it tries to fill—it is fetish with a vengeance.

The built body allays anxiety *because* it refers to its filling of the gaps it fills while it is filling them. Rambo doesn't just "kick ass," he announces that he is kicking ass; Schwarzenegger's various epic personae—Conan, the Commando—tend to be deliberately strong and proactive instead of reactive. The built body's specter of totality works because it combines an image of wholeness with a consciousness of the process by which that wholeness victoriously supplants lack. The deliberately pumped body combined with narratives self-conscious of their disavowal function (this includes both the narrative of bodybuilding and the heroic narratives that deploy pumped protagonists) simultaneously provide a narrative of the law revived *and* the narrative of the agent who knowingly revives it. This agent becomes the Law's savior as well as the hero of culture; he is the order that salvages order.

The fetishlike qualities of the built body, thus, work as a literal fetish or a doubled or layered fetish, while also functioning as a fetish of the fetish. If the fetish represents a formula of "I know, but all the same . . .", then the fetish of the fetish would be "I know I know, but all the same . . ." By referring to its own fetish operation, the built body embodies a phallicized law (the phallus as the end of desire) by impersonating the phallus that saves patriarchy. But the built body's culturally compensatory politic also employs the fetishized body as a lure away from the knowing disavowal it enacts. While we might know we "know but all the same," the body's spectacle is freed to perform the fetishistic disavowal all over again. Where, however, a consciousness of the fetish in its physical manifestation would seem to disenable disavowal (can knowing disavowal permit continued disavowal?), consciousness of the fetish actually permits such disavowal to work even more completely in the place from which the built body is consciously perceived as a fetish. Seeing the bodybuilder as fetish permits a fetishization of our own knowledge of the fetish; a clever discernment of fetish in the bodybuilder's hyperbole disavows the discerning viewer's lack, as fetish compensation for that lack is manifested in the register of knowledge instead of phallic objects.[23] This means that bodybuilder narratives (of both kinds) are multilayered fetish operations whose stake is both a disavowal of castration and a disavowal of the failure of the Law as that which organizes phallic dispensation in the first place. The fetish replaces the Law in appearing to reorganize the phallus, but overdoes it by multiplying the phallus and the fetish all over the place.

The bodybuilder serves nicely as the physical and imagistic correlate to cultural defenses against sexual difference that also have taken the form of a fetishization of the fetish. For example, in the 1970s and 1980s, film theorists hypothesized a metaphorical fetish operation that defends against and recuperates sexual difference and functions as a control mechanism in cinematic representation. Laura Mulvey's famous understanding of the female figure as fetish in narrative film sees scopophilia as one of the mechanisms by which male castration anxiety, catalyzed by images of the female figure, is contained by building "up the physical beauty of the object, transforming it into something satisfying in itself."[24] This female fetish is "intrusive," playing against and disrupting the "unity of the diegesis," but at the same time healing that disruption by covering over the breach introduced by the advent of the female figure (18). Beauty building is an imaginary operation conducted on the female image instead of the male, aided by narrative, but presenting both the

73

threat of castration and its assuagement in the woman *CUM* phallus. In Mulvey's terms, the male bodybuilder would doubly allay castration anxiety by "transforming" a spectacular male body (presumably not threatening in the first place) "into something satisfying in itself" that plays with instead of against the "unity of diegesis."

Christian Metz locates a fetish matrix in the belief structure of cinema as a whole, interpreting viewers' delight in the "equipment of the cinema" as their defensive disavowal of cinema's essential "absence" of reality (74). Metz's view of the fetish privileges control anxiety over castration trauma: an admiration of cinema's controlling techniques disavows the absence behind cinema's presence—the fact that the film image stands in for and veils the absence of reality. This is not unlike the way superheroes' consciousness of their superheroic effect actually constitutes a large part of superhero narratives' control compensation. In addition to image and narrative, knowledge constitutes the defense, one enabled by the spectacle of equipment (Arnold's big muscles and weight equipment, Bond's gadgetry) augmenting the spectacle of the body. This redoubling (body, equipment, consciousness) actually literalizes the layered fetish, the fetish (tool, machine) of the fetish (phallic object) becomes a disavowal of a lack of Law (patriarchal order) instead of a lack of phallus (castration).

While feminist film theorists such as Mulvey analyze and critique cinema's reiteration of phallic politics, other film theorists see the fetish as a desexualized aspect of the cinema machine. The disparity in these critical perspectives suggests that sexual difference is still pivotal both to the operation of the fetish and to understanding the extent to which phallic presence (or absence) is bound up with notions of control (itself a synecdoche for law). Rose criticizes Metz and Jean-Louis Comolli for displacing fetishism from the realm of sexual difference to the arena of cinematic plenitude. She sees this displacement as an intellectualized disavowal of sexual difference. Kaja Silverman reads male psychoanalytic film theory as a field preoccupied with castration, lack, and fetishism, where theory itself, as a mode of control, becomes as much a fetish operation as the filmic pyrotechnics proposed to control cinematic lack.[25]

Some critics' tendency to desexualize and universalize castration anxiety into a larger question of representation enacts a covert displacement of the fetish from the body and image of the woman to the apparently neutral field of technology. Fetishizing apparatus, however, curiously fetishizes what might be seen as a mechanical threat to human order. While the fetish is typically a substitute for the threatened object, here the threat itself becomes the fetish. Fetishizing the threat is a double disavowal that works like the fetishized fetish. Since the Law that demands castration is human and linked to a familial reproductive nexus, this human law is disavowed by the intercalation of the mechanical and its self-productive order. The mechanical functions as a fetish that disavows castration in the human order. At the same time, since the threat to human Law is the metonymy of the mechanical, making the mechanical the fetish transforms its metonymical threat into phallic metaphor. By situating the mechanical as the object of desire subject to human order and control, the mechanical fetish can disavow the threat posed by the mechanical in the first place. The mechanized phallus/metaphorized machine's self-productivity is reflected in the proliferations of layered phalluses. Hence, Bond's gadgetry and Arnold's big guns only increase their figural potency. Schwarzenegger's *Terminator* appearances play on this version of the mechanical fetish in combination with the built body in a superheroic paternal narrative.

In the case of film theory, ignoring sexual difference (and its concomitant castration anxieties) in favor of overdeveloped equipment is not only a grand species of disavowal, as Rose observes, it is also a fail-safe mechanism that defends against the idea of castration, by layering fetish upon a masculinized ground, in a drama of spectacular reassurance that disavows disavowal as well as contradiction and ambivalence. The emphasis on control that accompanies this gender displacement suggests that layering the veiled and fetishized penis onto a metaphorically and metonymically phallacized physique is an operation orchestrated to control control—that is, to control the disposition of knowledge (theory), the phallus (power, fulfilled desire), and the very ground (no difference, masculine) through which these play. Some theorists' moves of grand displacement foster the illusion that problems of sexual difference are no longer relevant or even operative. Not only does this overcompensation avert even the emergence of castration anxiety, it permits its relief without any recognition of the fear. And while we might understand its hyperbole as a signal of the huge anxiety it tries to disavow, self-consciousness tends to parodize such anxiety, appealing again to a superior control. Schwarzenegger's *Last Action Hero* (1993) perhaps does this for all of his films, and not too successfully, since its stake in parody is always clearly elsewhere—in Schwarzenegger's other films, for example, or in the largely compensatory functions of action films themselves.

Through a mechanism similar to that performed by some male film theorists, the image of the male superhero bodybuilder manages both to subsume and displace any "feminine" figuration that might be a source of anxiety. But the feminine that may be a source of castration anxiety is also a necessary component of the prohibitive paternal Law. Introducing the mechanical as a fetish displaces the feminine and replaces it with that which actually directly threatens the Law-of-the-Father. But in replacing the feminine with the mechanical, the masculine also subsumes the feminine to become the total human in relation to the now-mechanical Other. Arnold becomes a mother. In this way, the mechanical actually performs its threat to the Law by negating human sexual difference, and at the same time, appears to uphold the law in its assumption of the binary difference of Otherness. In other words, the

75

advent of the machine fetish (predictable in mechanical reproduction's twentieth century trajectory) redistributes difference from intra-human sexual difference to a human/extra-human difference in ontology.

Disavowing sexual difference, the fetishized mechanical enables a "pure" field of masculine signifiers around the renegotiation of the paternal metaphor, a homogenous field that looks much like the homogenous field of the male builder's body. This technology—Metz's "equipment" (74)—cannot help but slide into the realm of the generic masculine, propelled not only by cultural stereotypes, but also by the way theorists regard the apparatus as an illusory locus of control, as a phallic substitute.

While this associational regendering is circular and illogical, the subtle displacement of the fetish from the female image and from the realm of sexual difference into a wholly "neuter" (masculine) field effects a change in the function of the fetish itself. For if, as Teresa de Lauretis points out, "'woman' is constituted as the ground of representation and its stability," what happens when that ground—the ground of representation, the ground of the fetish—becomes wholly masculine? Does it remain masculine or is its relative position governed by a heterosexual logic that still requires the feminization of the ground?[26]

Despite the many phalluses and machines and equipment, the feminine never quite disappears. If the bodybuilder's body is itself a fetish—is something to be looked at that assuages anxiety and provides the illusion of control, it is analogous to the female figure to which Mulvey alludes. The bodybuilder's made-for-spectacle appearance manifests the stereotypically "feminine" attributes of a heterosexual logic: it is excessive and narcissistic, and it poses for men. And if the bodybuilder's muscles, like the female figure, also provide a secondary ground for the location of another, more truly Freudian, fetish object in the phallic fingers of muscle, isn't the bodybuilder's body feminized in relation to the tiny, mid-body too-literal bulge at the fetishized center of display? In other words, doesn't the muscled body become feminized in relation to the hidden phallus it mimics? I would suggest that it does, but this hint of the feminine is necessary both to the larger narrative of patriarchal salvation and to the fetishized disavowal of castration. Even in a machine/human dialectic, a feminine spark is necessary to fuel the fetish mechanism. Carefully controlled and recuperated, the feminine provides a crucial element of the bodybuilder's ideological operation. Analogous to the hero's grinning acknowledgment of anxiety, the feminine supplies visual evidence of a threat already subsumed, a meaningful field for phallic action in a heterosexual logic (a heterosexual field that is also a necessary contrast to the bodybuilder's play of phallic homo-eroticism). Through an appropriation of the feminine, the Tiresian bodybuilder manages an image of totality: male, female, hetero, homo, man, machine—and, lately, father, mother.

Shifts in the representational role of the bodybuilder reveal some of the cultural gender politics that play through and are contained by the bodybuilder image. Before the 1970s, the muscle man image was aimed at men who believed themselves somehow inadequately masculine (in binary logic, feminized); it overtly appealed to weak, thin, "sissy" types through the bourgeois narcissism of self-improvement narratives. Because of links to narcissism, display, pornography, homoeroticism, and homosociality, bodybuilding skated on the edge of stereotypical femininity. But at the same time that the bodybuilder became a narrative protagonist, female bodybuilders entered the scene (or were actually allowed to be seen in the scene), superficially heterosexualizing the sport and serving as the locus for displaced gender anxieties. As Klein points out, when bodybuilding became more mainstream, images of bodybuilders were carefully constructed to include heterosexual bodybuilding couples; featured males were often paired with females to (re)assure us of the male builder's masculinity, but also to create the image of a singles' scene and/or "family" atmosphere.[27] Bodybuilding's shame was no longer the suspected femininity of posing muscle-bound studs, but, rather, the potentially hideous masculinity of female builders. Through the agency of the female bodies that intervene, muscularity is defined as completely masculine, and the long-raging arguments over the proper form of muscle women center entirely on the conflict between masculine muscle and ideologies of femininity.[28]

The decoy of the female bodybuilder appears to rid the male bodybuilder of gender impurities, but it actually enables the male image to subsume and contain femininity as part of a masculine performance. The presence of the less muscular woman recuperates spectacular narcissism as a masculine prerogative. At the same time, women builders distance males from a muscularity that has become a separable feature wielded by both men and women. This distance between control and muscle in turn sanitizes the pleasurable look at the male by making muscle display objective and "homosocial" (like admiring corvettes) rather than overtly homosexual.[29] Protected from conspicuous homoerotics (instead of consumption) and appropriating aspects of the traditionally feminine, the male bodybuilder is designed to be looked at, his very appearance catalyzing a politic of avowal and control analogous to Metz's conception of the fetishized cinematic apparatus. While the bodybuilder's fetished fetish politic seems to be totally masculine, the bodybuilder also and *at the same time* incorporates the feminine as a way of embodying *all* in a digestible socially symbolized masculine form. The bodybuilder's very negotiation of the seeming contradictions between feminization and masculine totality enables the built body to function as the delusion of wholeness and completeness and as the model for how the feminine can be usefully appropriated.

Layering masculine on masculine, fetish on fetish, the built body is not only the disavowed, anxious fetish of its residual feminized ground, but also the highly defended, avowed, triumphant imaginary phallus itself upon a masculine ground. The heterologic of sexual difference is transformed into the alternative terms of phallus/penis, man/machine; the body's masculinity also subsumes femininity in an act of imagistic appropriation and muscular redefinition. In its illusion of self-completion, of desire fulfilled, the bodybuilder's body becomes both fetish and ground, the masculinized, phallic ground that appears to make the fetish itself, and its attendant anxieties, finally unnecessary by seeming to incorporate the two. The bodybuilder plays out the disavowal game on masculine turf, where what one looks for is behind the magic door—a certain drama that cannot disappoint because of the perpetual metonymical loop that welds body to phallus, phallus to masculinity, masculinity to control, control to the presence of the phallus, feeding the eye through a series of homeomorphic displacements. The fascination of the image lies in the loop's perpetual tracing of the arc of phallic fulfillment, the vision of something there, making the fetish seem to disappear in circuits of oscillating fulfillment as the connection between body and phallus is continually made and unmade. There is the appearance of no disavowal here because there is the appearance of no absence, just a continuous anticipation of presence. All is as it should be, all is all, the phallus is on the phallus in a regressive, presexual hallucination of difference that licenses the spectacle of masculine homologic as a locus of power.

The bodybuilder is to be looked at, admired, loved *because* he is in control; his control is manifested in the gorgeous pyrotechnics of the body made phallus even while it retains a soupçon of femininity. Because his spectacular body, while phallic, never makes the mistake of showing its phallus (except in Schwarzenegger's one indiscrete moment in *Spy* or Serge Oliva's porn career), the phallus contained on the body shines out in its magnified muscular glory. Like the cinematic apparatus, however, the bodybuilder really lacks the substance (phallus) it appears to have; more show than strong, the bodybuilder is what Clive Rives calls, "a condom filled with walnuts."[30] The bodybuilder permits the fetishist's dream: a gaze on the veiled phallus through the metonymy of the body, a phallus amplified to the height of desire, a corporeal phallus whose relation to the penis has been stabilized, balanced, and totalized, and whose body is the automatic veil of what also appears to be in plain sight. The built body is a literalized metaphor that remetaphorizes the literal. Literalizing the phallus by corporealizing it, the built body becomes a metaphor of the penis.

The bodybuilder's spectacle enacts a tautological illusion of plentitude, completion, and seamless control that effaces the very gap by which control and its premises are challenged. The bodybuilder's image, like the cinematic apparatus, is an illusion machine bent on destroying the traces of its illusion making while it emphasizes evidence of its effort to create what we see.

Caught in the act, the bodybuilder becomes the ultimate imaginary assurance for an anxiety that has been made to disappear while we watch. But what is the cultural use of this over compensatory, fetishized fetish in an era of disappearing Law? Why this shift to the body from Pop art's ploy of the name?

The Arnoldator

When this redoubled, overcompensatory muscle man becomes the already overinvested protagonist of narrative film, his spectacle plays a very different role than the fetishized female figures about whom Mulvey theorizes. In their narrative and spectacular strength, bodybuilder protagonists are apparently the opposite of the female fetishes presumably necessary to cover narrative gaps and challenges to masculine hegemony. Instead, bodybuilders proliferate the sites of narrative mastery—in the body, in the narrative, and in a consciousness of the narrative—so that narrative tension itself should by rights disappear and the protagonist's victory become a fulfillment of the already fulfilled. But the muscle man's fail-safe fetish mechanism merely displaces tension from the superficial "might is right" clashes of the story to the narrative's margins—to the hidden anxieties that motivate the deployment of a muscle-bound hero in the first place. In the Newtonian universe of cultural anxiety, this giant, armored, winning, phallic thing must assuage some even greater, more heinous, hidden terror than mere castration anxiety. The clue to what this is lies in 1970s and 1980s muscle man superhero narratives' obsessive repetition of an anxiety about patriotism, patriarchy, and paternity.

79

Superhero narratives have persisted in comic-book form (the form that corporealized superheroes with a muscularity that approaches that of modern bodybuilders) since 1938; their prewar appearance suggests that their initial function was to reinforce an image of American national masculinity and potency against the forces of "evil" (i.e., Hitler and the Japanese). Many of these superhero protagonists were either extrahuman (i.e., The Human Torch [a synthetic being], The Flash, Captain America [a presteroid steroid hero], Plastic Man [a toxic-waste mutant]), resurrected (The Spectre), or extraterrestrial (Superman). Batman, the second superhero to appear, was a human with the extraordinary motivation of vengeance for the needless death of his parents.[31]

The 1950s advent of the televised *Superman* combined muscle with righteousness in defense of "Truth, Justice, and the American Way." More costumed than muscular (though George Reeves was a 1950s version of a muscle man), the television Superman's hyperbole consisted of the extraterrestrial powers necessary to correct the impingements of megalomaniac villains. While the television Superman was appropriately serious in his redundant rectitude (the problem of being the son of two fathers), the more campy 1960s *Batman* series contributed both parodic consciousness and excessive gadgetry to a completely human, if excessively wealthy, protagonist. Like the Pop art that it employed and copied, *Batman*'s parody tracked the excesses of consumer culture, reappropriating them to its own self-conscious style. Both Superman and Batman's hyperbole necessitated the duplicitous Clarke Kent and Bruce Wayne. What their secret roles suggested was the hidden power of normal men, or the normalcy of extraordinary men. In either case, their assumption of a costumed superheroic persona is the sartorial precurser to the layering bodybuilding enacts.

As superheroes became progressively more neurotic in the 1960s and 1970s (Superman goes crazy, for example), their hyperbolic invincibility was gradually displaced onto more "realistic" protagonists in more realistic narratives.[32] The 1970s and 1980s literalization of the superhero cartoon relocated hyperbole in the physical body and persona of the protagonist. No longer split or even really neurotic (or human), the protagonist becomes larger and more humanly powerful as bodybuilding itself becomes more effective and as the sight of built bodies becomes more acceptable and necessary. While Superman and Batman concentrated on justice in a period of still-reigning (if waning) paternal metaphor, realist superhero protagonists suddenly must defend nations instead of wronged individuals, battling villains who have the combined powers of the machine and international criminal combines. The shift in the natures of protagonists and antagonists signals a shift in the anxiety these superhero narratives compensate for, as they cease rectifying a just system and begin to reconstruct a system that is missing.

Cinematic renditions of cartoon protagonists, more realistically realized and epically developed, continued sporadically through the 1980s and 1990s.. The *Superman* films (1978, 1980, 1983, 1987) and the *Batman* extravaganzas (1989, 1992, 1995) maintained the line of hyperbolic virtue. Their coexistence with muscled human protagonists provided precisely the kind of metacommentary on overcompensation that makes superheroes effective. These humanized cartoon protagonists necessarily completed a system in which the muscle protagonists took a relatively more "serious" and credible position. Without the continued coexistence of the cartoon men, the muscle men might look like cartoons. The cartoon protagonists also carry on a slightly different kind of cultural work, perpetuating the vestige of Law, while muscle heroes enact its figural replacement. The late 1980s and 1990s emergence of new cartoon superheroes such as the Transformers, the Teenage Mutant Ninja Turtles, and the Power Rangers bespeak not just savvy marketing techniques aimed primarily at children, but also signal the final hybridization of hero and machine.

The two strains of narrative film that feature muscled human protagonists in the late-seventies and eighties are the Stallone specialty, muscle-protagonist-overcomes-social-odds films such as *Rocky* (I [1976], II [1979], III [1982], IV [1985]) and *Rambo* in its various versions (*First Blood* [1982], *Rambo: First Blood Part II* [1985], *Rambo III* [1988]). Focusing on an underdog who is invariably identified with a pure, clean, populist, somewhat nostalgic America of self-made men, Stallone's films linked the muscular body, masculinity, and patriotism, often in reference (either overt or covert) to the Viet Nam War. The Stallone subgenre works to align patriotism, the work ethic, and masculinity, presenting them as a kind of national salvation, a defensive healing of the slights to American manhood suffered by the war's ignominious loss. "By assuming a monolithic and stable identity between masculinity and patriarchy," Susan Jeffords observes, "patriarchy manages to shield itself from real challenges to its structure of dominance" (181). In Stallone's films, masculinity's coming to muscularity is the story of the son; his rite of passage into manhood is the salvation of his patrimony and the assurance of continued patriarchal dominance. The muscled son makes up for the father's sins (and omissions), cleansing patriarchy and providing an optimistic promise of continuity, nostalgically assuming there is a continuity to continue.

Stallone's affiliation of superhero, muscularity, and America builds upon and localizes the ideological conflict between good, strong, morally sound men and bad, strong, morally weak men that also characterizes of Schwarzenegger's earlier primitive superhero films such as *Conan* (1982 and 1984), and *Red Sonja* (1985). But in his 1980s' films Schwarzenegger becomes both father and son, merging the two in a unified front that defies and unites generations, expunging the father's crimes while installing a new and better father in his place. This better father also has better brains to match his physique; the body becomes a metaphor for increased intelligence. In *Predator* (1987), (the film most like *Rambo*), Arnold battles an invisible alien being in the jungles of a Southeast Asia permeated by the ghosts of an indecisive war. Displaced into the cleverly unseeable alien being, the specter of lost-war humiliation is turned into triumph as Schwarzenegger nukes the alien out of existence and purges the jungle of its ghosts.

Beginning, however, with *Commando* (1985), almost all of Arnold's films contain overt paternal problems, from commando Arnold as the father rescuing his kidnapped daughter, to the nuclear father issue central to the *Terminator* series, to special agent Arnold rescuing his daughter in *True Lies* to *Twins'* (1988) humorous tale of artificial insemination to Arnold's surrogate paternity in *Kindergarten Cop* (1991) and literal maternity in *Junior*. Even *Running Man* (1987) images Arnold as the savior of culture as he exposes the conspiracy of simulation and corruption by which teleculture (the false patriarchy) is organized. *Running Man* established, in more technoid terms than Stallone's films, the difference between the good muscle strong man and the bad muscle strong men who, aligned with the bad, fake patriarchy, work as the game show's "enforcers" or its corpulent, corporeal minions.

The connection between simulation and the corruption of patriarchy (as both a reproductive filial order and an ordered nuclear reproduction) occupies the position of antagonist in most of Arnold's 1980s films. The simulated media of *Running Man* is related to the cyborg technology that creates the *Terminator* as well as the technologies of artificial insemination that produce the twinship of Arnold and Danny DeVito and then abjure responsibility for it. This simulation culture is not just a generic surface but a conspirator with a technology of paternal repression and substitute reproduction, technologies that expose the difference between progenitor and progeny and reveal the very tenuousness of the relation between creator and creation, father and child. At the same time, the muscled body becomes mechanized as Arnold plays the Terminator cyborg, the human appearance of the "skin job" machine veiling a metal skeleton and hydraulic muscles. The revelation of these machine innards makes the machine a metaphor for human muscle, while Arnold, the connection between cyborg character and human bodybuilder, becomes the metonymical agent of connection between human and machine. That Schwarzenegger the actor effects a transition from being a defender of the Law to enacting its destruction to embodying its metonymical resurrection traces a 1980s trajectory from the drama of paternal demise to the triumph of its reconfigured salvation.

In Arnold's mid-1980s films, the father is clearly lost, "alien-ated," as Vivian Sobchack observes, and the nuclear family is in jeopardy.[31] The world is threatened by beings and images—cyborg terminators, media simulations—generated outside of the family, errant reproductions no longer either referential or fixable. Social relations are no longer governed by the tattered and metaphorical Law-of-the-Name-of-the-Father; this disfunction in the paternal metaphor occurs at the same point in time when it is technically possible to determine with certainty who the genetic father of a child is. When the father becomes biologically certain, the metaphor and its magical ordering principle are reduced to parody, or worse—maternity. In *Running Man*, a game-show host who engineers social order in terms of Nielsen ratings represents a mock paternalism. In *Twins*, paternity is a parody of multiplicity and technological potency. In the *Terminator* series, father is either mother, the very temporary filial Reese, or the future son in the first film, or the cyborg and the child in the second. With this travestying of the paternal metaphor, the father as metaphor must be representationally regenerated, not because there needs to be a father, but because there needs to be a metaphor. It is, after all, the process of metaphor—of representational substitution as opposed to literal truth—that enacts social control and perpetuates the generational immortality that allays the most profound fear of loss—death.

The threat to the paternal metaphor in the 1970s and 1980s results in the creation of metaphorical fathers through narrative gambits that symptomatically take the form of battles against reproductive incursion and the intrusion of reproductive machines and technology. Where earlier in the twentieth century, the battle had taken place on the more metaphorical field of artistic creativity (as Benjamin and Pop indicate), in the 1970s and 1980s, the battle itself is increasingly focused on literal paternity as it is aligned with patriotism and as it veils patriarchy. The monstrous replication of both pseudohuman machines and of layers of reproduction (as multiplied representations), which merge into the realm of pure simulation, become the bad parody of paternity that must be salvaged by the hypermasculine, overphysical phallus figure as part of the process of paternal remetaphorization. The doubled layering of fetishized muscled bodies is multiplied again, moving the muscled figure from the realm of fetish and spectacle to the arena of pure simulation that emphasizes stereotypical masculinity as a way of cementing the masculine and the paternal in the position of the metaphorical father. Hyperbolizing the literally muscular masculine in what becomes a parody of the fetish (and its terms) enables a separation of the now too-literal biological father and the associated and obviously exaggerated superficially masculine from an emptied paternal position. This separation permits the reconnection of masculine, human, and reproduction in a metonymical refiguration of Law-of-the-Name-of-the-Father whose operation is no longer symbolized by the name but by a metonymical series of associations with reproduction itself. The metonymy of male/father/control/order supplants the metaphor of the name and the traditional order it represents, reinscribing a new simulation order secured by the image of control, an answer already had, an instant meaning, and the servility of machines that derive from contiguity and association rather than substitution.

83

"I'LL BE BACK"

Schwarzenegger's highly spectacular embodiment of the previously separate realms of paternity and muscle is perfect for this process of remetaphorizing paternity. His 1980s media persona becomes increasingly layered, increasingly reflecting the cultural workings of simulation—of images referring only to other images. Musculature is an image of masculinity already enclosed in its own phallic metaphor, its fetish also a "simulacrum," in Baudrillard's terms, that bears no relation whatsoever to any reality.[34] Additional layering of stereotypically masculine signifiers onto the muscled body takes the simulation of the muscled body into the realm of hyper-real masculinity, or hypermasculinity, by virtue of the fact that it represents the reproduction of an already reproduced simulation of "masculine" metaphor. Mere musclemen, previously nearly naked, become hypermasculine when they wear motorcycle boots and leather pants, ride a Harley or a horse or drive a semi, carry a big gun, and smoke a cigar. That, in this guise, Schwarzenegger also sometimes represents a machine makes literal the hypermasculine's removal from its human signified. The conflation of Schwarzenegger's muscle and machine wrenches the cyborg from the techno-natural hybridization suggested by Donna Haraway to the status of a will—the will of the male over nature.[35] The combo of muscles and machine removes the masculine completely from nature so that the now metonymical metaphorical father can return, displaced from paternal uncertainty into that which certainly salvages and orders the future of humanity.

Using the cyborg Schwarzenegger in his fullest reduplicated hypermasculine guise, the *Terminator* series exemplifies the complexities of the myth of paternal return as it is imbricated in and figured by hypermasculinity. That *The Terminator* is a film bound up with paternal issues has been convincingly discussed by both Vivian Sobchack and Constance Penley.[36] For Sobchack, the *Terminator* series plays with the politics of the nuclear family by splitting the paternal figure into its Terminator and Reese components. Bifurcating the father enables the emergence of more extended, permanent, time-defying versions of the tripartite nuclear family that "deny the existence of the single-parent family—even as they project it"(25). Penley traces the time paradox narrative of the films to primal-scene fantasies, where John Connor, the privileged son and metaphorical father, can engineer his own conception. But the unavoidable presence of the hypermasculinized muscled body in the extended *Terminator* narrative suggests that beneath the fragmented family and the filial fantasy, another metaphor is born whose terms are the figurative correlate of the hypermasculine body.

Terminator I and *Terminator II* comprise a single narrative in which the uncontrollable mechanical reproduction of machines is undone through the strategic use of nuclear human reproduction; the hypermasculine machine is the agent by which paternity becomes the metonymized figure of perennial order, surmounting and replacing the reproductive chaos created and overseen by Sarah Connor and Dyson, the inventor. *Terminator* enacts the demise of the Law-of-the-Name-of-the-Father by having the son Connor literally name his father while not taking his name. The reversal and failure of paternal law is linked to the intervening aegis of the reproductive machines; their interposition has disenabled Law, creating a gap that permits the child to father himself by designation. The adult Connor's deployment of the father's naming function is not an usurpation, but a strategic redeployment of human rule in a last-ditch effort to defeat machine culture. The metaphorical Law of the Name, however, is no longer primarily metaphor, as Connor employs it (that is to cover over an uncertainty), but metonymy, as Connor names a certain father figure (who is really a son) whose only uncertainty is success. The machine Terminator represents the order that has ground out paternal metaphor, supplanting it with the metonymy Connor grasps as a last-ditch attempt at paternal salvation.

While the first *Terminator* frantically attempts to recuperate the paternal function with the desperate filial persona of Reese, *Terminator II: Judgment Day* images a world where the child/father Connor is clearly in control of the rules of a new culture. Having turned the cyborg to human use, the mythical man

Connor is doubled by his very corporeal son, whose mastery over the Terminator/protector indicates a successful trajectory from no order to machine aegis to human appropriation of the machine as a way of refiguring the paternal function. The paternal metaphor is sutured by paternal metonymy, a metonymy played out in the curious son/father synchrony of the Connor figure. *T2*'s antagonist is the even more metonymical monster, whose polymorphous, polyalloy mimicry hyperbolizes metonymy. Becoming what it touches, the T-1000 is no longer a cyborg or even a metonymically functioning machine, but a pure instance of metonymy scooting through and deranging the field of narrative positions as it takes the place of Connor's foster parents, a policeman, even Sarah herself. While Connor's deployment of a reconfigured paternal metonymy is ordered, the T-1000 is unreliable and crafty, the perfect simulation enemy to a newly reordered culture whose metonymical refoundation provides an antidote to simulation's nonreferential slide.

This subtle but dramatic shift from dying metaphor to metonymy not only accompanies the literal literalization of the paternal, it also dramatizes the logical and recuperative end of the trajectory of machine threat in the first period of full-blown computerization. When computers become integral to human thought processes, the brewing crisis becomes acute. The elements already present in representations of crises of Law—monstrous constructed beings, mechanical reproduction, temporal dysphoria, proliferated simulations—come together in the *Terminator* series, which arranges them in a narrative by which the machine is returned to human service, by which Butler's nineteenth-century anxiety is finally rejoined.

On the surface, the two *T*'s look like modern versions of the Frankenstein myth combined with the chase motif of the Mummy film. In a sense that is exactly what they are: beings produced like Frankenstein's monster in an usurpation of paternal prerogative that exact revenge for human overreaching. But while Frankenstein's monster is a human creation gruesomely patched together from cadavers, the Terminators are the products of an overliteralized mechanical reproduction—machines reproduced by machines. The offspring of an Order that gains control because of technology outstrips human control, the Terminators' single-mindedness makes them displacements of an urge to kill that was originally installed as a part of the human defense network.

In the first film, the Terminator's mission is to kill the mother; in the second, it is to protect the son by killing everyone who threatens him, but, particularly, parental figures. The shift from mother to son (from a metaphorical paternal order in which the mother is the metonymy to a metonymical fraternal order in which there is no longer a distinction between father and son) is bound up with the Terminator's future relation to the son. In the first film, the son/father Connor has vanquished the machines, but must overcome one last challenge to human victory, which is located in the primal scene—the

85

prototypical moment of human versus mechanical reproduction. In the second, to avoid the mechanical demise that still awaits in the future, the son, who now controls the machines, must subject the machines to a fiery, elemental death where they become one with the metallic matter that has comprised their substance. The future relation of man and machine must reach back to avert the 1980s crises caused by an incorrect relation between man and machine. In the 1980s, humanity was still trying to be metaphor in the face of machine culture's metonymy; the future teaches humanity to become metonymy, to synchronize harmonically with the machine while all the time appearing to mold machines to human values.

The *Terminator* character is also the overdetermined representation of reproductive anxieties. A machine clone, multiply reproduced with interchangeable parts, its mass-production origins embody the fear of a loss of identity and individuality linked to an Huxleyan specter of genetic tinkering and bottle babies as well as mechanical reproduction's potential fascism (in this case, a conservatism so threatening as to be annihilating). The cyborg's indestructibility figures the horror of uncontrollable multiples that result when reproduction is removed from its "natural" one-on-one paternal insemination to the apparatus of engineered birth or machine mass production. The Terminator's ability to reproduce accurately any voice reflects a reproductively linked anxiety about unstable identity, where no one can tell who is who (or human) anymore. Its hypermasculine layering conveys a spectacle of excess, of a hugeness linked to the impossibility of its humanity, its control, and its invincibility. Through the figure of the hypermasculine machine, masculinity in its most exaggerated form becomes detached from the male, a parody of itself, revaluing by comparison the fragile real males—Reese, Dyson—who disseminate possible futures.

Another clue to the film series' dramatization of a shift to metonymy comes in its time-travel premise. While time travel may depend upon what some critics call a spatialization of time (i.e., its metaphorization), time travel relies more on the discreteness of temporal moments. In other words, spatially metaphorized time is analogue and linear; jumping from one time to another requires digital separability and discontinuity. While it might seem that time-travel narrative is simply a rearrangement of linear narrative (and for the purposes of narrative production, it is), the concept of temporal displacement (or displacement in time) is a concept dependent upon temporal discontinuity and the failure of cause-effect inevitability. Temporal discontinuity actually allows Connor tentatively to refigure the paternal metaphor as a paternal metonymy that becomes the momentary salvation of a failing culture.

By binding a narrative made self-conscious through the trope of time travel to questions of reproduction and nuclear holocaust, the *Terminator* series equates the menace of reproductive technologies with the extinction wrought by nuclear war. Recovering the narrative of human paternity is the only antidote to this dual horror, and it must be retroactively installed in a nostalgic quest for the mother (and through the mother the father), where the successful struggle to create a second originary narrative of the nuclear family replaces and obliterates the nightmare narrative of machine hegemony (and it turns out, nuclear war) created by humanity's escape from paternal aegis. But the family's express confrontation with reproductive artifacts (both mechanical and human) suggests that the stakes—continuity, operative paternity—are far greater than a simple human fear of technological monsters. The fear is about order itself, about the shape narrative/history will take.

In the context of the appearance of narrative open-endedness and the reproductive excess of too many machines, the two films in the *Terminator* series constitute responses to two different but related reproductive fears. *Terminator I* dramatizes an anxiety about human nonreproduction and the connected fear of no more father, as Reese is transported back in time by John Connor to protect Connor's mother Sarah and, coincidentally, to help conceive Connor. The film becomes a race between the Malthusian machine and John Connor's prospective father. The agents of nonpregnancy depicted as a lethal hypermasculinity, human salvation in *Terminator I* comes through the specific agency of an undeterred, heroic, self-sacrificial, lithe, and lean human father, who, as agent of his son, enacts the sacrificial death of the father to preserve the son who figures hope for human survival. The sacrifice of the literal father (like a previous sacrifice of a son) elevates the father's motive—continuity—reserving the now empty father's place for the son as the self-cycling figure of perpetuity.

87

Terminator II recasts reproductive anxiety as a concern over the loss of the nuclear family—and, specifically, over the empty place of the father, which has not yet been assumed by the son. Without a protective father, the human savior John Connor is doomed. Returning this time as the shielding representative of the adult son, the Arnold Terminator functions as both sheltering dad and malleable child to the prepubescent Connor, who becomes father/son to the machine as he has become father/son to himself. The Terminator is a better father than any literal version, Sarah Connor muses in her retrospective voiceover. Fighting the second Terminator, the T-1000, the Arnold Terminator rescues Sarah Connor from a mental institution and reorganizes the nuclear family unit as a fighting team that can stave off the last threat by machine. Still prenuclear holocaust, the reestablishment of a nuclearlike family of Terminator-father/son, mother, and son/father vanquishes the well-meaning Dyson, African-American progenitor of the machine family, who destroys the machine incubator/factory and himself, averting nuclear war. But Dyson's sacrifice does not stave off the necessary shift from paternal metaphor to filial (and fraternal) metonymy that comprises the films' cultural work. As Connor orders the destruction of the dangerous gametes of future machine self-repro-duction, the cycle of hegemonic technology is broken, its ordering principle displaced as the new figuration of human stability. Although with the death of the Arnold Terminator, the Connor family again lacks a literal father, the place of the father has been preserved for all mankind in the son who engineered his own procreation.

The built-body cyborg of the imaginary is the fulcrum for this figuration of Symbolic change; in a sense, human culture comes to embody the cyborg configuration of machine covered by skin. Continuing a human order with human procreation, human culture after *Terminator II* is no longer bound by the symbolic power of substitutive metaphor, but hides a metonymical system of constant displacement in better harmony with simulation culture and dig-ital and machine technology. But the incongruity of skin and metal matches the films' narrative incongruities; reconfiguring the Symbolic is a necessarily incongruous act (or an act of rectifying incongruities).

A part of this incongruity, the self-contradiction of the Arnold Terminator's opposing roles in these two films might seem to confuse the function of his cyborg hypermasculinity. In *Terminator I*, the Terminator is the techno-freak that threatens to obliterate the paternal function. The Terminator's hypermas-culinity seems to threaten rather than reinforce the paternal place, though its ultimate role is to lose out in the battle with the sensitive, intelligent human male so that the liberating possibilities of human paternity can be vindicated for the benefit of the son. In *Terminator II*, the Arnold Terminator takes the place of the absent human father, his hypermasculine presence reinforcing the son through contiguity. Merging the human and sensitive to the strong machine effects a kind of hypermasculine graft that makes the father (and the son) invincible; the paternal machine becomes the son's prosthesis. Becoming human extensions, machines are the extensions of humans who have some-how been impregnated by a machine logic that enables them to continue in the apparently unblemished surface comfort of patriarchal order.

In all of this, it is difficult to separate Arnold Schwarzenegger from the Arnold Terminator. The coalescence of his *paterfamilias* roles in media and in film, the ubiquity of his gap-toothed grin, the preponderance of his bulk make him more an icon than an actor. The *Terminator* series works because Arnold carries with him the very qualities that guarantee the ascendence of real men. When Schwarzenegger says, "I'll be back," he's not just talking about more Terminator films, he's also mouthing the battle cry of the father lost in the reproductive confusion that ensues when paternity becomes a literal, traceable fact. Embodying the alliance of potency and masculinity, Schwarzenegger promises a return to a former nuclear felicity—a kind of cure-all domestic policy that promises health, righteousness, and a finally triumphant American way. But more important, the new paternal metaphor is no longer just a name, but a social position necessary to ward off death—the death of the father, the death of the father's power, the death of America, the death of a capitalist, white, male world order. Arnold's signature "I'll Be Back" becomes the paternal metaphor itself, encapsulated in this repetitive, perpetual promise of return, a return that will, however, never again be metaphor, but the metonymy whose chaining order is linked to the specter of proliferation as Arnold comes back and back and back . . .

THE PHALLIC MOTHER

The *Terminator* films do not resolve the dilemma of the paternal, but provide an uncanny tracing of the Symbolic's cultural trajectory in the 1980s. Returning to nuclear-familial terms, the refiguration of the Symbolic must eventually also reconfigure the mother, who has always represented the metonymical term in patriarchy's metaphorical operations. Sarah Connor's transformation from slim girl to muscled heroine parallels her future son's evolution from human victim to machine commander. Her embodiment of a compensatory defensive musculature completes the cycle of human reconfiguration into the metaphor of the machine, and also anticipates the actual transition that takes place in the 1990s, when the built male body itself finally becomes the mother. Although Apollinaire's play anticipates this paternal/maternal solution as well, in the 1990s, the maternalization of the muscle man is not the comic incongruity one would have suspected, but rather a "natural" development of the metonymization of the paternal metaphor itself. While the Symbolic system may shift to a more metonymical function, the literal father is disempowered by his literalness; societal controls (laws against adultery for example) enacted in order to secure paternity no longer have any use in protecting against illegitimacy. The father, thus, must become metonymy to procreate, not just as a contributor but as the embodiment of metonymical (i.e., certain, identifiable, manipulatable) procreation itself.

89

This is what *Junior* enacts. But *Junior* is already anticipated by *Twins*, whose anxiety about mechanized human reproduction presents one trajectory from the metonymical paternity of six fathers to the nuclear family represented by the search for the mother. The good son, Arnold, seeks nuclear-family felicity by tracking down first his twin brother, Danny DeVito, and then their mother, dispossessed of her offspring through a researcher's lies. Throughout his search, the naive Arnold twin's belief in the virtue of family is indomitable; seeing the family as curative, he cures the family, redirecting it from its technological malaise (separation, ignorance, disorder) to a functional and productive unity. The rescue of the family is paralleled by Arnold's rescue of his twin, who has become embroiled in an industrial-espionage plot. Industrial secrets recovered, family reconstituted, the son reforges a paternal order, not in the name of the father (who has become so multiple as to be both unidentifiable and useless), but within the generous credulity of the pure and loving son. Proof of the stability of this new filial order is the film's final vignette of the happy family, the two sons both fathers of twins, happily wheeling their progeny around an amusement park. The son gets the family back on track after the mess made by the fathers.

While this might seem a postoedipal story, it is really an alternate oedipal saga. But the new oedipal trajectory is comedy instead of tragedy. When the father (or fathers) is too certain, the question of identity no longer drives an oedipal search or exacts paternal prohibition. The exiled son (Arnold grew up on a desert island) must not seek his father's killer but instead his mother, whose identity has somehow become uncertain. Transformed into the protagonist of a victorious narrative instead of into the chastised tragic hero, the son is the only one who can reconstitute Symbolic order. The mother's metonymy becomes a substitute for an ordering principle, stabilizing the field for the return of the father in the guise of the son.

It is only a tiny step from the son's recuperation of the mother to the son's becoming the mother, himself embodying the metonymical reconfiguration by which the paternal is resecured. Apollinaire's pregnant Dad is still a father; the unseemliness of Frankenstein and Apollinaire comes from the incongruous mix of paternal metaphor and literalized reproduction that unveils and reduces the phallus. The hypermasculine son, however, with his fetishized fetish body, can occupy the position of mother because the paternal metaphor has been literalized. With nothing in the place of the Father but literal fathers, the son's overcompensatory phallic demeanor looks like the Law organized around the metonymy that extends from fetish to fetish. Because the built body has already reappropriated the feminine, it easily reappropriates it on a larger scale. Layering just one more fetish (the pregnant abdomen) on the built body just makes the male body look even fuller but no less masculine.

Nonetheless, the overly fetished protagonist is the only male who could conceivably carry the child. His extraphallic fetish, even when clothed in conservative business attire, compensates for the potentially castrating vision of the abdomen extending beyond the priapus. Like beer bellies, the pregnant abdomen becomes another phallic sign, a signifier of redoubled fullness. While the film *Junior's* dance with nomenclature plays out the paternal's resignification, the protagonist's body, as it has in superhero films, reduplicates the narrative, signifying a righteous return to order that restabilizes Law.

It is also no accident that "Junior" is the name given to this salvation, since the new site of paternal reconfiguration is the son, not in any belated Christian gesture, but as the protagonist in a reconfigured oedipal where the son doesn't want to have the mother, but wants to be her. Combining son and mother produces a new paternal, one that operates like the mother through the masculinized veil of the son. *Junior* is actually a quite canny reading of the process by which the name of the father comes back in a son who is physically metonymical to mother and nominally metonymical to father and imagistically cyborg (or at least in control of mechanical reproduction).

If Lacan's observation about the impermanence of the oedipal acknowledges the possibility that the Symbolic itself can change, and if that change might occur through and in the symbolic remnants of triadic structuration most often represented by the nuclear family, then it is, indeed, possible that the Symbolic, and not just the cultural imaginary of the Symbolic, has already been changing. The dominant metaphor of tripartite prohibition represented best (but not as often as tradition would like) by patriarchal culture may have shifted to a permissive metonymy figured by the extended or fragmented family's quadrated structure as well as by the mass metonymies of a computerized technological function. Instead of the tripartite Mom, Dad, and baby, we have, as *Junior* unwittingly illustrates, the four-term formula Dad/Mom; Mom; DeVito, the in vitro facilitator; and child, or in the film's parallel plot, Mom, sperm donor, DeVito, and child. Despite its implicit restructuration of the nuclear three that doubles the paternal locus, *Junior* returns resoundingly to the familial triad at the end of the film; four makes three, reproductive metonymies result in the veneer of time-honored normalcy as Arnold marries the scientist and recreates the nuclear family. It takes two metonymical Pops to rebuild the appearance of one time-honored metaphor.

But it may be that *Junior* is too little, too late, that the march of metonymy is already so advanced that it actually represents a shift in the Symbolic that has been happening for at least as long as metonymy has reared its displaced head. Like Apollinaire and the Dadaists, the digital signaled the end of Pop almost before it got started. Pop is dead, but as both Freud and Lacan remind us, the only good father is a dead father and the son is a different story altogether.

91

The End of the End of Pop

To what ends do I make this analysis? Should I read Arnold's maternity as a strategic refiguration of the paternal in the face of Symbolic change or does Arnold's refiguration merely prove the strength of a Symbolic that still situates the father as the figuration of law? Does the pregnant father represent a different order? It may be that the end of the trajectory I have traced is the totally predictable performance of a system such as psychoanalysis that might reproduce its own terms. But if psychoanalysis is itself a symptom, then the father become mother is significant in the way it refigures the terms of the oedipal and contains anxieties about continued reproduction. One way to understand the maternal paternal is as a defensive regrouping of reproductive technologies within a still paternal aegis. Another way is to see it as trying to retain a kind of gender organization that is on the point of collapse.

If reproduction no longer requires the participation of two parents, the oedipal nuclear tripartite structure of father/mother/child is opened up. Genders no longer necessarily align with reproductive roles, which means that the figuration of law with the father is no longer sustained within the pragmatic structures of childbearing and rearing. It also means that the function of the father may become entirely extenuated; no longer prohibitor, the father becomes a contributor in a scenario of multiple conceptive helpers, while prohibition is gradually replaced by deferral. This literal vision of the future reproductive technologies offers does not necessarily mean that the process of prohibition will stop completely or that psychic development will alter radically.

In this sense, understanding the bodybuilder and the maternal father as attempts to compensate for symbolic change means seeing the conservatism of their ploys both in psychoanalytic and cultural terms. Attempting to salvage an endangered status quo, they also refigure the paternal as a more metonymical (as opposed to a metaphorical) function. In so doing, they seem to conserve a patriarchal Symbolic. Seeing this compensatory mechanism, however, also means seeing the potential for opening up the oedipal, for recasting its gendered terms and eventually dispensing with gendered binaries altogether in favor of a more varied, multipositional spectrum anticipated by reproductive technology's separation of gamete production from incubation from parenting. Even though reproductive technology is designed to produce traditional nuclear families, its breakdown of gender and reproductive role means that the nuclear family no longer (if it ever did) reflects any necessarily "natural" paradigm.

The end of Pop, then, is no tragedy, if we even have further capacity for tragedy; it is the signal of the birth of comedy, not as the conservative fecundity of familial reparation, but as the buffoon ethic that fools with the contiguous links in a metonymical chain that might loosen sometime in the next millennium.

LAW IN THE AGE OF MECHANICAL REPRODUCTION

chapter 3

LEGISLATIVE INTENT

While Pop art, Arnold Schwarzenegger, bodybuilding, and superheroes compensate for a loss of the paternal function by reinscribing a heroic paternalized son, the law itself is perhaps a more symptomatic site of alterations in Law as that embodies the Symbolic. This chapter undertakes three facets of cultural compensation around Symbolic shifts reflected in law and litigation. The first is the anxiety manifested by conservative worry about the proliferation (and cost) of litigation and the loss of "law and order;" this isn't so much a philanthropic misgiving about the social cost of a frivolous justice (overblown liability for ladder accidents, for example), but is, rather, an anxiety about the disappearance of a righteous, hierarchical, traditional Law in favor of a multiplicitous, multifarious, media-induced gang of overly literal litigations that make the law (Law) a travesty, divest it of power, and swerve ever further from an imaginary Way Things Should Be (Patriarchy). The second is how statutory law attempts to define literal paternity in an attempt to recapture a Law-of-the-Father in place of the now all-too-literal Name.[1] The third is how law's spectacularization attempts to compensate for Law's lack, its transition into laws, and a perceived loss of Order (as opposed to the loss that founds the Symbolic in the first place) as litigation goes from spectacle fiction to futuristic and (symptomatic) man versus machine trials to obsessive real-time trial broadcasts.

If the Law-of-the-Name-of-the-Father is the typifying instance of a substitutive Symbolic order, then the paternal metaphor's increasing links to a literalized paternity and its replacement and refiguration with metonymy would disrupt the substitutive relation between Law and laws. If the Law-of-the-Name-of-the-Father is a metaphor that substitutes for a gap, then interfering with the operation of metaphor as that has underwritten tradition, the devolution of property, kinship, and specific, literal prohibitions, social relations, and gender codes, would mean disrupting all forms of metaphorically patriarchal social relations. The transliteration of the metaphorical Name into a literal figure has not happened all at once; the transition from the "gravitational pole" of metaphor to that of metonymy has been gradual, easing towards metonymy's proliferation and association with the quotidian dominance of the mechanical and the digital, the advent of world-inclusive systems of production and distribution, the separation and sequestration of production stages, and the dominion of media simulations. In all of this, the Law-of-the-Name-of-the-Father is itself a Symbol instead of a motivation, a symbol whose imaginary correlate appears to be under the siege of large-scale cultural shifts in order and epistemology.

Changes in Symbolic Law (metaphorical order) are manifested not only in cultural images of failing paternal order, but in the representation of and functioning of the law itself. Law, as increasingly devised and codified by legislatures and regulatory agencies, is less and less Law (making a connection where one does not exist) and more a form of multiple-site regulation (hence, the conservative complaint about the proliferation of federal regulations and "government"). Lacan notes that "when the Legislator (he who claims to lay down the Law) presents himself to fill the gap, he does so as an imposter."[2] Generating rights, protections, and prohibitions that seem independent from any larger, overweening principle, regulation appears to balance interests within a capitalist patriarchy, but actually proliferates often compensatory rules in a beset ideology. If capitalism isn't quite working, fix it with statutes; if organized crime presents too much of an effective alternative to the governmental father, fabricate elaborate criminal statutes (conspiracy, for example) to hamper it. This regulatory expansion also applies both to the religiously guarded principle of local determination (States' rights) and to the proliferations of public agencies and their separate regulatory functions on all levels. Shifting from a grand old Law to tiny ignoble rules isn't the old, familiar narrative of a reduction in the majesty and splendor of things past, but the narrative of a progression from a sustained substitutive Symbolic to a law that becomes increasingly compensatory, Imaginary, and metonymical through the proliferation of laws, the increased regulation of production and reproduction, and the spectacularization of police work and the legal system.

Superman versus _____

In his clever, anxiety-laden parody on the state of contemporary litigation, columnist Stephen Bates imagines a series of lawsuits and criminal trials against Superman. In his short essay "United States v. Superman," Bates sketches the panoply of actions that might hinder the superhero's efficiency as defender of the "American Way."[3] For example, cases against criminals Superman has apprehended are reversed because "Superman has failed to obtain a search warrant before using telescopic vision," or because "though Superman had obtained [a] search warrant, he then travelled backward in time and conducted search before warrant's issuance" (31). Beset by litigation, Superman must also defend actions in unfair competition and negligent failure to act as well as a violation of the pit-bull ordinance (Krypto).

While Bates's catalogue of fantasy cases is mildly humorous, and although it is intended to point out how ludicrous the restraints are against law-enforcement officials and "free enterprise," what the essay more effectively manifests is a deep anxiety produced by the suspected loss of Law. Bates's use of Superman as his exemplary figure is not coincidental, but an appeal to a figure who already compensates for a loss of order. In sketching just how beset this paternally compensatory figure is, Bates reveals just how much law is feared to work against Law. By hyperbolizing both the figure of justice and litigious possibilities, Bates renders legal checks and protections ludicrous barriers to a smoothly functioning paternal order identified as a union of police state and business.

Bates makes one symptomatic mistake that confirms his deep Law-of-the-Name-of-the-Father anxiety: he confuses Superman with the government that he had already confused with capitalist enterprise. More than half the cases he fabricates are only litigable causes if they involve government action. Configuring the extraterrestrial Superman as a "quasi-state actor" hints at the extent to which the government is already confused with a superheroic big Daddy figure. In Bates's terms, the proper father (the government) is the figure who upholds what we all "know" is right in accord with the conservative Constitution (the Father of all Law). The bad father is the liberal government that doesn't protect patriarchy, that lets its concern for a few minor Constitutional clauses (such as the Fourth Amendment) get in the way of its real paternal function of protecting not mothers and children, but fathers themselves. Contemporary American law is a fake Pop, too permissive, too soft, too fair to interests that don't count. The example of Superman's legal inundation shows just how much.

Bates's parody is graphically encased within L. Gordon Crovitz's startling 1991 analysis of "How Law Destroys Order."[4] Arguing that "a legal system that fails to protect order signals flaws in the law itself," Crovitz hits the nail on the head without ever knowing it (28). Analyzing how courts have interfered with order in law enforcement (giving the defendants their constitutional rights, for example), interfered with business contracts, and come to the bizarre conclusion that words might not mean what they say, Crovitz mourns the wrong-headedness of what he calls, "liberalism's social experimentation with the courts." As a result of all this judicial blundering, Crovitz argues, order has gone to hell. Evoking the nostalgic (and misled) narrative of a halcyon police force that "once enforced the law" (28), Crovitz confuses cause and effect, but in a way that exposes the understandable error of an investment in a Law that has quietly passed away.[5] While the incredulous Crovitz can't believe that Supreme Court justices would "wave away evidence that from Elizabethan times [vagrancy] laws had been crucial to maintaining order," what Crovitz doesn't understand is that order maintains laws instead of the other way around (28). Without the Law that constitutes an order, laws cannot resurrect the tranquil vision of propertied patriarchal harmony Crovitz laments.

Both Bates and Crovitz symptomatically reveal the diminution of paternal Law; like Rip van Winkles who have awakened after one-hundred years, the avowedly conservative columnists can no longer find their vision of order in a system that has had to employ Superman to try to hold onto the Father as long as possible. And while Bates confuses Superman with the government and Crovitz sees the government as interfering, effeminate (they go after white-collar criminals now), and misled, both still seem to want there to be a Father somewhere, clothed, as usual, in a conservative suit. The judiciary is comprised of bad, disrespectful sons who do not and perhaps cannot carry on the father's name, at least since the 1960s, when it began issuing these bad decisions.

The right wing Bates and Crovitz are not, however, so far from those liberals whose wrong-headed agendas they decry. The "liberal" emphasis on Consitutional protection of citizens' rights Bates and Crovitz criticize also hinges on a belief in Law, this Law the Constitution's metaphorical principle of Due Process. Bates and Crovitz complain about what they see as a too-literal application of Due Process principles; to them, the Courts' various readings are absurdly exaggerated. Crovitz characterizes Justice Douglas's limitation on vagrancy statutes in *Papachristou v. City of Jacksonville* (1972), for example, as castrating law enforcement, making "cops and prosecutors . . . fight with one arm behind their backs" (28). Crovitz's argument that vagrancy statutes are useful tools for fighting drug dealing and crime appeals to a belief in the identity of police and Law. Seeing vagrancy statutes as overbroad, Justice Douglas appeals to a different fantasy of a benevolent, fair Constitutional Father who protects the innocent until they are proven guilty. The point is that both visions wish for (and try desperately to engineer) a return to Law and blame one another for its loss. What is seen as legal nonsense from either side (permissive loopholes or overly repressive police function) is actually an effect of the loss of Order itself. There is no Law grounding either police action or citizen protection; there are only sets of self-contradictory rules that spawn an increased litigation whose spectacular televised presence lets us believe that the Law is still there.

THE FATHER'S NAME

Bates and Crovitz employ parody to cover their despair about a deplorable loss of order and good sense—what might just as easily be seen as the tragic loss of tragedy itself. One cannot mourn the Father, since the Father is already dead; one mourns one's mourning, reduced in the early 1990s to a whimpering about legal illogic. This grousing is more like the unrestrained sibling rivalry between tattletale children who have no one to tattle to. Their complaints are not unlike former Vice President Dan Quayle's constant (and equally whiney) overliteralization of the paternal function in his book *Standing Firm.* (Is it possible to be any more symptomatic?) Quayle believes that only a return to nuclear-family felicity with good, strong fathers will ever heal an America prone to drug use, crime, and disrespect for property.[6] Lamenting "too many laws" that interfere with competition, "too many lawyers" who raise the cost of product-liability insurance, Quayle's answer to all of America's problems is to free the market and market "family values."

The odd coincidence of these topics—free enterprise and family values— in the 1992 section of his autobiography signals their shared paternalistic assumption. Removing government "interference" (read, regulation) in business appeals to business's self-governing function—it can "father" itself through the analogical maxim of "What's good for business is good for America." A return to "family values" would likewise stop government interference in the fabric of daily lives so that families will be forced to return to patriarchal self-government. Familial self-government means (a) getting off of welfare; (b) supporting the law that families should be headed by a literal father supposedly somewhere between Ward Cleaver and Quayle himself. "Fathers," Quayle preaches, "are important to a child's life—both financially and emotionally. A society that promotes the idea that a father's role is irrelevant breeds irresponsibility" (322). An absent father means bad breeding, the breeding of government care for paternally abandoned families. Quayle visibly makes the mistake Lacan warns against; he mistakes the literal father for the Symbolic one, thus locating order in the family instead of in larger cultural metaphorical formations of property, kinship, and tradition. The conservative tragedy becomes literal but anachronistic, as are conservative solutions. To avoid making the same mistake as Quayle, it would be best also not to mention here such familial problems as child abuse, the need for two incomes, the earning disparities of women, the lack of child care, the lack of affordable medical care, and other problems that the presence of father wouldn't allay.

The loss of the family is the loss of tragedy and vice versa since the western "sense of tragedy" has been understood in terms of the family since Aristotle: in the oedipal association of Desire with the mother and in the correlation of Law and the paternal metaphor. Creating a realm of tragedy and death, the three terms of the familial configuration function metaphorically as the Symbolic signifiers structuring the psyche (or the structure of the psyche is understood in familial metaphors). Despite individual family breakdowns and historical changes, the metaphorical mother and father continue to function symbolically as long as they remain in a relatively stable relation to one another, even as familial functions are undertaken by others. The sense of tragedy linked to the nuclear family fades, however, when parental signifiers no longer closely attach to the three-term configuration by which the child learns Desire and loss. This loss of tragedy is what Quayle's insistence on a paternal presence tries to stave off; it is an inevitable side effect of the loss of a governing metaphor identified with the fathers as literal versions of the Father's Name.

98

While the twentieth-century American imaginary literalization of the father seems to hinder the Law's function, disturb order, or threaten mass psychosis caused by foreclosure of the Name-of-the-Father, what Lacan suggests by the loss of a sense of tragedy is, I think, the loss of the metaphorical correlation between concrete familial terms and the structuration of Desire and Law they represent. This may happen as our "nuclear" family "form of society" gives way to other caretaking configurations (which is, perhaps, the proximate cause of the cultural outcry against the family's perceived decline). But that giving way, in turn, is partly produced by shifting modes of production, economic conditions, media simulation, and information technologies. The perceived loss of the family is a symptom of the loss of the myth of the patriarchal family rather than the loss of any coherent nuclear grouping. The foundations of Symbolic order shift as does its closely tied relation to the claustrophobic nuclear configuration that foments the intensity of tragedy. This nuclear family is then misunderstood as the locus of paternal and societal repair. As Lacan warns, "to speak the Name of the Father is by no means the same thing as invoking paternal deficiency."[7]

But within a legal system that, as Crovitz and Bates suggest, is running on empty, where would one intervene to salvage order? Can the Symbolic as metaphor ever be recuperated or do we ever only grasp the literal as its substitute? The confusion between the Symbolic Law-of-the-Name-of-the-Father and the literal father is a logical symptom of law's malaise rather than its cause, while at the same time the ability to discern the father undermines the Name's metaphorical function. If the Name is the operative mechanism of law, then, in one very literal logic, the strategic use of the name should recuperate law. A judge in Columbus, Ohio, for example, "recently denied a request from an unmarried mother who wanted her child's last name switched from the child's father's to hers. 'He contested it, and we did not accept it,' Belskis said. 'To do so would violate the father's rights.'"[8] To what?

This now overly literalized naming functions not so much as the symbol of generational continuity in the child as it relates to some unspecified right now relocated to the father. But what is this "right"? The "right" to a return on his investment? The "right" to paternal power over the child? The "right" to a narcissistic pleasure in nominal self-continuity? The Ohio case was not a matter of custody or support (functions that might be perceived as literally paternal), but a challenge to the apparently symbolic meaning of naming. Suing for the mother's name galvanized the anachronistic response of salvaging not the order or even the functions represented by the father's name, but the father's name as Name displaced into the register of the certain, redundantly certifying the already known as the all-too-empty symbol of a faded but hastily re-revived order.

99

"A Verdict on the Paternal Function"

Since the late 1960s, a rising feminist consciousness has challenged the symbolic gendering of the family drama's roles and is, thus, partly responsible for the erosion of the sense of tragedy in so far as that sense is literally dependent upon the sustenance of familial roles. By questioning the "natural" correlation between female and Desire, on the one hand, and male and Law, on the other, feminist critics publicly exposed what is not superficially apparent: that the gendered structuration of Law and Desire is a shaky metaphor in part because the "reality" of biological genders cannot sustain the Symbolic roles into which they are cast. The literal father cannot live up to the role of the Father, nor can the literal mother sustain any of her fantasmatic personae. Because of the metaphorical gendering of Symbolic functions, the intersection of a more literalized gender and law reflects both the already existent lack in the Symbolic and its slow shift to metonymy.

Feminist praxis instigated legal reform by challenging the relation between biological sex and gender stereotype as a way of addressing the law's differential treatment of genders. If there is no "natural" basis for disparate treatment, the argument goes, such inequities should be corrected according to a greater Constitutional principle of fairness. Opposition to equal rights has been clearly premised on a desire to conserve patriarchy in the guise of the exhausted gendered metaphors of order ("a woman's place . . .), nature (women are naturally weak and emotional), or religion (God made woman from man); resistance to equal rights only makes sense if the Law is understood as Patriarchy itself. The contradiction between equal treatment and the preservation of patriarchy echoes a liberal/conservative split around the character of the Symbolic Law. Liberalism looks to the Law as order and fairness; conservatism looks to the Law as hierarchy, conservation, order, and propriety (patriarchy). No matter what one's philosophical position on "equal rights" is, however, when scrutinized at all, the imaginary connection between gender and gender role breaks down. The very act of questioning the "naturalness" of gender brings gender (and nature) into question, momentarily at least, undoing gender's fragile but stubborn ideological lineaments. Proponents of equal rights use the breakdown in the nature/gender relation to argue for equal treatment in everything from jobs to sports; opponents link a suspected lack of correlation between gender and gender role to contemporaneous cultural disorder, creating a cause-effect circle that locates gender disaffiliations as the reason for cultural chaos. The trick is, of course, not to see a nature/gender disparity as the problem, whether it can be corrected by equal rights or a return to patriarchy.

Seeing gender disparity as *the* primary problem prevents us from seeing the order that produces and sustains gender as the problem in the first place. Challenges to gender may actually result from a breakdown in order rather than cause one; feminist praxis may have already benefitted from the slow metonymical shift of the Law, which constitutes, what Lacan calls, the "order and norms . . . which tell the subject what a man or woman must do."[9] Its lack exposed, Law has already been dissolving into a series of metonymies since at least the 1960s when feminist activism arises again. Like Bates and Crovitz, who are still faithful to a Law long since "perverted" by liberals, opponents of equal rights see the distribution and enforcement of prerogative as the cause of disorder. But the Law's faithful are not just conservatives; they also include those who believe that gender parity is the intention of and will result in a just and fair Law. For both conservative and liberal, gender dysphoria is believed to be the cause of systemic changes rather than the other way around.

Feminist challenges to gender roles have forced the limited public deconstruction of familial metaphors in the realm of literal, statutory law where patriarchal authority, as Bates and Crovitz demonstrate, is imagined to exist.[10] Most of this deconstruction has taken the form of an ironic extension of previously gendered functions to both parents, splitting gender from gender role. In this way, feminist political practice works to purge statutory law of its gender bias, hoping that changing the law will force a shift in cultural comprehensions of the value and function of gender, which will, in turn, effect an end to gender bias in a larger cultural sphere. In other words, they hope to alter the cultural imaginary by altering what they believe is the Symbolic. That statutes are rewritten in ways understood to be gender-equitable suggests a belief that the authoritarian structure of the law is receptive, malleable, and inherently fair; it also demonstrates that gender ideologies might not be permanent, natural, or divinely decreed. Efforts at statutory repair have a political value insofar as statutory law is confused with Law—insofar as laws and the Name-of-the-Father are conflated—since revising the law's treatment of gender appears to be an assault upon the authority imagined to legislate gender value.

At the same time, the Imaginary confusion sustained between biological gender and its metaphorical function—the confusion that tends to meld the literal father with Symbolic authority—means that feminist efforts to effect statutory change work within the frame of the law rather than questioning the basis and structure of legal authority itself. In this way feminist efforts are still conservative. Statutory reform assumes a Law rather than treating the idea of law or Law itself; reform remains within the gendered parameters of Law and Desire, reinforcing the very idea of law (and Law) while trying to challenge its more literalized instances.

Despite the political value of feminist legal reform, legislative change does not finally represent the voluntary and enlightened alteration of the underlying cultural gender ideologies that continue to inform statutory application, enforcement, and judicial interpretation and threaten constant regression into gender dualities. Instead of correcting or changing patriarchal Law, which is what defines the Imaginary vision of social change that drives reform, statutory change responds to an absence in Law itself, proliferating laws and increased statutory coverage to compensate for what is, in its all-too-visible presence, disappearing. If the Law-of-the-Name-of-the-Father no longer dominates the Symbolic, if metaphor no longer sustains tradition, then more laws are needed to fill in the gap, to try to force the appearance of order. In this context Bates's and Crovitz's railing represents a denial of Law's demise.

If the decline of Paternal Law is the problem, this might account for the fact that many of the legal reforms that appear to endow gender equity have actually backfired, turning out to be of more practical benefit to males.[11] One reason for this ironic return of male supremacy in the guise of gender equity is that in confusing statutory law with Symbolic Law, efforts at gender equity treat symptoms rather than the underlying gender drama that bifurcates and metaphorically genders Desire and Law in the first place. Another problem is the stubborn strength of gender metaphors linked to structures of Law and Desire—the intrapsychic gendered structuration drawn from cultural law. A third is the fact that the proliferation of laws around gender and reproduction is compensatory rather than reformative in the first place. Such laws are designed to erect the failing Law-of-the-Father as the champion of equality as a way of retrieving its own terms.

There are two correlative issues here, representing the flip sides of the same problem. On the one hand, feminist efforts at legal reform seem to result in benefits to males and only vague political gains for women without any corresponding systemic change. In fact, statutory changes are always threatened by repeal and modification as exemplified by fifteen years of attacks on affirmative action. On the other hand, order itself seems to have failed in some way, requiring increased statutory activity to sustain the system. In both conundra the problem is Law: its lack, its literalization, its confusion with laws, the nature of compensatory strategies already active (the reemergence of the father, the resurgence of "family values"), and a cultural imaginary long ensconced in the naturalized truth of patriarchy.

It would seem, then, that any feminist attempt to alter laws would be difficult as long as laws were confused with a literalized Law-of-the-Name-of-the-Father, since a literally gendered father reifies gender and links it to substance and order. Taking advantage of Law's failing would require an onslaught upon the reluctant release of this gendered Symbolic as it makes a transition to a more metonymical order. Such a project would take as its focus shifts in Law rather than the specific laws and attempt to recast the gendered metaphors that appertain to the originary drama of the mirror stage where gendered metaphors are allied with structuration. As Ragland-Sullivan maintains in her analysis of the structuring function of Desire and Law: "Though the specific meanings attached to the structures of Desire and Law vary according to personal experience and historical context, the structural effects are themselves Real and shape both personal trajectory and history. The 'enemy' which feminists must confront, then, is neither class structure nor patriarchy per se, but the mimetic mirror-stage processes of fusion and difference by which the human subject takes on its nuclear form between six and eighteen months of age" (269). Because the Imaginary is resilient and compensatory, mimetic mirror-stage processes resist change. On a cultural level, the mimetic processes of the Imaginary occlude Symbolic rifts in much the same way the Imaginary fills in for the foreclosed third term in psychosis. Hence, Pop art's renaming, or bodybuilding, or superheroes can seem to fill in—in fact, can make it seem, on the level of a cultural imaginary, that nothing has ever been missing. The very processes of compensation and redefinition themselves continue to gender and sustain the illusion of a system that has already broken apart, providing the structures of difference that ground primal and Imaginary processes.

One difficulty in confronting Law (apart from its unconscious oedipal ensconcement) lies in being able to distinguish between the Law's metaphorical appurtenances and its ordering function, since even our ideas of the Law are already Imaginary, that is, gendered and metaphorical. Despite the fact that Law, as Lacan has stated, is not a hidden force moving behind the scenes, it is, nonetheless, difficult to approach the Law as Law; this book itself demonstrates the tendency to represent Law in a more limited, schematic idiom. The operation of the Law can be found only by implication as it performs within structure; as a structure, the Law is a relation determinable better in its functioning than in any direct representation. Only strategies that either expose Law as metaphor or unveil the Law's lack via shifts in structural relations would tend to reveal the links between metaphorical gender, Desire, and the Law. As Lacan observes, the potential for this revelation already exists in the fact that the paternal function is always inadequate; he states: "Even when in fact it is represented by a single person, the paternal function concentrates in itself both imaginary and real relations, always more or less inadequate to the symbolic relation that essentially constitutes it."[12]

As statutory law compensates for Law's emerging visible lack (particularly in response to what appear to be gender questions directly affecting social forms), it reveals both lack and the slow shift of the Law-of-the-Name-of-the-Father. The gradual disengagement of Law and paternal metaphor in American law is exposed in at least two ways. One way is through the inadvertent rift in the metaphorical relation between the law and Law produced as a side effect of feminist legal reform as it attempts to introduce gender parity. Statutes, in other words, no longer necessarily represent patriarchy; this is what Bates and Crovitz are loudly ruing. The ensuing gap between gender role and gender exposes the operation of basic kinship laws central to Law that are otherwise effaced by statutory formulation; it is only in this environment that the father's name could even be questioned in the first place. The exposure of kinship laws—evidenced most dramatically in child-custody cases between biological and adoptive parents—makes evident the inconsistency between Law, reproductive certainties, and social conditions, which, if noticed, allows for a consciousness of the gendering of Law and the operation of metaphor as well as a recognition of the changes in technology and social form that create the dissonance.

Another means for exposing the paternal metaphor's demise is in the ease with which the biological paternity can be performed by biotechnological paternal substitutions such as artificial insemination; the overliteralization of the paternal betrays its metaphoricity in the cultural imaginary. Because of this paternal overcertainty, statutory law must fill in the gap by defining paternity as its metaphor recedes. These two mechanisms—no need for the Name and too many statutes—operate together, often inseparably, and are evident in the texts of legal codes if such codes are read as effects of the operation of a cultural unconscious trying desperately to find a renewed paternal function to moor a fading order.[13]

Law is to law as . . .

The exposure of Symbolic lack is paradoxically possible because of the presumption of a metaphorical relation between Symbolic Law and the law enacted by statutes and legal codes. That is, all laws are imagined to refer to and stand for a coherent principle of relation. This relation is neither fairness nor truth, since those are masking ideologies, but the fact that the Law as metaphor already stands for and is structured as something with something missing. As Stuart Schneiderman cannily observes, "The function of the Name-of-the-Father is its subversion."[14] The fact that Law covers a gap already indicates its lack. Bates and Crovitz and feminist proponents of legal reform all presume a metaphorical relation where law corresponds to an Imaginary Rule that supplies systemic consistency, but each envisions a different Imaginary Law (fairness, patriarchy) that defines the nature of the substitution. Neither liberal nor conservative questions the function of metaphor itself; both cling anachronistically to the vision of a complete and whole system without which order is not perceived to be possible.

The tie that sustains the relation between statutes and an Imagined principle of Law is, indeed, metaphor, which is represented by the same paternal metaphor that binds Law to the metaphor of the Father's Name. Law is imagined to be to law, as Father is to father, and Phallus to phallus. But any failure of either the paternal or the metaphorical follows rather than initiates the rift in the legal system itself. Since the Law already enacts both a lack and its compensation, its rift is simply exposed by the literal, overly scientific suture of father to child. The Symbolic Law presumed to determine social ordering, division, and identity in any culture where lineage and names are connected is already not coterminous with the tradition of common and statutory law by which Americans codify the relations among themselves. Spinning through Imaginary permutations created by operations of cultural narcissism and compromise, civil law is an Imaginary version of the Symbolic Law that disappears within its fabric.

The tradition of common and statutory law, though presumably Symbolic in its effect, is literalized in its practice. Engendered primarily in the cultural Imaginary as the narcissistic image of a jurisprudential self composed of competing self-interests, political machination, compromise, and an image of social weal, statutory law and its accompanying trail of case-law interpretation is metonymical in its power and practice.[15] Attached more to event (social problem, loophole, public policy, contemporary cause célèbre) than to a reasoned systemic logic, legislated law produces a system that mimics order, but is more congruous with the contradictory multiple needs of various societal, political, and cultural interests. Hence, the seven-year spread in legislated ages of adulthood; for the purposes of marriage and driving, sixteen, for debt, contract, and military draft, eighteen, for drinking alcohol, twenty-one, for declaring economic independence to qualify for higher-education loans, twenty-three, for trial as an adult, variable. These are metonyms rather than metaphors, since they are related to various, contradictory interests and ideologies of reproduction and consumer culture rather than to any sustained understanding of the meaning of age or adulthood in relation to a larger ordering principle. Veiled by statutory arabesques, Law has operated just like the Name: as an unconscious ordering principle whose effects only appear either as the explanation for legal gaps and inconsistencies or in those things assumed to be incontrovertibly true (children have fathers; people die). Because the Law-of-the-Name-of-the-Father has underwritten the Symbolic order defining identity and family, it is in civil laws that govern such matters—reproductive and paternity statutes—that the operation of Law and its lack have become most immediately apparent.

Most state statutes treating reproduction address questions of pregnancy termination and involuntary sterilization. Statutes governing questions of paternity constitute the obverse case, admitting and inscribing the exact difficulty of proving the connection between father and child while providing the means to establish a connection. Because part of the current ideology of human reproduction is that reproduction is an absolute and completely inalienable right even to those biologically or physically incapable of reproducing, this culture would not countenance statutes that defined when one could or should reproduce, though the state does provide laws that set the conditions for when and how the process of reproduction can be terminated, including abortions and sterilizations. This selective statutory coverage makes sense if reproduction is seen as "natural," and the voluntary termination of reproduction is seen as "unnatural."

A legislative obsession with laws that treat certain aspects of reproduction and parenting and not others already reflects the presence of an urge towards perpetuity and immortality understood as proceeding through undisturbed processes of mating and reproduction, or what would seem to be some version of the Law-of-the-Name-of-the-Father. In this sense, reproduction is a metaphorical extension of the language of kinship and identity that forms social order, the "primordial Law," which Lacan defines as "identical with an order of language" and without which "no power is capable of instituting the order of preferences and taboos that bind and weave the yarn of lineage through succeeding generations."[16]

SPERM RIGHTS; OR YOU HAVE A RIGHT TO A RETURN ON YOUR INVESTMENT

Simple inconsistencies in reproductive laws reveal the operation of this Law whose deeply ingrained gendered metaphors compete with attempts to erase gender difference or equalize the law's effects. Exposed in two guises—(1) kinship exchange principles that govern marriage and family; and (2) the interest in immortality and perpetuity reflected in property ideologies that displace the Law of kinship and social order into real estate—the effects of Law masquerade as ideologies of genetic prudence and ownership. For example, the self-contradictions of abortion statutes sometimes reveal ideologies of lineage and real property that refer to Symbolic Law. Older, pre–*Roe v. Wade* (pre-1973, prefeminist) statutes often betray the operation of the Law whose underlying presence is the only way to account for the statutes' internal inconsistencies.[17] The differences between older statutes and "reform" statutes that tend—in the process of appearing to equalize gender disparities—to efface the underlying operation of Symbolic Law expose the futility of changing law without approaching the lack already inherent in Law.

Abortion laws are riddled with the conflict they are codified to sort out; the interests of the mother, for example, may conflict with those of the foetus, especially when the life of the mother is threatened by the pregnancy. Already the site of displaced issues of access to women and birth control, abortion embodies the crux of the family crisis as the mother, appearing to usurp the role of the Law, threatens to separate from the child in defiance of a father who is already nominally absent from the statute. The premature oedipal conflict represented by abortion (Moms cuts off baby before Dad even has time to interfere) replays the drama of separation and prohibition with the wrong characters at the wrong time. Abortion laws attempt to recast this oedipal conflict in its proper terms—mother desiring child, father protecting it and dividing it from its mother, only at the proper time, in his name. The foetus's interest in abortion laws, despite a cultural identification of the foetus with principles of perpetuity and fecundity, is not necessarily identical with the interest of either parent, but rather is identified with the interest of a social order bent on perpetuating itself—through the child, through the "correct" configuration of familial power. The dilemma of abortion, while focused on a battle between mother and foetus, is the locus of a displaced battle between an individual's desire not to procreate versus a social Law represented by the absent Father who demands reproduction.

This broad conflict does not really refer to the pragmatic difficulties of pregnancy or to the plethora of social issues surrounding birth and women's health; it does, however, explain why those concerns are so easily dismissed, since they are beside the point in terms of Law. In abortion laws, the issue of gender and Law created by the possibility of abortion is deflected into specific statutory self-contradictions related to, but also masking, a Law of social order that, of necessity, privileges procreation as the illusory defence against mortality. The configuration of abortion statutes reenacts in concrete reproductive terms the metaphorical functions of the Law-of-the-Name-of-the-Father. Abortion statutes generally omit mention of the father, an omission that might be seen as a progressive recognition of the woman's authority over her own body. The statutes themselves, however, treat the mother as a medium rather than as a subject with will, enforcing not a philosophy of maternal choice, but rather the authority of the state to perpetuate procreation in the *name of the father*, who is, of course, absent.[18] The literal lack of reference to the father in the statute preserves the absent father's right; the Law is present through the statutorily effaced Name.

Some older abortion statutes contain self-contradictions symptomatic of the Law that reside in the law's attitude towards the foetus, which is inscribed as a kind of property right in the name of the absent father instead of as a life to be nurtured and protected. For example, the Delaware statute on abortion titled "Limitation on termination of human pregnancy" (24 *Del. Laws* section 1791) makes sense only in the context of the Law of kinship exchange and its concomitant extension into property rights. The basic rule in Delaware is that "no person shall terminate or attempt to terminate . . . human pregnancy" except under certain listed conditions such as the likelihood of the mother's death or a risk of permanent physical or mental injury to her if the pregnancy continues, the "substantial risk" of birthing a child "with grave and permanent physical deformity or mental retardation;" or if the pregnancy resulted from rape or incest. In any of these circumstances a pregnancy can generally only be terminated during the first twenty weeks of gestation.[19]

The statute's exceptions to the rule of maintaining pregnancy appear to balance the interests of the mother, foetus, and the conspicuously absent father. The primary purpose of the law is apparently to protect the foetus: the product and perpetuation of the Law. The pregnancy may be disturbed only if its continuation would kill or severely damage the mother or if the foetus itself is so damaged as to not be a foetus—as to not present the possibility of perpetuation. But despite its ostensible focus on the foetus, this abortion statute also reflects a more compelling interest discoverable through a reading of the statute's disparate treatment of the exceptions of rape and incest. Apart from health issues, the only other exceptions allowing the termination of a pregnancy are if the foetus is the creation of an illegal act upon the body of the mother such as in cases of incest and rape. Incest and, particularly, rape refer directly to neither foetus nor mother, since the foetus is a foetus no matter how procreated, but rather to the violation of some other interest during conception.

The disparate treatment of rape and incest exceptions points to the operation of a subtext linked to Paternal Law. The Delaware statute laboriously spells out the kind of rape that will permit the termination of pregnancy as one "committed as a result of force or bodily harm or threat of force or bodily harm," and cites the proof necessary to verify it: "The attorney general of the State has certified to the hospital abortion review authority in writing over his signature that there is probable cause to believe that the alleged rape did occur . . ." (24 *Del. Laws* section 1790). If the pregnancy is a result of a physical crime, and if the law is designed to protect the mother against having to bear the fruits of a crime that has presumably already been committed, why so many mechanisms to determine the actual validity of the crime in cases of rape while incest as grounds for terminating a pregnancy requires no proof at all? Though the rights of the mother to resist violent sexual abuse may be at issue in rape, those rights are not necessarily at issue in cases of incest unless incest is defined as violence per se or unless the incestuous act is also a rape. While we might argue that society's interest in preventing incest and its adherently greater likelihood of genetic mishap makes incest an understandable exception, isn't rape equally heinous and equally to be prevented?

The contradiction between the statute's treatment of incest as an automatic exception and rape as a highly defended one can be explained only in reference to the Law of kinship exchange. Incest denies the exchange of women among men and thus breaks the Law by permitting the illusory fulfillment of intrafamilial Desire. The foetal product of a rape, however, is a part of the kinship exchange, though its presence threatens to subvert the order of patriarchal naming and genetic perpetuity by substituting under the name of one father the kinship line of a father with another name. The foetus of a rape can only be divested in the event that it is unfairly gotten—by violence or threat. The extra proofs required to certify violent rape refer to the confusion attending the metaphorical gendering of the Law, which appears to enfranchise all males with procreative rights over females.[20]

What this inconsistency indicates is that, apart from any societal interest in procreation, what is at stake in the limitations on the termination of pregnancy is the vested right of the invisible father, whose individual genetic investment stands in for the paternal metaphor and is protected at all cost except the life or health of the mother. The exceptions protecting the foetus—limiting abortion to only those circumstances that threaten the death of the mother or the possibility of a monster child—actually protect the interests of the father and through the father the interests of a social order premised upon the orderly reproduction of identifiable patriarchal generations. The rape/incest exception, then, exposes the extent to which the rest of the statute is bound up with the absent father, whose stake in the maintenance of the Law of kinship exchange is inscribed as a property interest—a right of ownership or control—in the foetal vestment of a right of immortality. In abortion laws, the foetus is treated as a kind of property right; aligned with the state and with the vastness of Social order, the foetus is inscribed not as the personal interest of what is not yet a personalty, but rather as the future interest of the Law situated in the place of the absent father, whose "theoretical" right in genetic perpetuity is assumed. Apart from the rape/incest contradiction that exposes kinship Law, the rest of the Delaware statute refers to the Law via the analogy of a property-like paternal right in the foetus.

Just as the literal father stands in for the Name-of-the-Father, the register of property is a systemic displacement and reinscription of kinship laws. Real property, like children, perpetuates the name-of-the-father, represents power and potency, and allays the certainty of mortality through the immortality of a social order inscribed in tangible assets. Among the most ancient protections in English common law, property law asserts a definitive connection between an owner and property, defining the degrees of attachment and control the owner might enjoy. Because there is no necessarily "natural" relation between an owner and (historically) his property, perhaps the most important feature of property law is that it provides an unbroken chain of title within which owners enjoy a visible, legally inscribed connection to property where none is otherwise readily apparent; perhaps its most dangerous feature, a product of legal overcompensation, is the range of property prerogatives provided to owners who zealously guard their interests through an array of remedies ranging from actions in trespass and nuisance to the assertion of interests in water and game.

In the Delaware abortion law, the anxiety-allaying principles of property become the "paternal" anxieties of reproduction, transferring the clearly metaphorical function of Law from the realm of the permanent to the register of the all-too-literally reproductive. Both reproductive laws and property principles focus on the property (foetus). Despite the fact that property laws make certain an uncertain connection between owner and land, property rights' attachment to the property makes the rights of ownership incidental to the thing owned. Locating the source of rights in the property itself makes those rights permanent rather than personal, producing endurance and continuity. In turn, this permanence endows the owner with more potent and absolute protections in the form of nearly unassailable rights to "quiet enjoyment" and testamentary disposition. This displacement from owner to property ironically fails to affirm the connection between owner and property that is one source of anxiety. But the failure of that affirmation suggests that the source of anxiety is not only the difficulty in proving a connection between owner and land, but is also some fear of the failure of continuity, immortality, and perpetuity itself. This second anxiety returns to ideologies of reproduction as the literal mechanism for continuing the "name," "the line," the genetic survival of an individual. In this way, property law intersects with the Symbolic Law of kinship from which it has been displaced, revealing the hope and the failure of property law to fulfill forbidden desire through the surrogate of real property. The law that creates property is linked to the Law that dictates that one cannot own anything except a connection to the Law of social ordering that simultaneously inscribes, immortalizes, and spells mortality.

It is in the guise of displaced property rights, rather than in a consciousness of kinship Law, that battles over reproductive rights are fought. Not only are property rights linked to tangibility, they stand in for the operations of the Law they both occlude and enact, though the property version of the Law provides a far greater illusion of control and possible fulfillment. In this sense, property principles embody the wish forbidden by Law and Desire. The debt that effects a bond to the Name-of-the-Father in Symbolic Law is transformed in property law from a debt to the illusion of right, often, but not necessarily, premised on a mortgage debt and existing with the threat of foreclosure. The real debt of property is not mortgage, but rather the need to pass the property to someone else on death: it is an adage of property law that land can never be without an owner—the chain of title can have no break. The realizable desire of real property is full ownership represented by full payment of the mortgage; testamentary law fills in the debt of the land by reiterating kinship laws in the annals of property deeds. Real property, and the laws governing its control and transference, provide an illusion of plenitude and fulfilled desire, with the delusion of much greater permanence than money or any other mode of exchange that might be seen as mimicking kinship exchange.

As the displaced, but operative site of kinship Laws, property ideologies provide a partial explanation for certain inconsistencies in cultural attitudes reflected in laws about when life needs to be protected, whose right it is to protect, why the female is regarded legally as the blank page rather than "co-owner" of the life she carries, and why the male, whose investment is protected, is nearly invisible in statutory provisions. If part of what is at issue in reproductive legislation is the property rights of fathers, understanding abortion prohibitions (and passions) as the protection of property interests reveals the extent to which much of the anxiety surrounding reproductive rights arises from the jealous assertion of property instincts rather than any desire to preserve or protect life (a proposition reflected in the failure of law to provide for the quality of the rest of a newborn's life). The subtle presence of property ideology also helps account for some of the hysteria that surrounds issues of abortion, birth control, artificial insemination, and surrogate motherhood. While human life issues have rarely ever been the impetus for war, the endangerment of property interests often has been. Whether bellicose irrationality is perpetrated in the name of god, country, or race, encroachments on property and the protection of property interests—borders or oil—instigate battle.

Post-*Roe v. Wade* abortion statutes efface the presence of kinship Law and property ideology by delaying the "vestment" of the foetus to the second trimester of pregnancy. The Massachusetts abortion statute titled "Abortion; pregnancy existing for less than 24 weeks" plainly states: "If a pregnancy has existed for less than twenty-four weeks no abortion may be performed except by a physician and only if, in the best medical judgment of a physician, the abortion is necessary under all attendant circumstances" (112 *MGLA* section 12L). Gone are the rape and incest exceptions, dissolved into the category of "attendant circumstances." But curiously, the decision now rests with the physician, the arbiter and delegate of the Law, which has been displaced from property to medicine (just like literal paternity). A second Massachusetts abortion statute, titled "Abortion; pregnancy existing for 24 weeks or more," restates the state's (father's) and foetus's interest in the continuation of the pregnancy: "If a pregnancy has existed for twenty-four weeks or more, no abortion may be performed except by a physician and only if it is necessary to save the life of the mother, or if a continuation of her pregnancy will impose on her a substantial risk of grave impairment of her physical or mental health" (112 *MGLA* section 12M).

Taking these two laws together, feminist reform has only effected a delay, which subsequently continues the father/foetal's own interest (as opposed to that of the mother, who is presumed to be an adversary) with greater latitude (no rape or incest exceptions, no question of a damaged foetus), now vested in the person of the physician who represents, through ethical imperative, the interests of the State. Simply declaring the foetus a nonentity for a few months defers the alignment of the foetus with the father of the Law. But the first trimester delaying tactic that appears to depend upon definitions of when life begins invites opponents of abortion rights to affix personalty to a foetus from conception, thus sealing the realm of the Law and maintaining an unbroken chain of title—not in the name of the Father (though often in the name of God) but in the name of "life," already a self-contradictory principle that caches the now literal father.

111

While the trimester delay shifts the balance of control over the pregnancy from patriarchal property interests to an appearance of maternal control over her own body, what it actually does is textually obfuscate the continued presence of a hysterically insistent Law, while merely deferring its effects in relation to the foetus. While this appears to be a slight liberalization, providing some margin of choice and/or escape from the laws of social order, it does so only by delaying recognition of the personhood of the foetus, which triggers the Law, remaining thus strictly within the order of Law. The compromise merely delays both a "showdown" over the question of life (or really over the problematic overliteralization of the father), which might itself reveal the operation of Law in its self-contradictoriness (life means death), and the recognition of the Law abortion laws anachronistically represent.

The interests of the State also reemerge at different sites as these apparently straightforward statutes are undone by a plethora of corollary laws that limit the amount of government support that can be used to finance abortion procedures, restrict facilities, free physicians from any obligation to perform abortions, and require—in the reappearance of patriarchal property rights over children—parental consent for abortions performed on adolescents or spousal consent for married women. The remainder or difference that exists between the earlier and later abortion statutes is precisely the apparent gap between Law and laws—between the overt operation of kinship Law stumbling through issues of rape and incest and the veiling of that Law through delay and the proliferation of statutes that combine to reassert the Law in ways even more symptomatic of the proprietary paternal metaphor of the Name-of-the-Father. This latter proliferation, however, also signals the compensatory mechanism of metonymy as such laws reveal multiple, contradictory rationales (quality of familial life versus forcing [rather than permitting the termination of] teenage pregnancy).

Understanding the kinship basis for reproductive laws alters our conception of those laws and provides the potential for a shift in the abortion-rights battle from the dismal and misleading lure of the "pro-choice" versus "pro-life" dichotomy into an open query about the status of reproductive laws, their relation to gender and to ideologies of property and perpetuity. Such conscious examination brings the relation of Law to law into open question and, thereby, begins to confront the authority and operations of Law itself. If we go further to confront kinship Law with its property-law displacement, the gendering of the former becomes visible in contrast with the formal operations of the latter, disimbricating Law from its gendered metaphor and revealing the nature of the social stake in Law.

In one way, abortion laws are nothing more than the preservation of sperm rights as synecdochical of the ideological maxims of capitalism. While there is little public forum for such analytical processes, practicing them will enable feminists to confront the law in unexpected places, bringing to the fore more trenchant issues than those currently under discussion. If sperm rights constitute a governing metaphor, why not fight for birth control? Openly questioning, for example, the interest of the foetus's father (an interest that has recently emerged in abortion lawsuits that attempt to restrain the mother's legal choice to abort), situates the question of the parents' relative roles in reproduction openly as an issue of gender and parental right. Exposing paternal interest as only nominal and financial undermines the paternal myth Quayle elaborates. If fathers are forced to support offspring without the privilege of naming, the illusory control of patriarchy would be fractured and the societal performance of paternal metaphor might be derailed.

Naming the Father

Abortion statutes garner the contradictory tensions of cultural anxiety about the failure of Law understood as the failure of religion, patriotism, economic strength—the failure of the advantage of world exchange—precisely because they are bound up with the Law in a way that challenges literal, imaginary versions of the paternal metaphor. While Stuart Schneiderman asks, "Why can feminism not just live with the idea that the function of the Name-of-the-Father is its own subversion," the Imaginary of a culture caught by questions of gender inequities schizophrenically codifies changes in gender relations at the same time that it zealously maintains—and, in fact, encourages—its strict, but confused notion of the Father.[21] The increased incompatibility between Law and the law is the effect of and continues to effect a crisis in order that is played out around reproduction and paternity. The metaphor sustaining and sustained by the Law is both eroded and aggrandized by laws, creating a tension that threatens to disimbricate the Symbolic Name-of-the-Father from just plain "names"—that threatens to make conscious and visible the Name-of-the-Father's self-subversion. That this might enact a desirable feminist praxis is clear; but another, perhaps more tragic, effect is to force a judgment, to bring Law and Desire into the open in a momentary impasse such as that inspired by the conscious consideration of the rights of the foetus's father.

The quiet site of this metaphorical dislocation is paternity statutes, which appear to provide women with more choice in broad correlation with shifts in other reproductive laws. Paternity statutes reaffirm in forthright terms the relation between father and child. While reproductive laws shift to permit a margin of choice (or a suspension of the Law), paternity laws become increasingly definitive, expanding the rights of fathers as well as certifying the certainty of the paternal/child connection. This occurs at the same time that DNA testing promises paternal certitude, the potential of a provable, inalienable link between father and child that replaces or augments the metaphor of the name.

113

In paternity laws, as in abortion statutes, the child's rights become the State's Right, which, in seeking support for the child, combines judicial procedures for determining paternity with procedures for affixing a burden of support on the father. Paternity statutes (formerly known as bastardy proceedings or illegitimacy proceedings, now often referred to as parenthood laws so as to continue the tendency to omit the name of the father) contravene the commonly held common-law tradition that fathers bear no responsibility for the support of children born out of wedlock. Part of the rationale for that traditional principle is in response to the former impossibility of proof; part is also connected to upholding forms of kinship Law by refusing recognition of those children born outside of the kinship order represented by marriage, unless the father himself formally recognized the child as his. Common law, predictably, presumed that the husband of a woman who has given birth is the father of the child.

Paternity laws that formalize procedures for proving paternity codify a judicial search for the literal name of the father in the name of the State and in the ostensible interest of both mother and child, whose financial burden is thus relieved.[22] Paternity laws, thus, reduplicate the Name-of-the-Father in their literal search for the name of the father, reducing the metaphor of social organization into the subject for microscopic scrutiny through evidentiary blood tests, tissue typing, or DNA tests. The appearance of statutes openly called paternity statutes reflects a feminist interest in gender equity by making both parents of the child equally liable for its support.[23] Paternity statutes also greatly reinforce a tie that previously existed metaphorically, shifting the operation of kinship Laws from questions of exogamy (whom one marries) to a certainty about identity (I know who Dad is). The effect of this literalization of paternity is the reinforcement—doubling—of the paternal presence: the almost parodic conflation of Law and law. While Schneiderman may ask why feminists don't simply let the Name-of-the-Father subvert itself, feminists watch culture duplicate the Name-of-the-Father in a way that identifies the literal father with the Symbolic Law, forestalling its self-subversion even as it self-subverts in proliferations of paternal "proof" that obscure the difference between the Name-of-the-Father and the father's name. The debt owed to the absent father becomes the absent father's debt in the form of child support, reducing the paternal metaphor to a matter of social conscience, which might have the effect of reducing Law to law (the subversion Schneiderman suggests).

Paternal certitude contravenes the metaphorical connection between Law and the Name-of-the-Father by making grossly visible the State's attempt to make a literal connection between an outlaw father and his child. But this metaphorical reduction may also swerve away from the Law it otherwise undermines precisely because it is so literal, appearing to preserve the paternal metaphor in its privileged place. On the surface, then, paternity statutes tend to reify paternity and to suggest that, indeed, the connection between law and the father should and can be made. But this occurs on a literal rather than metaphorical level and, as in the reform of abortion statutes, the difficulty of feminist praxis has always been to force a separation of Law from its Imaginary effects in law.

Breaking the Phallic Bounds

Paternity statutes such as the "Uniform Law on Paternity" appear in relatively recent history, in the context not only of feminist reforms, but also in the wake of improved biotechnology that enables paternal proof. Such laws are both symptoms and harbingers of a change in social form, attempting a last-ditch salvation of the paternal metaphor on the level of social action. This happens at the same time that another threat, biotechnology, endangers the phallic function by disengaging the father from the reproductive process. As Lacan observes, "Will we have to be overtaken by the practice, which may in the course of time become common practice, of artificially inseminating women who have broken the phallic bounds with the sperm of some great man, before a verdict on the paternal function can be dragged out of us?"[24]

The "phallic bounds" are broken when principles of genetics become detached from acts of procreation, uncoupling the phallus from its procreative role and from the chain of signifiers attached to the Law-of-the-Name-of-the-Father, which operates without the phallus. Reproductive technologies remetaphorize the father as the figure governing the joining of genetic material. This is the obverse of paternity laws, which literalize the paternal metaphor by naming the father. These two paternals—the genetic and the denominated father—enable one another in a binary tautology that oscillates between metaphor and metonymy. When reduced to a metaphor, the paternal metaphor reveals its metaphoricity—the real emptiness at its place—which may disimbricate the paternal metaphor from Law. This is, indeed, the danger Lacan may see in artificial insemination which disturbs not only phallic function, but also the "social form" of the nuclear, reproductive family unit. If this is the case, then feminist reform may utilize technology to effect the breaches that shift gender metaphors in more "equitable directions."[25]

The remetaphorizing of the literalized paternal metaphor occurs in the environment of a displaced Law—the Law of medicine, whose increasingly microscopic machinations effect a procreation premised on a series of metonymies and displacements instead of the traditionally metaphorical and romantic coming together. While biotechnology may threaten a shift in the paternal function, Law intervenes to transpose biotechnological threat into an extension of the right of the father. Given the dual potential of no need for a literal father and the possibility of a "mythical" biological father in reproductive practice, the threat to the paternal function is not surprisingly allayed by recourse to property and contract law that affixes the right of control in the name of the father and absorbs biotechnical products within kinship laws. Two instances of biotechnological reproductive practice—artificial insemination and contract motherhood—have catalyzed the rescuing operations of laws that take the place of and try to return the paternal function.

Like the issue of the unborn child's father's rights over the foetus, contract maternity challenges the hidden singularity of the father's claim on the foetus, confronting the Law's necessary attachment to the father through the disposition of the child. This suggests that in addition to the multiple-front challenge possible in matters of abortion, other reproductive laws also afford sites where the paternal metaphor may be brought into question as an issue of the necessary right of one gender over another. Breaking the phallic bounds disrupts an entire chain of signifiers: from phallus to father to the father's name to the Name-of-the-Father to the Law. For this reason, feminist reform might profitably look at the system of law, rather than at specific laws, bringing into play the gaps afforded by artificial insemination and surrogate motherhood.

In any case, the trajectory of social change, affected by increased biotechnical control over reproduction may accomplish what feminist praxis by itself cannot. Dislocating the father at the site of conception threatens to become the tragedy of tragedy. Unlike the tragedy of Oedipus, whose question of identity answers society's debt for the murder of the father, the future Oedipus may locate identity and debt in a place other than the biological father whose connection to him has been mediated by test tube. Dad might become mother in the fantasy of a Tiresian Arnold or Dad might disappear altogether, dislocated into the metonymical comedy of multiple parents. As Roseanne describes it in 1995, babies come from a Mommy, a Daddy, and fifteen fertility specialists. At this point of tragic waning, however, Law still scrambles to shore up the father (or father still scrambles to shore up law), the verdict on the paternal function is neither oedipal guilt, nor biotechnical dislocation, but a hung jury.

AUTHORIZED REPRODUCTION; OR THE SPERM OF THE FATHER

The image of father's sperm traveling bravely through untold gynecological terrors, fulfilling its purpose in narratives of inevitable success, proves the claim of paternity in increasingly microscopic terms, filling in every junction of cause and effect so that, finally, reproduction becomes a series of contiguous transfers, fact—science—at last. But in a metonymical system, gametes also become detachable elements, wieldable ingredients in a process that can be manipulated, as Aldous Huxley's 1932 *Brave New World* predicted. Eggs and sperm, detached from their corporeal and social contexts, become the raw materials of a mechanical reproduction. Displaced temporarily from the law of the family, flash frozen in suspended animation, thawed and floating freely in infinitesimal pools of nutrient liquor, gametes may be adjusted, mated, spurred to productivity in complete disregard for the gendered patriarchal regimen from which they have been momentarily released. It is only when one tries to put them back that there is trouble, as the metonymous foetus meets the jealously defended shreds of the Law-of-the-Father.

In the case of artificial insemination, the sperm of a man (not necessarily married to the woman who uses his sperm) is introduced extraphallically into a woman. The insemination itself is not artificial; what is "artificial" is the means of introducing sperm as well as the family configurations such practices may create (single mother, nominal father, and biological father). The law in cases of artificial insemination, though currently evolving and unclear, reflects the differing kinship emphases behind the shifts in paternity law. For example, a section of Washington State's "Uniform Parentage Act," titled "Artificial insemination," provides that: "the donor of semen provided to a licensed physician for use in artificial insemination of a woman other than the donor's wife is treated in law as if he were not the natural father of a child thereby conceived unless the donor and the woman agree in writing that said donor shall be the father" (26.26.050).

The law presents two different courses, the first, that the donor shall not be the father, upholds the law of kinship ties as they relate to marriage and the orderly descent of generations under the name of the father. Biology bows to Law. The second alternative, that the woman and donor can agree the donor is the father, emphasizes the genetic connections that supposedly underlie kinship order. Law serves biology. Either alternative fits into a kinship scheme, though the second permits both the emergence of familial permutations—the possibility of a single mother if the donor's paternity is rejected—and a way to correct those permutations—the donor becomes the father. In the possibility of no father at all, an option implied by this statute, lies one challenge to the paternal function: the child born without a nominal father who is not illegitimate. Because of the statute's inability to close such a scission, the possibility of a "fatherless" child begotten at the will of the mother disrupts kinship Law and the paternal metaphor, at least on the level of human reproduction. In the case of voluntary single mothers, however, the name-of-the-father appears intergenerationally (unless the maternal patronym has also been changed), effecting a return to the mother's paternal line.

Although the Huxleyian specter of bottle babies, cloning, and parentless childhoods looms over reproductive technologies, the dissociation of sperm and father does not in itself subvert the paternal function. Two lesbians who have a child through artificial insemination carry on the paternal function in the two-parent arrangement of their household. Artificial insemination of a woman with sperm other than her husband's vengefully illustrates the paternal function as the father's name seals the biological gap that, though certain (rather than uncertain), is still the gap the Father's name has always sutured. Gene splicing, the technology imaged in *Twins*, threatens biological integrity, but not nominal or familial formations. The fact that the literal father is not at issue in the metaphorical function of the Name means that all kinds of inseminatory permutations can take place without disturbing the paternal function. What disturbs it is the loss of the metaphor itself.

This Leggo approach to procreation would seem to defy the concept of the family, the literal father, and certainly the Law-of-the-Name-of-the-Father, enabling lesbian couples, infertile couples, and single parents to procreate. Limited by the not-yet-superceded need for a womb (though artificial wombs are certainly imagined), gamete manipulation seems to broaden our reproductive sites, spread the paternal function around, and adjust the notion of family. Best evidence of this challenge to Law is that the Vatican condemns these reproductive technologies, claiming they have sundered "flesh from spirit in an area where the integrity of parenthood demands that they be one. . . . Inevitably, something important, though unseen, stands to be harmed in the

117

process. And what stands to be harmed is human parenthood."[26] What stands to be harmed is the metaphorical system of the Law-of-the-Name-of-the-Father, that amalgam of flesh and spirit, that unseen order that sustains paternal aegis.

Confused with the literal family, which is in turn confused with social order, this Law becomes "Love," the metaphor that makes biology into civilization. "By removing the child from the personal context of conjugal love, as IVF [in vitro fertilization] does, a decisive step is taken which necessarily depreciates that love. . . . And to weaken this love which is the essential bonding act of the family . . . is to weaken the family. And since the family is the basic unit of society, what weakens the family also weakens the society" (DeMarco, qtd. in Overall 143). Disentangling reproduction from "conjugal love" in its most coital sense undermines this loving set of metaphors by taking away the single moment of invisibility and "magic." Attached to emotion, coitus becomes a metaphor; conjugal love that asks technological assistance supplants this coital metaphor with the factitious metonymy of highly visible technological manipulations.

As a literalized version of the paternal function, sperm's transferability enables the imagining of this gamete grocery. The techniques of reproductive technology are mainly engaged with the manipulation of sperm; in so far as sperm have become the all-too-literal metonyms of the paternal, reproductive technology has made that paternal even more metonymy than the fulsome frozen egg or the gestating maternal womb. Artificial insemination, in vitro fertilization, and contract motherhood all require the removal of sperm from its loving familial function to more mundane fertilizing operations.

The Vatican's anxieties would seem to be incarnated in the proliferating variety of coitusless reproductions. While adoption is simply another layer of metaphor (a loving family steps in for a "loving" act), these manipulated reproductions don't need metaphor and that is their threat. Since there is nothing to prevent sperms' use outside the boundaries of the larger patriarchal aegis of traditional family order, there is nothing except economics to prevent the establishment of atraditional reproductive units. With portable sperm technologies, lesbians and single women may procreate with sperm from males they know, from deceased mates, or from banks. Gift or commodity, sperm demystifies phallic magic, the "miracle" of life. The ensuing families are not, however, necessarily outside the paternal function. The whole point of some of this reproductive manipulation is to enable the disenfranchised (the literally fatherless) to join in the laws of familial order, the system of names and generations that reattaches despite the child's embryonic scene. Thus, lesbians who procreate and establish lesbian families do not necessarily undermine the Law-of-the-Father; often they embrace it, simply taking the father's place in an extension of the metaphor. The nuclear family lives, even if uncoitally constituted and without a literal father (and even though conservative ideologies deeply fear these extrapaternal formations).

While eggs are less portable, their detachment from their ovarian site has a similar demystifying effect on maternity. Eggs from a biological mother can be implanted into a gestating mother and the resulting child adopted by a third parenting mother. In other words, detachable gamete technology undoes the mother's characteristic metonymy, turning maternity into a substitutive, metaphorical task. While this return to metaphor seems theoretically comforting, the mother's loss of contiguity is the more vexed site, since maternity is the certainty that guarantees the paternal function. While contracting for gestation services would seem to enable paternity by allowing male couples, single males, and males with infertile wives or partners to have children, commodifying maternity destroys the material site of the paternal metaphor. For this reason, a rationale often identified as "the sanctity of motherhood," eggs and gestation services are more difficult to acquire and gestation contracts difficult to enforce. The Law will allow the circulation of the paternal, but suspiciously restricts its medium of support.

The paternal function can persist even if paternity is overly literalized and metonymized as long as the maternal remains a site of contiguous metonymy. If mothers are limited to a certainty premised on physical association, then sperm can function not as overliteralized and hence reductive paternity, but as an even more potent and pervasive version of the paternal. Now one can father anywhere and be able, theoretically, to identify one's offspring. The Law of the Name is, to some degree, enhanced by the circulation of the identifiable gamete, which, when recovered by a legal system that works to reconstruct the nuclear family, simply hyperbolizes this spermic metonymy as the new paternal metaphor. Maternity's commodification, however, seems to suggest the coexistence of an independent (i.e., nonpaternal), competing reproductive function. If both sperm and egg or womb are commodified there is no locus for metaphorical control. In other words, the reason the circulation of sperm is less disturbing than contract maternity or in vitro fertilization is because (a) sperm have already freely circulated; (b) maternity has already signified the paternal function in its metonymical complement. Altering maternity is a far more radical threat than accommodating the Symbolic to a paternal circulation that has already existed. This is because while social relations might have been envisioned as the exchange of women between men, what that exchange masked was an exchange of sperm; the movement of women signified—metaphorized—the movement of sperm, reassuring the paternal function through the systematized application of rules and names.

Bearing atavistic residues, commodified maternity creates patriarchal panic. Lesbian mothers are one thing (and they can be interfered with through various child-custody maneuvers), but contract gestation (known also by the odd nomenclature "surrogate mothering"—there is nothing surrogate about the mothering, it is a surrogate to the lawful medium for the paternal function) plays out the conflict between an enlarged and sustained paternal function and the threatened emancipation of its necessary maternal medium. Contract maternity consists of an agreement between a woman and a male or a couple that the woman will either consent to impregnation with the male's sperm (will, in fact, also be the biological mother) or will consent to the implantation of an in vitro fertilized embryo for the purposes of gestation. Her body is being rented as an incubator. Arguments against this practice include not only the traditional defense of family values, as supra, but also arguments that focus on the woman as the site of potential disruption. Contract maternity either exploits women in inequitable contractual relations—women are victims—or enables "feckless" women to exploit their reproductive capabilities to make an easy buck.[27] In either case, contract maternity is objectionable on the displaced grounds of its potential harm to women. But the argument believed to be the strongest prohibition to maternal freelancing is that contract maternity involves the sale of a child and people should not be sold.

These arguments about women and the sale of children are underwritten by ethical considerations that veil the patriarchal ideologies and systemic fears that sustain maternal conservation; they superficially presume a system of values about "life" that stands in the place of a more metaphorical Law. Both of the arguments about the relation between women and contract assume that, somewhere, there is a fair and equitable contract that assumes the continued operation of the equitable provisions of Law. Understanding the sale of womb time as the sale of a child implies an understanding of gestation as both the establishment of a relation between mother and embryo and the transformation of a saleable commodity (gametes) into an alienable noncommodity. This in utero transformation is the still extant correlate of a metaphorical paternity. If the Name of the Father transforms a baby into an heir and a located member of society and in the order of generations, the mother's gestation transforms genetic material from biological matter into a citizen with rights.

When a male (or couple) contracts with a woman for gestation and or gamete contribution, the father is buying his metaphor, a purchase that undermines any metaphorical function. In other words, the potentiality of genetic certainty is overguaranteed by contractual certitude. While the potential father would seem to be asserting his paternal function in an expeditious way, what he is doing through the contract is disenabling the paternal function by making the woman an equal partner. Enabled by the manipulations of detachable metonymies, the Law-of-the-Father that looked more like property law transforms into a contract, that in purchasing rights, reveals the exchange that constitutes paternity. This contractual paternal enforcement clashes with the more traditional metaphorical ethical law incarnated by the maternal's conservative preservation of the familial system. By retaining the specter of the metaphorical paternal in the mother's performance of contiguity, a fantasm of the Law remains.

Concern about the mother (either positive or negative) and about the child are in some ways screens for this never mentioned conservation of the Law itself. While "public policy" mitigates against the sale of children, and child-custody presumptions mitigate for the continued custody by the mother, what public interest is protected by refusing to enforce contracts for gestation of a foetus produced with the contracting father's (and sometimes a contracting mother's) gametes? And if gametes can be commodified, why can't the children resulting from commodity gametes be commodities? What transpires in utero that changes the game?

The pregnancy is the metaphorizer, the transition from biology to family. Severing procreation from rearing, the New Jersey Supreme Court refused to uphold a "surrogacy contract" in the Baby M case on the grounds that New Jersey adoption statues exclude "paid and enforceable surrogacy contracts."[28] Even though the baby was contracted by a man anxious to become a father, the sanctity of motherhood imagined as an in utero relation wins out over the father's interest in establishing what would be a very certain father–child relation. Severing procreation from rearing enabled the continuation of the maternal guarantee to the paternal function—it enabled the fantasy of metaphor—while it disallowed the contractual metonymy of the man's more literal attempt to purchase his paternal function. What looks like mother versus father is actually metaphor versus metonymy: "To assert that Mr. Stern's right of procreation gives him the right to custody of Baby M would be to assert that Mrs. Whitehead's right of procreation does not give her the right to the custody of Baby M; it would be to assert that the constitutional right of procreation includes within it a constitutionally protected contractual right to destroy someone else's right of procreation" (qtd. in Robertson 23).

John Robertson argues that severing procreation from rearing is illogical; but given the number of times, in this culture, that procreation is, in fact, severed from rearing (in adoptions, child-custody battles, child welfare), it would seem that even if the Court "misdescribes the scope of procreative liberty to form families with biological offspring" (23), it does so to protect metaphor, which has come to be increasingly enforced from the Law itself rather than from "Nature." This preservation of metaphor ironically stems from the same impetus that has instigated more legislative definition of legitimacy, that cultural correlate of the Law-of-the-Name-of-the-Father. If the Name-of-the-Father no longer functions reliably to define familial relations, then the Name-of-the-Father must be reinforced by the Law it underwrites. This occurs not only in statutes that define paternity, but also in those that legitimize offspring produced through artificial insemination. "Any child or children born as the

121

result of heterologous artificial insemination shall be considered at law in all respects the same as a naturally conceived legitimate child of the husband and wife requesting and consenting in writing to the use of such technique"[29] While, literally, AI children are illegitimate, since they are not the children of the mother's husband, the law extends to attach legitimacy on the basis of the maternal, rather than the paternal function, a basis itself veiled by the appeal to consent.

What is really at stake here, despite the potential for traditional, but non-traditionally parented families, is the family as itself the chief sustaining metaphor of Law. While discussions of reproductive technology occasionally nod towards the possibility of nonmarital fecundity, the issues of legitimation, ethics, procreative rights, etc., have an assumed familial context. And the family is still a screen for an embattled patriarchy. The law (and the Catholic church) are concerned with stabilizing the familial metaphor itself against the onslaughts of metonymical capability. As long as metonymy can be made to serve the family, generally through limitations on maternity, the threat of reproductive technologies can be allayed. While it seems that family forms are changing—and they are despite the law—the law represents an attempt at familial conservation. If we aren't going to have the "traditional" patriarchal family, then by God, the families we do have are going to follow the rules.

LAW'S SPECTACLE

A former carnival showman, *The Wizard of Oz*'s Wizard gives everyone in the Emerald City a pair of glasses with green lenses ostensibly to protect their eyes from the "brightness" of the city's glory (81). Looking through these glasses makes everything the prized color green, the money-colored value supplement that stimulates consumption. Viewed through the glasses, Oz has green people, sells green popcorn, and radiates a verdant joie de vivre. The tinted glazing between the consumer look and the commodity—the spectacle itself—renders the mundane desirable, and more.[30] Although, in the course of the novel, the lens trick is exposed (it doesn't appear in the film), the citizens continue to wear the glasses anyway; they know but all the same . . . Happy consumers in the Emerald City, the city itself is happy, graced by singing, spending, satisfied inhabitants who are quite content to look at the world, the tumbled facade of the Wizard, the devaluation of commodity, and their own disavowal as acceptable adjustments to urban life.

Disavowal is a common reaction to large-scale symbolic change in *The Wizard of Oz*'s tale of the Wizard's unveiling, departure, and replacement with the detachable-limb Scarecrow. Just as *The Wizard of Oz* performs the unveiling of the Wizard's power, so it dramatizes one mode of paternal compensation in its strategic use of spectacle. Both the glasses, which insure that the world still looks the same, and the staged spectacles of the transfer of power protect Emerald City denizens from recognizing qualitative change. At first a fatherly trick, spectacle now substitutes for the father who lacks. Upheavals in the Symbolic fabric of the city might occur, but the green is consistent, affecting and transforming everything that one sees, situating the eye as the agent of cultural constancy. Presumably marking transitions, spectacular ceremonies such as the one staged for the Wizard's departure actually suppress the recognition of change by making all symbolic upheavals appear to be simply another part of city ritual.

In the same way that Oz's literal spectacles provide an illusion of order in their emerald constancy, so a spectacularized law performs a similar function in contemporary culture, easing the anxieties of a consumer population whose paternal Wizard has been slowly unveiled for the last two hundred years. Television and films about law enforcement and practice, trials staged for television (*Divorce Court*, *The People's Court*), and, most recently, endlessly televised real-life trials saturate culture with the image of justice being served, coloring what we see, assuring us of the continuing vital presence of order. While cinematic law is spectacle on the order of Oz's reassuring ceremonies, pervasive television law works like Oz's glasses, assuring the quotidian constancy of law.

We might read America's preoccupation with law since the late 1950s as a symptom of the finally visible rift between Symbolic Law and law resulting from a breakdown in the paternal metaphor that has sustained Law's illusion. Personified by lawyers, law, already intrinsic to the American imaginary as manifested in detective fiction and cowboy drama, takes center stage in the visual imagination with *Perry Mason* (1957–1966).[31] *Perry Mason*'s 271 episodes endlessly reenact the victory of Law over laws as Perry regularly extracts the Truth from appearances of circumstantial guilt and physical evidence that have fooled the prosecutor and the police. Perry, in his wisdom, appeals to a higher Law characterized not by the superficial coincidences of events and their physical traces, but by Human Nature, whose correct interpretation does law's empiricism one better. Reassuring us that law courts are, indeed, sites where law and justice prevail, *Perry Mason*'s redundant confessional denouements produce the continual illusion of a connection among the paternal lawyer (Mason), spectacular trial apparatus, and Law as a Truth that unfailingly appears. Through Mason's canny interpretations of evidence, the Truth becomes the product of Law's process, even though the official prosecutorial apparatus (the law) invariably fails.

If it is true that *Perry Mason* "was created to publicize local scandals in the legal profession," it does that and more.[32] Playing law off against Law, *Perry Mason*'s 1957 debut countered police shows such as *Dragnet* that tended towards a documentarized reinforcement of the state legal apparatus. *Dragnet*, which now seems like a pioneering original from television's infancy, actually follows both a series of popular radio superhero crime fighters (*The Shadow,*

The Lone Wolf, The Green Hornet) and a radio tradition of dramatized audience participation "real" police cases where audiences were invited to help in capturing criminals (*The Eno Crime Club, True Detective Mysteries, Homicide Squad, Calling All Cars, Twenty-First Precinct, Mr. District Attorney,* and Jack Webb's *Pat Novak for Hire*). The latter constituted the first wave of the "reality" format that would again become prominent in late 1980s shows such as *Unsolved Mysteries, America's Most Wanted, Cops,* and *Rescue 911.*[33] Television's first law-and-order entries were *The Plainclothesman* (1949), *Martin Kane, Private Eye* (1949), *Man Against Crime, The Black Robe* (1949), and *They Stand Accused* (1949).

The 1951 *Dragnet* organized and consolidated television's somewhat disparate images of law enforcement, private detectives, and law into the single, businesslike, straight-arrow ethical figure of police Sergeant Joe Friday, whose style of deliberate nonromanticism (he didn't even have a girlfriend) and emphasis on fact and its ironically factitious delivery rendered law the unassailable province of the government. The show mimicked documentary realism ("The story you are about to see is true. Only the names have been changed to protect the innocent"), filming scenes on location and narrating an overly detailed attention to exact time, police language, a seeming restriction to "just the facts," and the court's disposition of offenders. *Dragnet's* style aligned a particular cause-effect narrative of calm, authoritarian fact-finding—a very literal law—with a law that inevitably justly punishes those whom Friday hunts down. The various social tragedies resulting from criminal activity (children who die in bathtubs because their parents smoke marijuana, the high cost of auto theft, the victims of burglary) provide a second-level commentary on the wisdom and power of law and the reason for order. But *Dragnet's* legal reinforcement ultimately confuses law with Law, mistaking the maintenance of order with the metaphorical principle that defines Law in the first place.

Dragnet, like *Perry Mason,* was conceived to solve an image problem, this one the image of police as corrupt bunglers.[34] While *Dragnet* spectacularly aligns police, laws, and the court system, and *Perry Mason* illustrates that the Truth-finding apparatus of court proceedings can realign law and a higher Law, both shows present law as an existent, stable, full site that fails only through human frailty. These shows teach respect for law by repeated and formulaic narratives of law's ascendancy. Even if agents of the law (lawyers, police) are fallible, justice is not. Law exists. Cultural disorder is, thus, not the fault of any lack in Law, but of a lack of respect for or understanding of the law.

Just like the detective stories upon which they are modeled, law shows liken legal process to the elements of a particularly oedipal narrative—problems of identity, investigation, and revelation of the right answer—delineating a law that follows a story instead of presenting the problematic dissonances of legal investigation. In fact, as George Gerbner comments, "If you can control the storytelling, then you do not have to worry about who makes the laws" (qtd. in Stark 283). Linking law to narrative couples a somewhat faulty apparatus to a tremendously familiar ordering principle; substituting narrative exigency for law's sometimes unpredictable peccadilloes translates systematic rifts and illogic into the currency of common cultural consumption. The very narrative nature of television's versions of law makes law seem eminently accessible to all who can read narrative—that is, to everyone. In this way, law shows substitute the specific tensions of narrative for both the metaphorical operation of Law and the real-life difficulties of law.

The display of this fantasized narrative law presents more than a particularly rewarding story; as spectacles of interpretive activity, *Dragnet* and *Perry Mason* painstakingly trace the deductive logic and mundane but orderly methods of detection (stakeouts, questioning witnesses, sifting through mounds of accounts to find discrepancies) whose concreteness appears to sustain legal process. The spectacle of collecting evidence is like watching someone put together a puzzle; it makes viewers collaborators in law's constant fact-based legitimation by inveigling their participation in the gradual solution of crimes. Law shows specifically invite (and even require) viewer interpretation of facial expressions, analysis of testimony, and knowledge of human nature through the deductive process of evidence collection and the spectacle of faces offered for examination. The court's emphasis on the face has even been offered as one rationale for the popularity of courtroom drama on television; television's close-ups easily render and personalize courtroom action.[35] Although we might explain the use of the close-up as an effect of the same motivation that instigates Law's spectacular reinforcement, the plenitude represented by the facial image aligns with the fullness ultimately attributed to Law's truth-finding processes.[36] Thus, by strategically imaging faces that signify answers, *Perry Mason* seduces viewers into a cooperation with the metaphorical trajectory of Law's truth in its spectacular narrative guise.

This ruse of participation, however, is neither the rationale for law's spectacularization nor its effect; rather, the very spectacle of "justice" glosses over the myriad gaps in reasoning, unlikely coincidence, and temporal convenience of the shows' investigations.[37] Spectacle, like Oz's green glasses, makes the narrative of law cohere, enabling disavowals of the shows' lack of verisimilitude in the service of law's continuity and illusion of order. Even though the system imaged is nothing like the real system in practice, we accept that narrativized system because it triumphs, because it provides an image of fullness and weal that real law seems to lack. "Television drama has thus given legitimacy to a process that does not warrant it, and has changed the public's entire conception of legal reality" (Stark 283). Law, which seems a reified Truth, is actually a spectacular commodity that functions to guarantee order in the increasing absence of Law. "The spectacle presents itself as something enormously posi-

125

tive, indisputable and inaccessible," Guy deBord observes. "It says nothing more than 'that which appears is good, that which is good appears.' The attitude which it demands in principle is passive acceptance which in fact is already obtained by its manner of appearing without reply, by its monopoly of appearance."[38]

Television law's "monopoly of appearance" obtains not so much "passive acceptance" as disavowal premised both on the viewers' participatory acquiescence in a system of visualized truth-finding and in the "green"ness of the field of vision, glossed by the added value of documentary realism in *Dragnet* and by the riveting persona of Mason and truth-bearing faces of *Perry Mason*. Spectacle's supplement emphasizes continuity, coherence, and value in the same way the fetish produces a defensive image of wholeness. Spectacularizing the legal system disavows its gaps, incoherences, mistakes, and failed narratives in the service of maintaining the specter of Law. But as that Law is increasingly destabilized, its spectacle must become more spectacularized by increasing its documentary realism, magnifying the opposition between lawyers or detectives and police, and/or layering on the pure glitz of an *L.A. Law*.

Beyond the Legal Principle

As the two variants of law's spectacle, law dramas replaced police shows in relative popularity in the 1960s. Steven Stark attributes the disappearance of police shows in the 1960s to the era's countercultural attitudes. *Batman*, which appeared in 1965, seemed the extreme parody of police bumbling, and Stark locates it as "the apex of countercultural rebellion on television" (252). But *Batman's* graphic associations with Pop art (Whoosh! Blam! Holy Over-Analysis, Robin!) suggest that its campy combination of superhero and cartoon is linked to the compensatory strategies of Pop and 1960s' superheroes. Like Pop art, Batman relocates the law from the sloppy mechanical productions of the well-meaning police to the stylish spectacle of costume and gadget; another superhero, Batman's supplemental excess reinforces a failing order.

The influx of self-conscious superheroicism most graphic in Batman also supplemented the image of mainly human legal defenders, who become versatile, cynical, clever, and stylish. Secret agents (*I Spy*, *Mission Impossible*), detective lawyers (*77 Sunset Strip*) replace the police as protectors of justice. Vested now in single figures or well-equipped teams instead of in systemic representatives like Friday, the law requires an almost vigilante attentiveness—an outlaw attention that circumvents law for the good of Law. But while *Batman* might have been a Pop parody of police drama, its self-conscious imaging of obviously compensatory strategies suggests that the larger transition to spies and private eyes, and the continued popularity of lawyers (*The Defenders, Cain's Hundred, Slattery's People, Judd for the Defense*, and *Owen Marshall*), was connected to an individualization of the paternal function as that had been linked to law enforcement in its various guises.

If police and lawyers are the spectacular representatives of the law and if the literal law they represent is already confused with Law, then both police and lawyers stand in imaginary place of the law—that is, they incarnate the paternal function. The police work as an institution; the institution defines the locus of imaginary law. Lawyers work within an institution, but rarely represent it. Instead, lawyers personify the law themselves, especially as they, like Perry Mason, constantly demonstrate that Law is not located in the system, but in a higher principle to which wise individuals (but rarely institutions) have access. The 1960s shift to a focus on individual (and noninstitutional) law enforcers may not be so much television following countercultural popular attitudes, but rather television enacting the same drama of systemic failure and compensation that Pop art performed. Police don't disappear from television, they become the incarnations of a system that is failing. The only way to salvage this failing system is to locate the paternal function in superheroic figures whose extraordinary cleverness, vision, and street smarts make them the saviors of a system gone wrong. This doesn't mean that law has disappeared, but that, as in Pop art, television has found a way to reappropriate law for the cultural imaginary.

In the late 1960s and 1970s police shows return, but are no longer populated by the boringly obedient Joe Friday's of the 1950s (though *Dragnet* and Friday do return briefly). The lawyer-detective super sleuth is relocated into the hybrid personae of police commanders such as Kojak, Steve McGarrett, Columbo, and Ironside (Perry Mason as a cop), or teams such as the trio of *The Mod Squad* who represent the system, but whose slightly maverick and still independent talents make the police force an institution that works despite itself.[39] Superheroic figures ensconced as the defenders of a justice gone permanently out of whack, the police in police dramas in the 1970s performed the function lawyers performed in the 1960s; they became the exponents of a justice that is beyond the system, compensating for a feared lack by reinstalling institutions such as the police as the locus of law.

While this revaluation of government clearly works as conservative backlash in the ideological field of post-Vietnam unrest, it also—and perhaps more transparently—works as a belated attempt to compensate for an increasingly missing law. One producer remarked, "I am a patriot. In the police shows that I do, I show the police in an idealized way. Without respect for the police, I think we'd have a breakdown in our society" (Stark 265). Or as another producer put it, "We were close to chaos, close to suspicion of institutions in the early 1970s. The blue line was there to preserve what was left, what was the semblance of what used to be one helluva government when it served the people" (Stark 266). The reforged connection between nation, government, police, and "the people" is an imaginary vision of a very full metaphor of law as standing between chaos and order. Revived, this law operates like a Stallone or a Schwarzenegger, a super body standing for us all against the chaotic forces of suspicion and disrespect.

Family Law

In the 1980s police and law dramas repopulate prime time, but with an appeal to a different televisual "realism" than the *Dragnet* documentary. While the protagonists of such shows as *Cagney and Lacey* and *Hill Street Blues* seem more like "normal" people, this new, more personal realism was another kind of spectacular ploy. The police become "real" people with "real" problems and families, working in a system that isn't perfect (they don't always win, they don't always catch the villain). This admission of law's occasional failure merely supports its illusion of authority and infallibility. Like the postmodern, law becomes the narrative that knows it doesn't know.[40] Appealing to the verisimilitude of law's failure references the law that the system hasn't served, working, as Perry Mason did, to reinvigorate law as a higher principle of justice.

Patrice Petro attributes the increased personalization of law enforcement in the 1980s to the larger number of women viewers.[41] The personal equals the feminine, but in a not-so-perverse way, the inclusion of traditionally feminine spheres in the realm of police work extends the overt and considered spectacle of law from the streets and the squad room to the patriarchal home. The humanization and familialization of the law respond to gender anxieties in a particularly insidious way. Gender—or really feminism—challenges an imaginary law of the father in more direct terms and is, therefore, a threat to be specifically defended against. As Petro observes, "in light of the real social and legal sanctions which continue to be imposed on women, it is clearly *patriarchy*, and not feminism, which consciously seeks to contain its own excesses and instabilities so as to redefine the Law in its own image" (59).

As feminism becomes a mainstream fact, women are increasingly televised, ostensibly as pleasing role models, but also as a way to recoup the patriarchal all over again. As both Judith Mayne and Petro have argued, 1980s' law shows directly address gender issues and, as Petro concludes, "reinstate patriarchal law with a vengeance" (57). Although Petro makes this argument in relation to daytime law shows with a judge (*The People's Court*), it is equally valid in the more complex atmosphere of *Cagney and Lacey* or *L.A. Law*, where women, serving as law's representatives, inevitably reinforce rather than challenge patriarchal order. Imaging women cops and lawyers with personal lives is a disciplinary vision that attempts to return overly enfranchised women to the patriarchal fold by juxtaposing their personal lives to law enforcement. The professional always wins over the personal (or if it doesn't it causes tragedy), demonstrating repeatedly the aegis of law over disorder, emotion, and a lack of discipline.

Cagney and Lacey's effectiveness as enforcers, for example, takes second place in relation to their relationships: to their jobs, their families, and to one another. Seen as humanizing and personalizing law, *Cagney and Lacey's* focus away from the law appears to leave the law alone while it invites it home. Chris and Mary Beth are law's handmaidens, occasionally seeming to wield power, but more often worrying about their relationship to a more literally patriarchal law in the guise of family. As they support one another in the precinct's ladies locker room, their focus is exactly on the way their job makes uncertain their relation to the world. It is as if they cannot both be the law and live within it at the same time.

More articulate in its fully drawn legal landscape, *L.A. Law* continues *Cagney and Lacey's* work in a slightly different direction. Mayne's compelling argument that *L.A. Law* tells "*its* stories by acknowledging, however subtly or indirectly, that men and women occupy radically different positions vis-à-vis the law" suggests another way law's narrative spectacle attempts to compensate for anxieties about law's failure.[41] Noting that the program, like all law shows, links law to storytelling, Mayne locates the figure of the swinging door as defining *L.A. Law's* wanting to have it both ways—wanting to appear to enfranchise women and treat feminist issues and wanting to reaffirm patriarchy and heterosexuality at the same time: "The doors that swing both ways are defined within terms central to feminist discourse," Mayne observes, "rape as the ultimate test of whether the law is patriarchal or not; female narration as difficult and marginal; the appropriation of feminism by men to recapture those privileges challenged by feminism in the first place; the definition of feminism as a threat to the heterosexual status quo" (35). By subtly subordinating feminism (or its apparent effects) to a patriarchal law presented as liberated, benign, and flexible, *L.A. Law's* gender dramas both defuse overt feminist threats to patriarchy produced by women's changing relation to the law and suggest that law has not really been irretrievably altered. The comforting Ozian spectacle of *L.A. Law* is not only the narrative lesson of its convoluted gender wars, but also its veneer of wealth, excitement, and power, which covers over law's problems with a glossy image of law practitioners' material well-being.

L.A. Law went out with a less than spectacular whimper in 1994, but its demise certainly did not mark the end of television's compensatory fascination with law. Even as *L.A. Law* reigned in the late 1980s, new, even more alluringly "real-life" police shows such as *COPS, Rescue 911*, and *America's Most Wanted* were aired. These seemingly innovative hybrids of documentary video and staged reconstruction hark back to radio's early "nonfiction" police stories such as *True Detective Mysteries*, which presented narratives of "real" crimes involving the audience in an ongoing manhunt. The late 1980s' combination of direct audience address and sense of eyewitness reliability actualized law enforcement in its gritty, tacky, classist detail, as it moored law within a barely varied, even more simplistic, infinitely repeated story. *COPS'* shows redundantly pursue perpetrators involved in car theft, drug dealing, domestic abuse, and robbery, catching and cuffing them, exposing them as devious, dishonest, and intellectually deficient, and standing triumphantly over them while delivering bare edicts of enforcement ("You shoulda stopped"; "Don't lie to the police." "You have the right to remain silent.").

Imaging the police as a working-class group of professionals, *COPS* and other such shows locate crime in the lower class, making enforcement the province of the worker and crime the habit of a seedy subclass. This class relocation extends law's aegis to all but the dissolute, reinforcing class, racial, and work-ethic ideologies and realigning a dissatisfied and disenfranchised working class with law. The shaky camera and sounds of breathing might make one feel like one is on the spot with police, but their often milling behavior (four or five officers standing around one subdued "perp"), deployment of force, and truly pathetic quarry reduce law enforcement to something more like playground politics. Shows like *COPS* and *Rescue 911* still revel in the ideology of law, mouthed in the homely philosophies of cruising officers, the admonitions of *Rescue's* host, William Shatner, or contained in their narratives' of routine triumph. Even in real life, the police win.

These super-realist spectacles occur simultaneously with the spectacle of cable-televised, real-time real court cases on Court TV and CNN. Enabled by changes in trial rules permitting cameras in court, court television moves from the moralistic narrativized productions of *The People's Court* to the apparently serendipitous excitement of actual ongoing, unmediated court cases. Competing with obviously (and somewhat clumsily) narrativized docudramas, real-time court seems to reject the earlier tactic of narrativizing law. Apparently going with the indisputably boring legal flow, real-time court cases displace the soap-operatic flamboyance of *L.A. Law* with a true-life flashiness that seems more realistic, compelling, and, if possible, melodramatic than television's fiction. If *Perry Mason* made law into narrative, court television makes narratives the extended subject of law; its appeal lies in the corollary narratives of the trial's participants that sustain its extended coverage of lengthy and often disjointed hearings. Narrative is traded for effect and commodity authenticity.

The televised trial of the Menendez brothers, for example, focused as much on narratives of celebrity, the lawyers' careers, and the lives of witnesses as it did on the actual narrative of truth finding. The rules of evidence become the principles of narrative exposition, allowing or disallowing parts of stories we already know exist. The court, in fact, plays against competing cultural narratives, regulating what can and cannot be officially told. In this sense, court television's law, localized into trial procedure and evidentiary rules, becomes again a prohibitive principle. But since the actual principle underwriting the trial's prohibitions was not rendered as part of a coherent system of reliability (the purpose served by the rules of evidence), trial procedure looks like the prohibitor (and enabler) of narrative itself. The narratives that are already known, or at least surmised, attach parasitically to the hyperrealized drama of narrative prohibition, filling in the trial's lapses in interest and demonstrating how the law gathers and controls disparate narratives under its powerful wing. The fact that such corollary narratives are necessary to the spectacle of the trial, however, signals a transition from the metaphor of justice that governs a narrative of truth to multiple narratives that coincide and intersect to justify law's spectacle. This narrative expansion may seem to extend law's aegis, but it also bends its metaphor into the metonymical commodity necessary for law's continued consumption.

Televised trials, though, have another way to present law's imaginary fullness. Literally filling time, saturating with detail, forcing the imagination into the contemplation of "real" events, the Menendez trial provided a material satiation in a commodity culture that could no longer discern between media reality and fiction. Law existed because law was there to see, there and always twenty-four hours a day. Infinite repetition, close-up, expert commentary, courtroom doldrums, the monotonous work of real trial law reified the law more than the excitement of *Starsky and Hutch* or *Hill Street Blues* or even the hijinks of *Matlock*. Real law in the age of spectacle is a spectacle of tedium; only tedium can appear to avoid the simulation that attends most spectacle. Consciousness of simulation as a nontedious value in general enables the illusion that the unspectacular spectacle, like a real trial, must not be simulated and must, therefore, be real.

As countersimulation, the Menendez trial still organized its multiple narratives through an all-too-literal oedipal scenario attended by Tiresian psychiatrists, unrelenting advocates, and a pair of ambiguous Oedipi. The trial's focus on the sons was no longer a dramatization of a long-lasting debt to the father, but of whether the sons had made the father pay his "debt" to them. Just as superhero narratives ultimately become the son's story, so law spectacles finally image the painful ascendancy of the son who has (allegedly) killed the father. The Menendez's mistrial performed a different law, one uncertain about the son's position, one that would not (either in the interests of justice or ideology) avenge the father. O. J. Simpson's even more obsessively televised capture and trial continues this saga of the son, the superhero accused of murder and tried in a procedure that is so spectacular, time-consuming, and expensive that a commodified justice may finally be exhausted by its end.

Televising real trials may, in fact, signal the depletion of the compensatory maneuver of a spectacle law. The television terrain shifts to medicine and back to police shows (*NYPD Blue*, *Homicide*) rendered more stylistically realistic through the use of cinema verité camerawork, graphic violence, uncensored language, and an even closer, dirtier, hairier, seamier image of what fighting criminals is all about. With beautifully written story lines, these police dramas compel attention to a fantasmatic real that extends so far beyond metaphor that its only figuration can be metonymy—its virtual reality attachment to a referent-less system where the illusion of the real is the only law left. These shows kill off their characters, violating the comforting rules of fiction that permit a continual mode of viewer disavowal. Their meaner, more businesslike, protagonists render the law a tough, real, literal force that wrests order in the streets of a culture whose rule has become disorder.

Also appearing in the 1990s lineup is *Law and Order*, a show whose style and idea are throwbacks to earlier television. It is, in fact, a throwback to *Arrest and Trial*, an early 1960s' combination of Ben Gazzara's pursuit and Chuck Connors's trial of the criminal; the show failed because in the 1960s' era of cops versus lawyers, "one of the show's stars had to be wrong" (Stark 254). In the 1990s, the police and district attorney have learned to work together cooperatively, sealing the various branches of law into a totalized institution whose lack is displaced into the nuts-and-bolts problems of obtaining evidence, getting around the constitutional fetters on police work and prosecution, penetrating the duplicity of witnesses, and countering the evil bargaining of defense lawyers. *Law and Order's* marriage of police and lawyers presents what appears to be a unified front where differences in race and gender, in opinion and politics, are subordinated to the job. This creates the illusion of an opportune system that can welcome multiplicity and still work. While one member of an investigating team can be conservative—even reactionary—the other can be liberal; while their commander can be a grumpy white man, she can also be an inventive black woman. The show provides the illusion that all opinions are presented, that all views are represented in a process where all is relevant.

Law and Order's seeming democracy of opinion illustrates how the spectacle law apparatus has produced a new order that refers not to justice, fairness, or any other legal metaphor, but to Law's lack itself. Its spectacle incarnates the transition from the Wizard to the Scarecrow, viewed through television's pixelated glass. Attaching an evolutionary series of perspectives about law to narratives based on topical cases, *Law and Order*, like court television, depends on a certain narrative parasitism, referencing and deploying wider cultural narratives. This parasitism is metonymical, working, as in the Menendez trial, to organize disparate narratives into a relation of contiguity. In this more metonymical context, *Law and Order* images a law that manages to attain order despite systemic hurdles or inconsistencies; its protagonists are the successful nemeses of systemic failure hampered by all of the nightmarish liberal handicaps Bates and Crovitz detail.

Demonstrating weekly a system that still works despite everything, detailing the lubricated coordination of police and lawyers, *Law and Order* is certainly a compensatory spectacle of law. But the order it images is a very different order from Perry Mason's confessional truths gleaned in an environment where only the police are the problem. Its metonymy works as a set of intricate and uncoordinated compensations that refer not to an overwhelming principle, but to the incident mechanics of accountability. Glossed by factoid subtitles giving the location and dates of the action (à la *Dragnet's* voice-over narration), *Law and Order* emphasizes the location and interrogation of witnesses, both in police interrogation rooms and in court. This interrogation is not like Mason's magic unveilings, but is more a painful delving to enable the completion of a chain of information sufficient to support indictment and then conviction. The show's narrative is about building this metonymical chain by which criminals can be linked to the crime.

Law and Order's narrative chaining culminates the transition from an appeal to a higher metaphorical Law that was unrealized but still referenced in 1950s and 1960s television shows to more direct compensations that protect against challenges to law that arise, not coincidentally, in the registers of gender and multiple differences. In the 1990s, hyperreal law enforcement dislocates law altogether in favor of the personal danger of its synecdochal representatives, who no longer reference justice with the zeal of Steve McGarrett, but who instead have become soldiers in a pervasive struggle to maintain safety in a nonsensical world—a world the police and lawyers can still make sense of. This new world order is finally metonymy, attached to commodity culture where a linked hypertext of narratives becomes the Truth sustaining a system whose metaphor has been lost.

133

LAW IN THE AGE OF MECHANICAL REPRODUCTION

Given this compensatory trajectory and transition from an appeal to Law to law as a chaining of narratives, what does it mean that the two most successful space-exploration shows both begin with trials? Conceived in an oddly legalistic frame, as if extension into the galaxy might spell chaos, the original *Star Trek* series began with the trial of Mr. Spock, who, against orders, had returned the gravely disabled Captain Pike to a virtual reality planet where he could live the illusion of wholeness. Outlawed because of the hypnotizing attraction of its hyperreal illusion, the planet presents the dangerous lure of living in a simulation instead of reality. Imagining virtual reality effects that are only now becoming possible, *Star Trek* envisioned the threat of their dangerous substitution of the imaginary for the real-life struggle of Star Fleet existence.

The Law in this inaugural *Star Trek* episode is a law of prohibition, a law that forbids fragile humanoids from an entrancement with lack itself, with sets of signifiers so totalized that their lack of real substance promises nothing for something (or something for nothing). The planet's systematic delusion is far too close to the Law-of-the-Name-of-the-Father *Star Trek* otherwise represents; in substituting the illusion of something for nothing, it reifies the law's own substitution, challenging Star Fleet's self-imposed limits.

Those limits are encapsulated in Star Fleet's "prime directive" of noninterference in cultures that are not yet aware of other life-forms. Rationalized as a way of preserving natural development, and hence variety, individuality, and the historical integrity of species and planetary differences, the prime directive is also a way of producing the illusion of power through its prohibition. Like the Law-of-the-Name-of-the-Father, the prime directive works in the absence of the agent attributed with the power; like the father, Star Fleet governs at a remove, gaining its power through the metaphor of the prohibited relations between its ships and planets. Its limits, while appearing to be a limit on a metaphorical exogamy with new kinship systems, are actually a taboo against something more like pedophilia. Star ships can't consort with the technologically and politically immature.

Nearly twenty years later, *Star Trek: The Next Generation* also premiered with a trial. The two-hour pilot movie is framed by the cosmic being Q's trial of humanity as personified by Captain Picard. Rudely playing with time-honored legal principles (such as the presumption of innocence and due process), Q's trial seems in all ways a travesty except for the very real power behind it.

Forced to recognize Q's puissance if not his perverse principles, Captain Picard succeeds in demonstrating that humans are, indeed, worthwhile and are not a barbarous, primitive species. He accomplishes this by sticking to the law, not Q's quixotic, self-serving version, but the time-honored principles of generosity, bravery, integrity, loyalty, and compassion that constitute an ethical Law. Proving that humans governed by principled Law are superior to Q's cruel whimsy, Picard sets the ethical tone for the entire series.

Like its precursor, *Next Generation*, too, is governed by the prime directive as well as an evolved tolerance for difference played out in its interspecies crew and myriad commonplace encounters. While the prime directive occasioned oedipal rebellions on the part of Captain Kirk, it stimulates clever circumventions on the part of Captain Picard. The Law-of-the-Father becomes the father's law, exceeded by an ethics of compassion that challenges the prime directive's absolutism. This shift in the treatment of the prime directive is linked to the relation between men and machines. While *Star Trek* negotiated the relation between humans and the computerized womb-projection ship as a relation between son and mother (Engineer Scott, in the fine tradition of seamen, always refers to the *Enterprise* as "she"), *Next Generation*'s hold on technology is far more commanding, as evidenced not only by the cyborg-eyed engineer Giordi's mastery of systems, but also by the presence of Data, the machine son of man. The mother-son configuration respects and fears the absent father's (Star Fleet's) law. When machines become sons, humans become paternal and the father's law is made literal. The compensation for this literalized paternity is *Next Generation*'s appeal to a traditional ethics that finally includes the machine in the order of beings, subject to human laws that, curiously, return once more to the issue of property.

The law is fairly pervasive in both *Star Treks*, constituting a constant frame of reference; trials hover in *Star Trek*'s imagination. Technology, however, intersects with law as it provides an ever-present, unimpeachable witness to human activity. The ship is a recording machine; its panoptic function verifies truth objectively. In one episode, the reliability of the machine witness becomes an issue in a trial that orders the hierarchy of man and machine. In "The Court Martial," Captain Kirk is on trial for having negligently caused the death of an officer. Relying on the ship's record of events, Kirk appears unquestionably to be guilty. But Kirk insistently remembers events otherwise and his clever lawyer thinks to question the reliability of the ship's recording apparatus. Finding a glitch in the computer system created by sabotage, the lawyer argues that the machine recorded events incorrectly—so incorrectly, in fact, that the officer Kirk is accused of killing is still alive and is the saboteur.

The *Next Generation*'s fascination with detection and law enforcement is manifested in various characters' holodeck fantasies (Data imagines himself as Sherlock Holmes, Captain Picard enters the seamy world of 1940s' private investigators) as well as in the occasional trial, most of which have to do with adjudicating issues of interspecies difference. Alongside galactic law is the series' continued preoccupation with Kling-on legal forms, juxtaposing what appears to be an anachronistically ossified patriarchal tradition to the liberated, principled, and quasiscientific legal apparatus of Star Fleet. And if the Kling-ons maintain what is so spectacularly the Law-of-the-Father (Worf, son of Mogh), Star Fleet seems to have maintained a more liberal ethical tradition that, at bottom, is an idealized version of present-day law where computer help and machine witness have again become mere tools in a humanoid search for truth. The Law, which made connections where none existed, has become a law of connections and provable contiguities if only we look closely enough.

In both *Star Treks* the intersection of human and machine in the "neutral" terrain of space seems to require the galvanic presence of law. Perhaps the unknown of space requires the compensations of a fully present legal system; or perhaps human dependence on an overly mechanical, digital apparatus incites the brooding omnipresence of the stable, traditional, now universalized Law. If the latter is the case, we return to the mechanical's threat to traditional production and reproduction in the early twentieth century. In fact the literal infiltration of machine into the human order has occurred with the "fully functional" android Data. Quite literally a mechanical reproduction, Data's sta-

135

tus as being is constantly challenged by Star Fleet's legal apparatus. In one episode, Data decides to reproduce, creating an android "child" based on his own positronic brain patterns. When Star Fleet claims the child as its property, Data's reproductive rights are challenged. But while humans can produce machines, the machine finally cannot reproduce itself. Data's child dies before her disposition is decided.

Data himself becomes the subject of an ontological inquiry into his own legal status in *Next Generation*'s "The Measure of a Man." Requisitioned for research purposes by an insensitive cyberneticist who proposes to take Data apart, Data refuses the request, claiming that his parts add up to more than the whole of his components and that his essence would be lost. Resigning from Star Fleet to avoid the order, Star Fleet retaliates by declaring Data to be its property. In a trial where one of the *Enterprise*'s chief officers must prosecute and the other must defend Data, the issue of Data's status hinges not on understandings of his consciousness, but on perceiving him as a new life-form. Appealing to anti-slavery ethics, Captain Picard, Data's defender, argues that the Federation will be judged on how it treats new "races." Making Data property would set a bad precedent.

The trial, while raising the question of the machine's status, answers it by recourse to a human law that absorbs all. Proving that law "does work," the disposition of Data as a sentient being and founder of a race subordinates the machine to the human order of law, species, and understandings of value and consciousness. Seemingly expansive and liberal, Data's place in the new order is to become a tenant in the old; saved by tradition, Data is saved from tradition as his ultimate difference is subsumed into a human order whose right is to subsume the father's proprietary rights.

In so far as these shows project contemporary anxieties into a future where they can be imaged as resolved, the presence of a traditional, functioning justice system, or of a higher law is a highly conservative compensatory tactic not unlike the compensation Perry Mason represents. But in this compensatory maneuver, machines comprise the spectacle by which law itself is compensated. Becoming the new subjects for law's operations, machines and multiple species difference are legislated into a paternal realm masquerading as benign and egalitarian acceptance. The clue to the continued existence of this paternal law is the issue of property, which continues to appear as the principle by which human order is determined.

Imagining law's trajectory as an advance to a compassionate Law, both *Star Treks* are concerned with ordering human and machine, humanizing and subduing the machine, overseeing its reproductions, and reserving the power to define life. Even if machine forms are declared life—Data, the hybrid Nanites that take over the ship's computer system, even the Enterprise itself, which reproduces a little ship—they are life within a human analogy, relegated to

136

human order, reifying a law of analogy by which the machines are finally, galactically relieved of their challenge to the Symbolic. While the law appears to advance from issues of property to issues of life, life's delineations are still an effect of property interests. Data is declared life, because self-consciousness cannot belong to anyone else; life and property appear to be finally divorced. But property still lingers, not as a threat to life, but as a threat to the machine. Machines that cannot be made analogous to humans are still property; the law still controls the threat *The Terminator* represents.

Anxieties about the self-reproduction of the mechanical are quelled by their subsumption within a human law that renders their reproductions analogous to the human. Reproduction, at first the threat, becomes the means by which the machines' menacing order is neutralized. Nostalgic, the two *Star Treks* image a Perry Masonic law existing in a time before the time when digital technology would propel humans into virtual space.

137

UNAUTHORIZED REPRODUCTION

Vampires' Uncanny Metonymy

chapter 4

SIBLING RIVALRY

John Polidori, a precocious young doctor and the irascible companion to Lord Byron on his 1816 European tour, spent part of the year with Percy Shelley and Mary Wollstonecraft Godwin Shelley in Geneva. A feature of that famous meeting was the group's decision to write ghost stories. Mary composed *Frankenstein* and Polidori finished the story Byron was to have contributed to the group's project. *The Vampyre*, a tale of tragic promises and ruthless destruction, supplied a complementary horror to Shelley's tale of creative usurpation. If *Frankenstein* disturbs the arrangement of divine Word and science, *The Vampyre* disturbs order itself, mingling death with life, immortality with mortality. Published in 1819 as a *Tale by Lord Byron*, *The Vampyre*'s success spawned five French plays and two German operas within a year.[1]

BACHELOR FATHER

Just before 1897, long after the fledgling *Frankenstein* and the 1819 debut of Polidori's *Vampyre,* Abraham Stoker, manager and secretary to actor the Sir Henry Irving, composed *Dracula.* Culled from both legend and literary antecedent, Stoker's *Dracula* proposes a reproduction turned on its head, or at least on its neck. Although both Frankenstein and Dracula envision single-parent homes, Frankenstein imagines himself a Godly father in a traditional if only slightly adjusted family, while Dracula is the *unheimlich* spirit who craftily inveigles a large brood from the ranks of the living. Supplanting the metaphorical relation between human father and child with a metonymical quasi-incestuous toothsome attachment between an *untertöt* progenitor and his child of the night, Dracula's postmortal, oral, infectious, parasitic technique competes with the mortal, coital reproductive regime. While the vampire may be an overly determined, magnificently metaphorical figure who represents everything from incest to hoary tradition, the common vein of its figurations is an anxiety about order itself.

A series of witness documents that feign original sources, Stoker's novel devises a verisimilitude that compensates for the vampire's menacing intervention into procreative and symbolic order. Just as Stoker's predecessor, Southey, buttressed his 1798 "lamiaesque" "Old Woman of Berkeley" with "an elaborate explanation assuring his readers of the reliability of his description," Stoker certifies his novel's veracity in a brief introductory feint: "There is throughout no statement of past events wherein memory may err, for all records chosen are exactly contemporary, given from the standpoints and within the range of knowledge of those who made them."[2] Contriving eyewitness testimony whose utter reliability comes from its temporal and spatial contiguity to events, Stoker heightens his villain's uncanny appeal.

It is not surprising that Stoker, a man of the theater, would write *Dracula* on the morn of the birth of cinema.

DRACULA IN THE AGE OF DIGITAL REPRODUCTION

If the vampire's first fifty cinematic years struggled with the specter of mechanical reproduction, then its last twenty-five years has negotiated the shift from the clumsy mechanics of physical metonymies to the light fantastic of electronic prestidigitation that clarifies, concentrates, and further empowers the mechanical's metonymic order. A chain of films from the late 1950s to the 1990s symbolically reiterates the vampire's move from theater to Stoker's postcinematic imagination, from romantic individualism to a decadent gothic that embodies the sweep of nineteenth-century industrial development.

That the vampire narrative evolves in direct connection to anxieties about mechanical reproduction becomes evident in a comparison between Polidori's early nineteenth century, prephotographic vampyre and Stoker's protocinematic Dracula. Polidori's vampyre is a man of the Word; his image and look are both dead, in contrast with Stoker's Dracula's spectacularly mortuarial appearance and lively eyes. Polidori's Lord Ruthven is marked only by his "dead grey eye," which "fell upon the cheek with a leaden ray that weighed upon the skin it could not pass" (15) and by his gazing "upon the mirth around him, as if he could not participate therein" (15). This Lord Ruthven, befriended by the innocent and attractive young gentleman Aubrey, takes a tour of Italy and Greece where he behaves with the greatest decorum towards all women, but, as Aubrey discovers, compromises virgins on the sly. He spreads familial destruction in his vampiric wake, but Aubrey does not know the nature of his companion's iniquity until he follows Ruthven and discovers his intention to ruin a young Italian girl. Foiling Ruthven's despoiling intention, Aubrey continues to travel with him. Set upon by brigands in a remote part of Greece, Ruthven is wounded by a bullet. As he dies, he asks Aubrey to swear that he will not impart any knowledge of Ruthven's "crimes or death to any living being in any way" (36). Thinking Ruthven will be dead, Aubrey agrees but is surprised to see the deceased Lord Ruthven resurface in London where with predictable vampiric perversity he courts Aubrey's younger sister. Unable to prevent the liaison because of his promise, Aubrey pines away in apparent madness as his sister marries Ruthven and is destroyed.

Focused around the gentleman's oath, *The Vampyre* defines vampiricism not so much as a postmortem blood fest, than as a matter of gentlemen's honor— a species of contract. Ruthven's behavior exceeds the bounds of the gentleman and dishonors families by spoiling their prospects for the exchange of marriageable (and live) daughters. Aubrey, on the other hand, represents an order where one's word is absolute, premised on an unspoken understanding that a gentlemen would never bind another gentleman to an immoral or dubious commitment and that conditions are what they seem to be. Aubrey pledges silence to Ruthven because he has no reason to think that Ruthven will not be dead. Ruthven's appearances always obscure his heinous designs; he personifies the noble interloper who perverts honor by misrepresenting capabilities and by appealing to the letter rather than the spirit of the gentleman's covenant. For Ruthven, the oath is an insurance policy that enables him to pillage the system by disenabling Aubrey's patriarchal function. Torn between competing imperatives, Aubrey sets his word above the protection of his sister; such is the ultimate operation of a law whose premier postulate is the principle of the prohibitive Word itself. Despite the danger his sister is in, Aubrey acts as a true gentleman. Ruthven, however, has already cheated the system, using Aubrey's ethics against him, inserting himself into the gentleman's order with his destructive and ultimately inhuman desires.

Like *Frankenstein*, Polidori's *The Vampyre* represents a disruption in the order of the Word as that represents the metaphorical symbolic order of culture. The

141

story's immediate and facile adaptation to the theater was instigated not by any inherently visual quality, but by an impetus to make the Word flesh, to dramatize, as in a court trial, Ruthven's ruthless and insolent abuse of the sacred foundations of homosocial relations. The staging of the gothic, while making this derogation of the word spectacular, also contained the vampire's transgression within the conventions of theatrical presentation and the far older tradition of theater itself. The point is that *The Vampyre*'s lexical fix presents an anxiety on the level of presentation—in the difference between word and deed, in a disturbance in the order of the Word itself understood as a principal of order among men.

While Ruthven's appearance conveys a cruel but stoic inhumanity that is not particularly spectacular, Stoker's vampire condenses and combines satanic signifiers and uncanny practices. Dracula's vampire has "peculiarly arched nostrils," hair thinning at the temples but profuse elsewhere, "the mouth . . . was fixed and rather cruel-looking, with peculiarly sharp white teeth; these protruded over the lips, whose remarkable ruddiness showed astonishing vitality in a man of his years" (24). He had pale pointed ears and "the general effect was one of extraordinary pallor" (24). Jonathan Harker, the law clerk sent to Dracula's Transylvanian castle to conduct business involving property the Count has purchased in England, notices a lack of mirrors, a general air of decay, and the Count's decided preference for the night. Upon further exploration he finds a room full of coffins and a chamber with three lascivious maids. He observes his host crawling down the side of the castle wall head first.

Stoker's feigned eyewitness accounts of Count Dracula as he moves from Eastern Europe to England produce the now familiar narrative of the undead nobleman who seduces his victims and drinks their blood to stay alive, who must return to the native soil in his coffin during the day, and who perhaps, like Ruthven, perversely seeks out the relatives of the very man he has hosted as his victims once in England. Ruthven's trespass was against contract; Dracula's transgressions are about property. While contract orders relations among men, property orders relations among generations, sustaining a version of familial or individual immortality in its stable devolutions. The female victims of these respective vampires go from being the third-party beneficiaries of a gentleman's contract to property analogues, whose fertile potential promises the continuation of bloodlines just as estates enable their material sustenance. The shift from contract to property represents a transition from the Word to generations, from the relations among men to an assault on humanity's propagation.

Having acquired property in Harker's neighborhood, the Count focuses first on Harker's fiancée Mina's friend Lucy Westenra, and when he has murdered her, turning her into a vampire who kills at least one child, he becomes interested in Mina, who has since become Harker's wife. Fortunately for Harker, the vampire expert, Dr. Van Helsing, a Dutch combination of science and ancient lore, has been called in on the case and with garlic, stakes, and crucifixes, they set out to find the Count's coffin and destroy him. But the Count, a master of displacement, has already left England and returned to Transylvania. Finally catching up to the train of gypsies conveying Dracula's coffin back to his castle, Jonathan and his friends kill him just before the sun sets, the body crumbling into dust and disappearing before their eyes.

The elements of Stoker's far more complex tale are more visual than Polidori's, condensing signifiers from the orders—law, the church, property, marriage—the vampire threatens. The novel's particular emphasis on law and property—the protagonist is a law clerk, he visits Dracula about a property transaction, Dracula knows English property law—encapsulizes the tussle Dracula's desire represents. Entering into the order of law and property, Dracula disturbs the law through its representatives, forcing their displacement and derangement, endangering their property and generational potential. Just as Ruthven used the contractual sanctity of gentlemens' honor for his own protection, Dracula uses property as both ingress and shield. His castles are sanctuary against probing eyes, housing the necessary native soil of his coffin refuge; he moves like a player on a board game, from estate to estate, avoiding capture.

Stoker's rendition of the vampire involves the perversion or twisting of the generational and religious traditions of western patriarchy. Both as vampiric signifiers and as defenses against his power, these twistings reflect a particular derangement of tradition. Like Ruthven, who perverted the word, Dracula perverts a system—the system of property that stands for the system of patriarchal generation itself. For example, he buys an abandoned abbey in England, turning the abbey into his own home; not only does he invade English soil, he appropriates the church. In response, Van Helsing employs the crucifix as a shield, the signifier of resurrection somehow preserving Christian order against the vampire pretender who makes the promise of eternal life into a literal practice. While Jonathan plans to marry Mina and her much admired friend Lucy is engaged to Arthur Holmwood (after turning down both Dr. Seward and the American Mr. Morris), the matings of these up and coming young folks are interrupted, first by Jonathan's trip to Transylvania and the injuries he incurs escaping from Dracula's castle, then by the Count's arrival in England.

Count Dracula's interest in England represents the invasion of an alien force, that, already residing within the traditional systems of property, family, and the church, destroys the fabric of order from within. Dracula's incursion forces the English to travel, to venture beyond their traditional bounds—into graveyards, to open coffins, to Transylvania on a wild chase. The zoophagic

Englishman Renfield, locked up in an insane asylum, offers the most spectacular evidence of the vampire's effect. Enslaved by Dracula, Renfield is telepathically aware of his master. Ingesting progressively larger species of animal, Renfield attempts to gain the life-giving power of blood that animates his master. But Renfield is a pathetic double to both Dracula and the English culture that keeps him locked up. He is an interesting addition to Stoker's narrative, embodying not the most dreadful effect threatened by the vampire—but, instead, its most piteous effect—the reduction of a human in the mad quest for eternal life.

UNHEIMLICH PROLIFERATION

The vampire's particular threat of unauthorized reproduction seemed to spur reproductions of the vampire, perhaps as a form of control or compensation, perhaps because the narrative of the vampire's destruction comfortably replayed a return to and reassurance about patriarchal order. The vampire's literary beginnings launched a spate of theatrical versions; in the twentieth century the screen rapidly took over for the stage.[3] F.W. Murnau's 1922 *Nosferatu* vampirically infringed Stoker's copyright, forcing a lawsuit with Stoker's widow that resulted in the destruction of almost all prints of the film. In 1931, Carl Theodor Dreyer's *Vampyr* and Universal's *Dracula* premiered, headlining a cinematic genre that would become increasingly populated. Vampire films and their offshoots appeared in crowded waves beginning in the mid-1940s, continuing through the late 1950s and the late 1960s. A 1970s boom sustained production until the early 1990s saw the revival of "classical" horror texts.[4]

Some critics locate the resurrection of the vampire film in Hammer films' 1958 *The Horror of Dracula* starring Christopher Lee as Dracula.[5] The first remake that followed Stoker's story but was neither a spin-off nor a sequel, *The Horror of Dracula* instigated a series of Hammer Dracula films that established Lee as the Dracula standard and inaugurated a repeated 1970s return to Stoker's story as the originary tale. *Count Dracula* (Lee as Dracula 1970), *Bram Stoker's Original Dracula* (directed by Ken Russell, 1978), *Dracula* (Frank Langella as Dracula, 1979), *Nosferatu the Vampyre* (directed by Werner Herzog with Klaus Kinski as Dracula, 1979) all followed the Stoker story with its particular threat to the order of property and patrimony.

The late 1950s remooring of Stoker's version refocused 1960s and 1970s wanderings through the vampire narrative's irresistibly attractive contiguities. The vampire's sesquicentenniary association with Frankenstein continued to reenact the complementary dramas of paternal usurpation and the perversion of order, the all-too-new versus the all-too-old, the oedipal arrogation of the father's power and the doggedly immortal vampiric plague that accompanies and vexes the son's snatch at paternal prerogative. The 1960s were host to a series of monster encounter films such as *Frankenstein, the Vampire and Co.*

(1961), *Frankenstein's Bloody Terror* (1968), *Dracula vs. Frankenstein* (1969), and *The Blood of Frankenstein* (1971). These latter-day pairings (which reflect the original Genevan pairing) deflect the ghouls' attention from the wider culture to an imaginary ogre realm where the threatening figures combat one another. Their joint venture, like contemporaneous superhero conclaves, produces a parallel world rather than an invasive (or rescuing) force. While superhero congresses eventually save humanity, monster bashes reduce threat to variety, the uncanny to proclivity, hyperbolized threat to hyper-hyperbolized excess. The monsters and their various threats cancel one another out. The group films were also a market ploy—more is better—that spurred interest in the monsters' power as a consumable spectacle whose commodity status nullified the more unconscious threats posed by each.[6]

Rival female versions of the vampire myth—Sheridan LeFanu's *Carmilla* (1872), Elizabeth Bathory—provided a related but different frame of menace, pestering patriarchy through the female's unseemly grasp at paternal privilege in a persistent series of both closeted and openly lesbian vampire films.[7] Flirtations with lesbianism, Medean womanliness, and vaginae dentata incarnate were wed to other perversions of the strictly coital—oral sexuality, necrophilia—or derangements of kinship taboos such as incest. In combination with the sexuality intrinsic to "straight" vampire depictions, these underwrote the sprinkling of vampire porn that burgeoned in the 1970s and 1980s—*Count Erotica, Vampire* (1971), *The Velvet Vampire* (1971), *The Devil's Plaything* (1973), *Dragula* (1973), *The Case of the Full Moon Murders* (1974), *Sex Express* (1975), *Suck Me, Vampire* (1975), *Spermula* (1976), *Dracula Sucks* (1979), *Dragula, Queen of the Darkness* (1979), *Gayracula* (1983), *Sexandroide* (1986), *Trampire* (1987), and *Muffy, the Vampire Layer* (1993). On the other side of the reproductive chain, vampires iconically transformed into aliens, Transylvania turning into the alterity of outer space, the alien vampire registering a quite literal threat to the continuity of the human species in an openly technologized field. The vampire is, in fact, the seemingly perfect metonymical medium for constant figural transition; vampires star in films about alien invasion, cowboys, Batman, Wolfman, Robocop, zombies, teenagers, rabbits, prostitutes, voodoo, circus performers, experimental surgery, dogs, hippies, witches, and Hercules.

The point of this brief vampire filmography is not to list the vampire's many permutations, but to indicate that vampire images work much like vampires themselves, spreading by a contiguous contagion. Although Stoker didn't own the vampire and couldn't control its spread, his particular narrativization of the vampire symptomatically arranged the anxieties it represented in the late nineteenth century. At the same time that mechanical reproduction's specifically metonymical reproductions of images (such as photography and cinema) begin to hold sway, the vampire figures an invasive conversion from

145

the order of generations to an antigenerational order, literally broadcast through contiguity, that threatens reproduction in both the human and the artistic sense. The reemergence of Stoker's narrative in the late 1950s and 1970s signals the emergence of some new reproductive threat, or some new challenge to an order that was in the process of changing.

If, in 1820, the vampire occupied the place the eighteenth century had prepared for it by making "folk superstitions a legitimate subject of literature" (Twitchell 33), the 1970s received the vampire's embrace with a fervor drawn from the predigital apotheosis of mechanical reproduction. By the 1990s, Dracula has become just another household name. As the Dracular death threat to order seems increasingly tamed by the commodity system (with its vampiric emphasis on empty consumption), so the vampire's stock seems to rise at the moment its technique has become common currency.

VLAD THE FATHER

Vampire films enjoy their third and most prolific wave in the 1970s. More openly sexual than the less bounteous and more subtle 1950s cadre, 1970s vampires inaugurate a renewed vision of unauthorized reproduction that branches into science fiction (*The Thing*, the *Alien* series), camp, pornography, and the neo-gothic excesses of Warhol.[8] We could speculate that the 1970s wave of vampire films images a paternal anxiety sparked by the rise of feminism, the increased sophistication of reproductive technologies, or, since the 1980s, AIDS; and probably all three provide some insight into the cultural fears of uncontrolled proliferation the vampire most recently represents. But the vampire still participates in its tandem connection to Frankenstein's tragic misprision of the paternal. If Frankenstein makes the symbolic paternal function too literal, the vampire confronts the metaphorical law of patriarchal order directly, combating procreation with contagion, mortality with sustained existence, genital intercourse with oral engagement, the Law-of-the-Father with the law of contiguity, and a talent for metonymical self-transformation that enables transport and escape.

The 1990s return to "classic" versions of *Frankenstein* and *Dracula* supplies yet another version of the twin urge towards overauthentication and the establishment of tradition that has marked the monsters' modern trajectory.[9] And yet the various threats to patriarchal culture and order that vampire figures embody are transformed through this 1990s neo-gothification from threats to refigured harbingers of the very patriarchal order whose gradual demise vampires had intimated. One of the most recent film versions of Dracula rather acutely reveals this defensive retransformation of the vampire. Coppola's *Bram Stoker's Dracula* is from the start overly marked by an anxiety about origination—about who its father is.[10] Claiming its pedigree even in its title (an overcompensation that does nothing to hide the film's rather gross deviations from the text), Coppola's film is thoroughly girded with originary moments. Inserting primal scenes of heterosexual love absent in Stoker's version that feebly try to rationalize Vlad's excesses, Coppola's *Dracula* provides a framing love-story rationale for the brave Vlad's denouncement of God and postmortem wanderings. This love story is actually the ghostly specter of the patriarchal familial status quo against which the vampire has always been a threat. Eliminating any sense of the *unheimlich*, the feeling of familiarity and over-closeness that makes the vampire a figure of fascination, Coppola's Vlad is a romantic hero whose parasitic appetites no longer directly challenge the order of patriarchal British culture, but rather pathetically parallel the human love stories into which Vlad interferes. This neo-romantic frame recuperates the vampire's threat to reproductive order by openly returning the now merely envious vampire to the patriarchal fold. The film's gaudy presentation of evidence to explain the vampire's sanguine proclivity humanizes the vampire, rendering him sympathetic rather than scary. The narrative of origins that has always accompanied the vampire has finally done its work.

The film clearly and resoundingly recuperates the vampire's threat in its conclusion. In Stoker's novel, the group of young swains whose women Dracula has threatened or killed chase and decapitate Dracula outside of his Transylvanian castle. In Coppola's version, Harker leaves his wife Mina alone with an injured Vlad, who, crawling to the foot of the chapel cross he had earlier desecrated, renounces his renouncement of God, becomes again mortal, and dies while looking at the spectacularly transcendent image of his wife and himself floating on the chapel's ceiling, a vision we see through his eyes. Grandly heterosexual, divinely familial, the vampire is returned to the fold he had attempted to destroy.

147

THE BOOK OF PHANTOMS

Coppola glosses his film with the patina of a century; the 1990s revivification of the vampire manifests a particularly urgent need to rehistoricize the vampire, to make visible its ancient pedigree. A recently published horde of scholarly books, vampire criticism, studies of vampire film, vampire encyclopedias, and Dracula histories insistently trace the vampire to the fifteenth century Vlad Tepes or Dracula, a Transylvanian ruler noted for his penchant for impaling his vanquished enemies on stakes. Dracula wasn't the first vampire and the conflation of his tyrannous habits and vampirism seems to have been Stoker's invention.[11] The 1990s exhumations of the vampire certainly do not stop at Dracula, but rightfully point to the folkloric origins of blood-imbibing figures from Lilith to the Indian Kali and the Lamia of Greece.[12]

While the vampire's folklore pedigree is ancient and his/her cultural presence traceable nearly to prehistory, the vampire's historians also attribute more "scientific" and medical derivations for his post-Enlightenment form. The vampire's chief characteristics—the survival of the "undead" corpse, the inspiration of "epidemic blood lust," and the perpetuation of sexual appetite—are traced to contiguous medical "causes," vampirism itself transformed into the product of sets of odd medical conditions.[13] In other words, the traits that make the vampire figure most threatening are explained as exaggerated medical anomalies, tamed through scientific explanation. For example, the vampire's fangs and need for a liquid diet reflect birth defects associated with syphilis; the vampire's facial features are the overdetermined symptom of nineteenth-century venereal fear.[14] The undead vampire's pallid complexion and uncanny rise from the coffin can be attributed to processes of decomposition—hypostasis (or settling of the blood), or the natural contraction of shrinking abdominal muscles.[15]

The 1990s proliferation of vampirabilia in print manifests the same documentary impulse that motivated Southey and Stoker; but rather than simply evincing some need for excessive authenticity stimulated by the vampire's unbelievability, the tendency to document and analyze vampires also comes from the need to fix the uncanny, to locate and control its invasion of order. At the same time, this most recent print obsession also represents an increasing fascination (and even identification) with the vampire's alluring provision of a hoary tradition that grounds and authorizes a more metonymical order. Its appeal augmented by its iconic relevance in an age of dangerous contagion, the vampire configures and makes acceptable a specific drama of symbolic transformation. Vampires are us.

This historicizing and/or factualizing reduction of the vampire's mystery occurs at the commercial height of the vampire's ascendancy. Where 1970s and 1980s vampires retained their unworldly charisma, their threat assuaged through such comedic renditions as *Love at First Bite* and *Transylvania 6-5000*, 1990s vampires are grounded in the reality of literalized history and scientific explanations. This 1990s' trend is, I suspect, not a compensation for the kind of unauthorized reproductive challenge to patriarchal order the vampire represented through the 1970s and into the 1980s, but rather a way of adjusting the vampire's intrinsically metonymical threat to order itself by reducing its figurative metonymy to the fully drawn cause-effect explanation characteristic of a metonymical order. This most recent authenticating adjustment begins, not surprisingly, in the vampire's 1970s renaissance, with the publication of Raymond McNally and Radu Florescu's book, *In Search of Dracula* (1972) and a series of documentaries that demythologize (or hypermythologize) the vampire figure (*The Historical Dracula, Facts Behind the Fiction* [1973], the 1976 *In Search of Dracula*, starring Lee, and *Count Dracula, True Story* [1979]).

By the 1990s, the vampire has become too much metaphor—for AIDS, for homosexuality, for decadent consumption. Like the pregnant father who appropriates the mother's metonymical relation to sustain the illusion of metaphor, the 1990s vampire, no longer uncanny or whose uncanniness has become a commodity, represents the normalization (or delusive remetaphorization) of a simulation commodity culture whose substitution of nothing for something reverses metaphorical law's substitution of something for nothing. The vampire's relation to the paternal function, which embodied the direct challenge of an intervening reproduction through contiguity, is transduced from threat to coconspirator in the resurrection of neopatriarchal figuration as the anchor of a metonymical system. Just as Arnold becomes a mother, Vlad becomes a too human, disappointed, would-be father who converts the uncanny into the pathetic, as Coppola's *Bram Stoker's Dracula* demonstrates, or as the recent emergence of the sympathetic vampire orchestrates.[16]

This recurrent factualizing, however, might also be a way to obviate the threat represented by earlier waves of vampire films, particularly those of the 1970s renaissance where the vampire's iconography and calculated reference to the turn of the century not only produced a sense of the uncanny, but also set out the specific terms of systemic threat around the figure of the father and usurped reproductions already disturbed by the emergence of digital technologies. That 1980s films such as the *Alien* series take up the vampire's iconography to depict alien interference with human reproduction seconds a reading of the 1970s and 1980s vampire as a specifically reproductive threat impinging on a patriarchal order that has allied itself with the very technology whose system has already spelled its transmogrification.

149

DRACULA'S SYMPTOMS

The vampire's entire apparatus—its threat to the orders of contract and property; usurpation of reproduction; version of immortality; proliferations; historical documentation and scientific explanation; iconic relation to death, insects, prehistoric creatures, rats, and even reptiles; charisma; and intimation of eroticism—signal the anxieties that spur the compensations enacted by Pop, bodybuilders, superheroes, and law's spectacle. The vampire is a harbinger of mechanical reproduction; its slow popularization followed the gradual shift from theater's highly metaphorical substitutions to cinema's mechanical metonymies. This transition in emphasis, which is total neither in any cinematic hegemony nor in the genres' complete devotion to one or the other order, has taken at least two hundred years.

The vampire's increasing share of the public imaginary not only proves its resilience as a complex and condensed signifier, but also suggests the coming of age of its threat to order. The evolution of the vampire is not so much marked by changes in its appearance, though there are more "human" vampires in the 1980s and 1990s, but by the increasing appearance of sympathetic vampire narratives that begin to delineate a vampire psychology from the vampire's perspective. Familiarizing and hence domesticating the supposedly soulless is evidence that the vampire figure already configures less the exteriorization of an internal threat (i.e., represents the threatening copresence of another order) than an increasing interiorization and management of threats of difference, variety, and alterity. Empathy for the vampire, the end product of the same kind of curiosity that has stimulated tabloid talk shows, is a species of identification. The uncanny is pathologized; pathologies are comprehensible and curable. In addition, the vampire's "otherness" can be a commodity only if its revelation in some way supports the status quo. That it has been a commodity since the 1970s is one indication that the threat the vampire had represented has been tamed, not because the vampire necessarily changes its signification, but because the system itself is altered, becoming more like the vampire itself.

But while the vampire's threat is assuaged by sympathy (or sympathy indicates the disappearance of threat), two symptoms on the level of the film image consistently appear in post-1958 vampire films that indicate the nature of the anxieties the vampire of the 1970s *untertöt* renaissance represents—and begins itself to assuage—in versions of Stoker's story. Stoker's *Dracula* is the standard of which other versions are variations. The centrality of the Stoker story is not just its historical precedence (actually LeFanu's *Carmilla* precedes it by twenty-five years), but its particular formulation of a central cultural anxiety about order and change. Vampire films of the 1970s, occurring at the same moment as other compensatory representations, demonstrate what is at stake in the vampire's particular narrative and iconography and hint at the beginnings of a vampire assimilation. Although most vampire films will manifest one or both of these symptoms, the Stoker narrative's relative consistency through cinematic history makes it a more transparent harbinger of both cultural investment and shifts in emphasis.

In the spate of 1970s' Stoker remakes, one symptom that reappears is the vampire's sudden and unexpected appearance in scenes where the vampire is approaching his victim for the first time. Occurring at least once in most vampire films, this sudden appearance implies either unnatural transport or a glitch in the visual field most often represented by the vampire's lack of reflection in the mirror. Not appearing in the imaginary or in what is established as the victim's field of perceptions, the vampire suddenly appears, contravening the laws of the physics of light and sometimes defying the laws of matter. Graphically connected to the boundaries of doorways and windows, the vampire's sudden appearance figures an anticipated narrative threat; but the suddenness of the appearance momentarily suspends narrative, gathering in—warping—attention and anticipation, disrupting the order of cause/effect and temporality as the vampire seems to be there before he/she is there, but after he/she has come. Enabled precisely by cinematic capabilities, the anticipated appearance of the unanticipated represents a version of the return of the repressed, enacting an imaginary version of the reality of death. The post–Stoker vampire is no longer a creature of the Word, but a phantom of the eye.

The other symptom is the return glance of the undead corpse, an unnerving motif in 1970s and 1980s vampire films. This glance is not simply the lifeless staring of unclosed eyes that reminds us of a death's-head; it is more the sudden and active opening of eyes that have been closed or hidden, filmed in such a way as to emphasize either their instant unnatural flying open or their unsuspected revelation, illustrating a precipitate change of state, an instant transformation from one thing to another, from inanimate to animate, from victim to hunter, from death to life. Generally occurring after the vampire has made itself known, this fleeting action in itself conveys the vampire's threat even as, coffin-bound, he appears to be a sitting duck for his now-avid pursuers. The glance's overdetermined concatenation of a literalized Gaze, the uncanny, and systemic reversal provides the intersection of individual and generation, life and death, absorption and differentiation as a second-tier assault on the viewer's unconscious. Occurring in cinema, the visuality of these symptoms takes advantage of and provides a commentary on the cinematic apparatus as itself an incarnation (or enmachination) of the reproductive threat that has produced myriad compensations in the register of the paternal.

These two symptoms both occur in 1970s remakes of Stoker's story that have finally fixed the vampire's specifically reproductive menace as an aggregate of sex and death. Less concerned with contract or property law, both John Badham's 1979 *Dracula*, with Frank Langella, and Werner Herzog's 1979 *Nosferatu*, with Klaus Kinski, go to the denuded heart of the reproductive matter and, specifically, in the case of Badham, to the literal father's failing aegis. Badham's *Dracula* emphasizes vampiric romance; Langella's vampire is an irresistible shape shifter whose goal is to woo ladies away from their fathers and prospective husbands. Klaus Kinski's Nosferatu embodies an overt sensuality curiously consonant with his cadaverous aspect. Both render Stoker's narrative in terms somewhat sympathetic to the vampire, who in both cases is finally entrapped by love. The tomcatting Langella Dracula spirits Harker's wife away, traveling with her in a coffin. They are discovered aboard ship where, in an odd but symptomatic twist, the vampire stakes Van Helsing. Literally snagged by a cargo hook wielded by the husband, Dracula is hoisted aloft into the setting sun where he ages, decays, and, finally, enigmatically flutters off into the dusk sky. Nosferatu, too, is caught by the sun as he stays too long at Mina's side.

These romanticized vampires emphasize the sensual and the adulterous, a deliberate and calculated interference with literal families as those come to represent patriarchal order. In both of these 1979 films, the vampire seeks either the unmarried daughter or the young bride or fiancée; his conquest of the female depicts an uncontrolled, extraphallic, competitive, reproductive chain that threatens patriarchal ideologies of biology and metaphysical order.

151

To get to the female, both vampires must somehow overcome patriarchal protections. Badham's Dracula aggressively masters male challenge through confrontation and the manipulation of property law. Nosferatu enslaves Harker
while he is still a visitor in Transylvania. While Nosferatu still wields enigmat-
ic but limited power, Langella's Dracula has a full arsenal of vampiric tricks
including the ability to self-transform into a wolf, bat, and penetrating mist;
he also stays awake during the day and employs a more "traditional" approach
to seduction.

Overtly courting their female victims, both Dracula and Nosferatu win a
willing compliance. Incarnating a curiously vivid reversal of both death and
reproduction, the vampire reproduces death in a simulacrum of life by means
of a copulation achieved in inverted terms. Employing an oral instead of a
genital intercourse, taking blood instead of inserting semen, the vampire's gen-
itive apparatus—the mouth—resembles a large-scale vagina dentata detumesc-
ing the body. The result of prolonged vampiric bloodsucking is an undead
corpse that embodies the reproductive reversals of the vampire act. Undead,
invisible in the mirror, it walks (or flies) the night, transforming itself at will,
and seeking to sustain itself until it is destroyed by the long overdue but reassuring penetration of a stake in the heart.

The emergence of the stake as the cinematic vampire killer's preferred tool
reveals the extent to which the Stoker narrative has become quite overtly
fixed on the challenge to order represented by the vampire's reproductive
inroads. While vampire lore declares that vampires may be destroyed by
beheading, by burning the corpse, and by being caught by the sun in addition
to the ubiquitous stake, the vampire hunters of most 1970s films (with the
notable exception of *Nosferatu*) at least try to employ the stake. A stake in the
heart figuratively reasserts the phallic power of the victorious patriarchal
order; its penetration counters the *unheimlich* penetrations of the vampire.
Instead of imaging a sparagmos that could reasonably dissipate the vampire, the
stake dramatizes, in the very image of his/her destruction, a resounding repen-
etration that rights the order the vampire has perverted. That *Nosferatu* abjures
the stake in favor of a liquidation by light is not only a consequence of the
extent to which Herzog's film follows Murnau's basic plot; it also dramatizes
the inefficacy of the protecting male (and the fidelity of his wife) as Mina
deliberately captivates the vampire until it is too late for his escape. Men don't
stake, women seduce and their seduction is finally more powerful than even
the vampire.

Most film versions of the Stoker tale, however, employ the stake and generally successfully. But Badham's *Dracula* reverses the process; Dracula impales the
paternal Van Helsing instead of the other way around, using the vampiric stake
against the patriarch in the film's final scene. Earlier in the film, Van Helsing had
used the stake to destroy his own daughter, who had been Dracula's first vic-

tim, the paternal prerogative dramatically visited on the errant female. While in Stoker's story the first female victim is an unrelated friend of Harker's fiancee/wife, Badham significantly introduces a familial economy—he is the first to make the literal father appear in the narrative. That Van Helsing is not initially present to protect his daughter, who is easily seduced by the vampire, suggests some paternal neglect for which Van Helsing pays with his own demise. While the father can try to right assaults to order, the father himself is failing. Badham's film, thus, enacts two versions of patriarchal discipline; Van Helsing's daughter revisits her father, which as we shall see later, adds an interesting but symptomatic twist to the vampire's rendition of the return of the repressed. The other version of discipline is the death of the patriarch at the hands of the vampire, who serves as an effective, if temporary, patriarchal avenger, killing the inept father before the father can kill him. In Badham's *Dracula*, the husband/son enjoys a limited triumph, tracing, as do other contemporaneous compensations, the ascendant narrative of the son.

Van Helsing's failures as a father accompany the film's more ambiguous ending. As Dracula (or his cape) floats aloft, Harker's wife smiles secretively. The vampire killer might be destroyed, but not the vampire—or vampirism—which may already have spread to a new generation. This less definitive ending is a far cry from Stoker's cathartic expungement; the film's literalization of the threat to the father not only parallels the literalization of the paternal metaphor, but also traces the failure of metaphor as the phallic stake and symbolic crucifix are no longer effective defenses or protection. While the film's suggestion of the survival of the vampire may provide a hackneyed thrill in the convention of the horror genre, the vampire's counter to patriarchy in its own terms—staking back—suggests its established presence as a more aggressive, less threatened entity. At the same time, the vampire's use of the stake also recalls Vlad Tepes, the original impaler; its innovation is disturbingly old. It has always been the repressed father.

153

Both of these late 1970s films manifest the vampire's two uncanny symptoms made increasingly evident by cinema's increasing ability to convey the erotics of sex and death. While the 1931 version, starring Lugosi, captured the vampire's hypnotic power through its focus on the vampire's eyes and the trancelike behaviors of his female victims, 1970s films cast even more charismatic, more traditionally "sexy" men as Dracula, exacerbating the vampire's seductive qualities. Dracula goes from Lugosi to Christopher Lee to Louis Jourdan to Frank Langella. Even more important has been the improved craft of on-screen seduction and the increased cultural permissiveness that has allowed the vampire's erotic quality to be more explicitly expressed. Thus, while Murnau's frightening apparition could only hover suggestively over his victim's body, Herzog's similarly alarming Kinski can more overtly convey signifiers of arousal in his trembling hesitation, in the closer, more obsessive view of his physical relation to his victim, and in the addition of sound effects.

The 1970s increased focus on erotic seduction emphasizes the vampire's threatening interrelation of sex and death. In this context the vampire figure more openly presents a twisted version of Georges Bataille's hypotheses about the relation of death, eroticism, and reproduction as these operate on the symbolic plane of sustained generation.[17] While the 1931 *Dracula* presented a focused, intently evil but polite hunter, 1970s versions recast the vampire as overtly erotic. Embodying a series of contradictions, the vampire's erotic survival and control of death is also, paradoxically, how it threatens the continuity Bataille asserts is promised by both death and reproduction. The vampire's unauthorized usurpation of reproduction, creating death from life and life from death at will and with little concern over its ghoulish paternity (or maternity), snarls the planes of sex/reproduction and eroticism/death Bataille postulates in his study of eroticism. While both Freud and Lacan assert a connection between sex and death in individual libido—a correlation overtly conveyed by the vampire—Bataille opposes reproduction to death and mediates them via eroticism.[18]

Bataille's notion of eroticism dancing just this side of the grave is a figurative death constituted by the loss of self in the physical and emotional invasion of the body. While the plane of sex/reproduction signifies the possibility of "discontinuous" beings created separately from their progenitors and sometimes requiring their parents' individual deaths, "death means continuity of being," since the denial of the individual heralds the continuity of the species. The vampire incarnates the obverse of this paradoxical configuration, figuring a literal "continuity of being" in its establishment of a contiguous reproductive chain that more often results in the death of the "child" than of the parent.

Thus, providing an alternative reproductive story—one that shifts the valence of the interconnection of death and reproduction, but maintains the alliance between death and eroticism—the vampire provides a visual and narrative example of a large-scale symbolic shift from a system where reproduction spelled a metaphorical continuity to a system that disenables metaphor in favor of the continuities offered by a metonymical, anti-generational erotics. In so far as patriarchy represents a law of generations sustained through the Name—generations that offer metaphorical continuity—the vampire threatens it, not only by directly attacking purveyors of future generations, but also by substituting a different, more literal continuity for generation's metaphor. Reproducing itself in a paternity fantasy, the vampire literally achieves continuity through death, but also literally enthralls its "creations" in an extreme possessive gesture of alternative fatherhood (and this includes female vampires who are the "patriarchs" of a competing order). The vampire's aegis—its figurative paternity—is never an issue in the vampire's reproductive quest, since its connections to its victims are already certain. But certainty also begets dependency, as the vampire relies upon its victims for continued nourishment and life. This vampiric symbiosis of a theoretically eternal life presents a wish-fulfilled (and order-threatening) vision of consumptive connection that can only be interrupted by the even more reassuring reassertion of the Name-of-the-Father with the crucifix and the phallic stake wielded by more literally paternal representatives of a rapidly failing order.

These representatives are, like the stake, indicators of what has become, since Stoker, the vampire's threat. Lawyers and doctors, husbands and fathers (instead of a mere gentleman brother), the vampire fighters epitomize an order of law and science that governs through logic and tradition. The law, as we have seen, is primarily metaphor—and in Stoker's Dracula stories is involved mainly with property. Van Helsing's and Seward's science is an enlightenment vision that, girding itself with technology and practicing careful observation, knows how to diagnose the vampire's presence and how to defeat it. Vanquishing the vampire, however, requires recourse to folk legend, myth, and Christian tradition. In other words, in order for science to quell the vampiric emissary of a metonymic system that is much like the completely metonymical system science would like to be, it must resort to the highly symbolic metaphors of crucifix (the church), the stake (the law), and garlic (medicine).

Science, which aims for the illusive lure of a metonymic certainty (a fully explicated cause-effect chain), presents no threat to the vampire; only metaphor is effective, and by the late 1970s, even metaphor begins to fail. While some critics envision the failure of technology as the expression of a technological anxiety, and others see the use of science as a triumph of the modern over a threateningly decadent past, science's inability to vanquish the vampire has more to do with the vampire's incarnation of a systemic anxiety that actually underwrites both of these contradictory interpretations of technology's efficacy. A fear of technology is an anxiety about a shifting order. The fear of an arcane past is an overcompensatory embrace of the new as if it were tradition; in this scenario, the vampire's version of tradition is less nostalgia than another version of the return of the repressed.

It is also worth noting here that the largest substrain of vampire cinema involves the variant narrative of Carmilla, whose predatory, sometimes lesbian conquests even more openly spell out the terms of the vampire's threat.[19] Where the vampire also includes an open commentary on gender roles and the specter of lesbianism, the threat to patriarchal reproductive order is even more explicit in all of the ways lesbianism threatens patriarchy.[20] Linking the vampire's nonreproductive sex and interruptions of order to lesbianism and homosexuality reiterates bourgeois ideologies about the necessary function of reproduction as a way to sustain family fortunes not otherwise grounded in property or old-order bloodlines.[21] In this context, the vampire, with its noble

155

lineage, begins to look like the frivolous upper class disenfranchising bourgeois industry—an older order interfering with the new. That the specific threat of this older order becomes linked to the female vampire more than to the male is related to the fact that female vampires' challenges to patriarchy are less systemic challenges than challenges to a system. While female vampires certainly represent the same aggressively metonymical production as males, maternity itself is already metonymical. The female vampire's threat is not her reproductive powers, but her aggressive usurpation of paternal prerogative, which is translated as a rift in a gendered patriarchal system instead of as a challenge to the system itself. In other words, gender politics alter both the inscription and interpretation of female vampires, even though female vampires are seen as intrinsically monstrous and castrating. The point is that female vampires *are* seen as monstrous; male vampires menace.

Unheimlich *Maneuvers*

In this *untertöt* narrative already riddled with symbols of a battle over the Symbolic itself, the symptom of the vampire's sudden appearance would seem, if anything, to present both the anxiety of surprise and the presentiment of a threat. The mode of instant presence, often accompanied by the discovery that the vampire has no reflection does more than just frighten; it enacts the uncanny itself. The vampire's appearance is not so much an appearance as a return; its immediacy bespeaks both the sudden and the familiar. The iconic demeanor of the vampire presents signifiers haunting in their familiarity, reminiscent of something not quite remembered. This sense is the feeling Freud sets out to explain in his essay on the uncanny.

Interrogating the uncanny through literary examples, Freud defines it as "something which is familiar and old-established in the mind and which has become alienated from it only through the process of repression." [22] Deriving this from Jentsch's idea of the uncanny as "'doubts whether an apparently animate being is really alive; or conversely, whether a lifeless object might not be in fact animate'" (226), Freud connects the uncanny to, among other things, the "old belief that the dead man becomes the enemy of his survivor and seeks to carry him off to share his new life with him" (242).

But Freud also connects the uncanny to the ocular—to the gaze and castration—in his discussion of E.T.A. Hoffman's story "The Sand-Man." Tracing the protagonist Nathaniel's madness to a tale told to him by his childhood nurse about a sandman who collects children's eyes, Freud traces how this tale is conflated with the child's father's occasional visitor, Coppelius. Nathaniel fantasizes that Coppelius threatens to pluck out his eyes and connects him to his father's mysterious death. Interpreting this knot of childhood material as castration, Freud reads the rest of the tale as the return of the repressed oedipal wish/castration in the guise of the optician Coppola, who sells the protagonist a telescope through which Nathaniel, from his vantage point on the tower of the town hall, sees the villain Coppelius and, in a fit of madness, throws himself off.

Freud carefully notes that not everything that "recalls repressed desires and surmounted modes of thinking belonging to the prehistory of the individual and the race—is on that account uncanny" (245). In other words, it takes more to constitute the uncanny than mere recall or even the reemergence of the repressed. He divides the uncanny into two categories: "An uncanny experience occurs when infantile complexes which have been repressed are once more revived by some impression, or when primitive beliefs which have been surmounted seem once more to be confirmed" (249). Only certain kinds of repressed material produce the uncanny; Freud's examples include material from the oedipus complex and feelings that one's thoughts have effected actions (wishing someone dead who later dies, for example). Both the oedipal and effective thought are linked to order and prohibition, the former to the onset of prohibitions, the latter to contraventions of social order. Both involve prohibited desires or desires for the prohibited.

In an extension of Freud's link between the uncanny and repressed oedipal material, Joan Copjec reads the vampire's uncanny as "an overproximity to the 'extimate' breast," the "extimate" the product of those objects—the breast, the gaze, the voice, the phallus, and the feces—from which "we separate ourselves in order to constitute ourselves as subjects. These objects are both rejected and internalized—"they are in us that which is not us."[23] "Vampirism," according to Copjec, "is located beyond this point where the child maintains itself in relation to a partial object, an object of desire. It is only at this point where the fantasy enabling this relation to the partial object no longer holds that the anxiety-ridden phenomenon of vampirism takes over, signaling, then, *the drying up of the breast as object-cause of desire*, the disappearance of the fantasy support of desire. The drying up of desire is the danger against which vampirism warns us, sending up a cry for the breast which would deliver us from this horror" (34). Vampirism, in other words, is bound up with the reemergence of an otherwise repressed reminiscence of separation and the potential loss of desire linked to castration and the onset of the oedipal, which forces the internalization of extimate objects.

157

Copjec bases this reading on what she sees as the iconic prevalence of breast feeding in images of vampirism. This locates vampirism's uncanny in the image of the vampire's sucking activity. Nothing, however, would prevent the same uncanny phenomenon from occurring in relation to any extimate object, especially if those objects, like the breast, have been prohibited by the intercession of the third term or the Name-of-the-Father. The subjective splits enacted by castration—"If you want Mommy, I'll castrate you"— as the dominant symbolization of prohibition might all provide uncanny material depending upon the form of the material's presentation. For as Freud points out, the material itself is not necessarily the uncanny, the uncanny is a particular representation of material—the redoubling of Coppelius and Coppola in relation to vision, for example, where material that already represents the repressed is itself represented in a way that again parallels (or re-presents) its repressed content. Hence Nathaniel's repressed connection between blindness and the death of his father is uncannily recalled by the provision of a vision prosthesis (a new phallus) that enables him to see his father's killer, who, rather than simply being a killer, represents Nathaniel's own repressed wishes for his father's death.

If the vampire alerts us to the return of an extimate object, and if, as Copjec notes, the vampire "confronts us with an absence of absence—an Other—who threatens to asphyxiate us," with "a bodily double that we can neither make sense of nor recognize as our own," then the uncanny moment when the vampire suddenly appears, both looked for and unexpected, both unreflected and doubly present in self and shadow and fixed on its victim, is the moment of the return of repressed material. But what repressed material? Is it, as Copjec suggests, the repressed extimate breast or the bodily double? Certainly, providing the image of breast feeding might reconstitute the breast and our desire for it momentarily, but I suspect the vampire is more complex than that. In the image of the vampire as breast-feeder, the viewer is situated as a third-person voyeur watching, it would seem, some sort of primal scene. When the vampire suddenly appears in film, however, its image appears as if to the viewer directly. What that typically medium close, reverse shot image provides is an image of being looked at, of simultaneously having something to see and being suddenly and openly seen. This suggests not the breast nor even the double, but the gaze.

As another extimate object, the gaze is "a kind of staring at us from the outside world."[24] "Neither apprehensible nor visible, a blind gaze that is erased from the world," this gaze preexists, correlated with the subject's "given-to-be-seen"(139). "The subject is seen . . . there is a gaze which aims at the subject, a gaze we cannot see because it is excluded from our field of vision" (139). Or as Lacan puts it, "I see only from one point, but in my existence I am looked at from all sides."[25] "The world is all-seeing, but it is not exhibitionistic—it does not provoke our gaze. When it begins to provoke it, the feeling of strangeness begins too" (75). The gaze is "not a seen gaze," Lacan comments, "but a gaze imagined by me in the field of the Other" (84).

The vampire's sudden appearance signals not the vampire's "given-to-be-seen," but ours, transfigured through the way the sudden appearance of the vampire correlates with our sudden sight of it. The alliance of appearance and gaze has the effect of doubling the gaze; we see the look itself and we see ourselves being looked at. Unlike the image of breast feeding, which momentarily reconstitutes a repressed object and the desire it represents, the gaze of the gaze simultaneously reconstitutes a repressed object and exposes the usually imaginary gaze as a Real presence. We, too, are present in all our seenness, a seenness linked not to the drying up of the object of desire, but to the necessity for the repression of the omnipresent, the asphyxiating Other who appears too suddenly and concretely. The instant reification of the gaze represents both the gaze's continued operation and its prohibitive function. The vampire's sudden appearance constitutes the unseen as the too-seen, making the gaze's regulatory effect both visible and an effect of being seen.

In both 1979 versions of Stoker's tale, the vampire suddenly appears in his female victim's room. In *Nosferatu* the woman at the mirror sees the door open slowly and close, although there is no image of anyone entering. When the door suddenly closes, the vampire's menacing shadow is visible on the wall. Clawlike hands raised beside its head, the shadow does not match the image of the vampire, which appears suddenly in a reverse shot as the woman turns to look. Seeing herself seen by that which she could not see, the woman is momentarily shocked, as are we, by the mismatch between the shadow image and the image of the vampire. Not only should the vampire not be there, the shot of his face breaks the rules of continuity. He is closer and at a different angle than he should be, defying cinematic convention momentarily. But that passes as Nosferatu murmurs an apology and the more traditional continuity editing recommences.

In the Badham *Dracula*, Dracula appears at the woman's bedroom window as vapor. The woman sees the vapor, but when she looks again, she suddenly sees the upside-down face of the vampire staring in at her. This shot breaks continuity also, but only in so far as we see no transition between vapor and vampire. Like Méliès' films, the vampire makes a too sudden transformation that draws attention to the break in continuity; this break signifies a glitch somewhere in time and space that is displaced into the figure of the vampire itself. The momentary disorientation rights itself as the vampire enters the window. In both cases, the vampire invades space where he should have no ingress and, simultaneously, shatters the sense of continuous time and space afforded by continuity editing techniques.

By penetrating the bedroom, the vampire would seem to personify a voyeurism that invades the inner sanctum. And that is exactly what the gaze is—a given-to-be-seenness that correlates to a look from the world. The vampire, in a sense, is the world that looks. But the vampire's look is a forbidden look—not that it shouldn't be looking, but that we shouldn't be seeing it look. Just as the gaze is not the look, but a given-to-be-seenness, so the vampire's prohibited look is not a prohibition of the vampire, but a prohibited seeing on the side of the victim (and the film's viewers) that represents repressed desire. As a vestige of the normally absent Other, the vampire personifies prohibition

159

as that turns on the interdiction of the repressed the vampire figure recalls. The gaze cannot be seen, the film should not look back.

In contravening law in this case the order defining the direction of the gaze (and expectations regarding the operation of the cinematic apparatus)— the vampire does not present an outlaw instance of potentially fulfilled desire, represented by the return of the repressed in the form of a formerly desired extimate object (a vision of the gaze) to be seen by the film. Rather, the vampire both instigates and fulfills the desire for prohibition itself; that is, the vampire represents the simultaneous presence of the forbidden and the interdiction that prevents our access to it. We see an image of the gaze we should not see, and cannot have, in the very figure of the vampire who both gazes and prevents us from having the gaze. Like Nathaniel, our repressed is recalled by the repetition of the terms of repression; the extimate gaze is prohibited by the interfering third term even as that third term subsumes the gaze in the guise of the Other. The vampire's appearance replays the appearance of the third term that forces the repression of the gaze at the same time that the vampire represents the gaze of the Other who has forced a repression normally invisible to us.

As in Nathaniel's case, the reappearance of this vision leads to death, the death represented by the figure who represents our own death wish and murderous proclivities. In this sense, the vampire represents the desire for death— a literal death as the real term of limit and the figurative death caused by a loss of self, overabsorption, or the short circuit of seeing and being seen, of a simultaneous subject/object position. It works like the figure of Death in Ingmar Bergman's *The Seventh Seal*, who appears suddenly and unexpectedly even though anticipated, or like the anamorphic object in the foreground of Hans Holbein's *The Ambassadors*, which represents, as Lacan notes, "a skull," "the subject as annihilated in the form that is, strictly speaking, the imaged embodiment of . . . castration" (88–89).

As the extimate gaze, and as the figure embodying its annihilative prohibition, the vampire does not represent the incest with which it is sometimes associated; rather, incest becomes a figure for the kind of symbolic contravention the vampire's prohibition embodies. Breaking the Law-of-the-Father, the vampire represents the father's return as the third-term figure prohibiting any return to the mother, just as it simultaneously figures her return. In its equally masculine and feminine iconography, the vampire, thus, personifies both the figure of the forbidding father and the lure of the forbidden mother. Or, to state this in nonfamilial terms, the vampire represents the return of a turning point where what was once had as an infant is simultaneously offered and forbidden. This is the very point of oedipal separation, of castration and subjective splitting, of the initial operation of the Law itself. Conveyed through the gaze, the vampire figures the reprohibition of the prohibited, the uncanny return of the subject's entry into law and desire as the law of desire comes to the victim.

As the gaze and the prohibitive/alluring Other, the vampire links neatly to Freud's analysis of Hoffman's story. If the sight of Coppelius, the father killer, instigates suicidal madness in the protagonist, then the uncanny is a return not of the father's killer, nor of the father's killer as a double of the self (as the fantasmatic father killer in Hoffman's clearly oedipal scenario), but of the father, through whose demise the protagonist got back his threatened sight. The protagonist sees because his father is dead; seeing the figure who constitutes the mask for his father's demise produces the uncanny. As a specifically visual phenomenon in Hoffman's story and in vampire films, the sudden and unexpected view of the returned figure—the killer who masks the paternal victim as well as the father's killer—is enough to destroy the viewer—at least momentarily.

As the overtly dead and returned, the vampire already embodies most of Freud's formula for the uncanny. While the return gaze and correlative to-be-seenness shatter the imaginary, the bodily reappearance of the dead inspires an uncanny linked to the return of the figure—father/mother—whose metaphorical order has been destroyed by the vampiric figure who masks and embodies his return. The vampire is Coppelius, the eye-threatening father killer, the figure reseen through the visual prosthesis, the figure who doubles, simultaneously, for self and for the other whose absence is no longer absent, made present by the incarnation of order awry, the dead walking, not only the dead father, but also the agent of the father's demise. In this sense the vampire becomes the oedipal double—the projected figure of wish fulfillment and the reminder of guilt.

161

That it is Van Helsing's daughter who returns in Badham's *Dracula* presents an interesting twist on the return of this repressed oedipal scenario. As Van Helsing plumbs the damp and curiously open depths of his daughter's grave in search of her undead corpse, he sees her image reflected in a pool of water. The coming into focus of the daughter's image—the image of a face that is where it shouldn't be—is another instance of a rift in the rules of vision and the operation of the cinematic apparatus. But this reflection is certainly not the visage of a parental figure or the Janus-faced specter of the point of castration. Rather, the daughter's reappearance reminds the father of his failure, of a split. Van Helsing's search for his daughter replays "the image of the approaching child, his face full of reproach and, on the other hand, that which causes it and into which he sinks, the invocation, the voice of the child, the solicitation of the gaze—*Father, can't you see. . . .* "[26] Van Helsing recalled from his neglect by the child already dead, who like Freud's example of the child in the burning coffin, represents a split in the father, whose sleep is continued by his dream of the real.

Incarnating a split in the father, the undead daughter is proof of the father's failure, his powerlessness against death and against the invasion of an alien order. The daughter's undead continuation means that paternal limits are exceeded; the split father has been foreclosed. The vampire daughter is the figure of his foreclosure, returning as if in a vision, to certify this paternal split—the father who is absent, the father who dreams. The daughter, thus, exists as the undead, because the father didn't exist as the Law, because the paternal function had already failed. Staking the undead daughter's corpse is a Pyrrhic exercise, too late to efface the failure by which it was produced.

If we connect this symptomatic moment back to the vampire's more narrative threats to patriarchal order, the sudden appearance of the vampire becomes the moment of a breach in the system. This breach makes visible what patriarchy itself normally occludes—the repressed desires upon which its prohibitive function depends. Law depends upon a desire for the preoedipal even as prohibition may found that desire. Representing the paradox of the necessary but prohibited desire and the desire for prohibition, the vampire embodies the glitch—the fulfillment of the desire for prohibition—that founds the system. This glitch, like the gaze, cannot be seen since the order of metaphor—of the Law-of-the-Name-of-the-Father—has already stood in the place of that glitch, substituting an ordering nothing for the previously too-full something of the child's relation to the mother or caretaker. Revealing the glitch on the level of the function of the image produces a momentary rift that shakes the system the way the vampire's narrative of a metonymical challenge to metaphor defies the larger symbolic system.

But just as the vampire challenges, so it reaffirms. It may expose a glitch, but it also covers it up. It may defy prohibition, but it is prohibition itself. Even though its reappearance—return of the repressed—of both mother and father in the guise of the gaze would seem to present, suddenly, too much, a truly "asphyxiating Other" that would constitute systematic overload, the vampire also contains such overload in its self-contained short circuit, which it grounds through the narrative of an all-too-human seduction. The vampire's instantaneous drama of desire and prohibition is countermanded by another drama of desire, where the prohibited again becomes desirable, where the system of prohibitions is back in place. By wooing, the vampire reinstates the proper relation between subject and object in the illegal, extramarital but nonetheless proper frame of Law—a Law he reiterates in his separate, but very paternal order.

Gaze Again

The vampire's other symptom, the return glance of the undead corpse, is the evidentiary moment of a literal continuity in a vampiric postmortem existence; the vampire's continuity signifies the potential discontinuity of the

human species as virgins are converted from potential human mothers to purveyors of the undead or as young men are weakened and captured. The vampire's operation actually requires two looks (as opposed to the gaze his sudden
appearance enacts the unrepression of): the hypnotizing look by which its victims are seduced and the vampire's startled coffin gaze. The first look is an
embodiment of scopophilia, seductive and powerful, arresting action, subvert-
ing will, achieving control, disguising and enabling the perverted coitus that
follows. This sexualized look signifies desire, displacing the victim's desire to
the vampire's actions in a barely disguised projection designed to be penetrat-
ed: the victim really wants the cheap continuity offered by the vampire, desires
the nonphallic oral act, eschews the human phallus in favor of the vampire's
deadly glance. Through the look, the vampire plays on the unconscious, on
his/her victim's death drive as that is manifested through a reproductively
inappropriate, short-circuiting sexuality.

Earlier cinematic renditions of vampires such as Murnau's *Nosferatu* and Tod
Browning's 1931 *Dracula*, with Bela Lugosi, employed somewhat primitive, but
nonetheless deliberate special effects to render the vampire's look both captivating and threatening. Murnau used makeup to accentuate Nosferatu's heavily ringed eyes; the eyes and the stiletto-nailed fingers dominate his image.
Browning fixes a key light on Lugosi's eyes, giving them an odd radiance and
obscuring the rest of his features. The eyes of both of these earlier vampires are
the centers of their hypnotic power as well as the signifiers of their other-
worldliness.

163

The look from the vampire startled from its daily sleep is the sudden,
shocking, uncanny look that reverses the order of life after death. Unlike
images of the vampire's seductive eyes, the corpse's unexpected return glance,
introducing a radical and parasitical other, threatens an Other consciousness.
By literally exposing the inanimate as animate, the vampire's opening eyes are
uncanny, signifying a look that might reenact a too literalized gaze, the doubling of seeing oneself being seen with the look one sees. That one look is
horrible because it signifies a separate consciousness, an alterity that rips us
from plenitude to loss as it, like the vampire's sudden appearance, projects the
too-instantaneous vision of the gaze, the Other, the simultaneous and contradictory moment of castration and failure of Law. But because its context is
more narratively limited, the opening of the eyes works slightly differently
than the vampire's sudden appearance, representing the emergence of slightly
different repressed material.

In both *Nosferatu* and *Dracula*, the vampire rests in his coffin with open eyes;
opening the coffin reveals the open eyes, the coffin lid acting like an eyelid, a
screen whose removal already breaks the rules of grave decorum and, in so
doing, permits the vision of the unseeable. While the first sudden appearance
of the vampire occurs before it is identified as a vampire and as the vampire

presents itself, this second eye-opener occurs as the law enforcers seek the vampire. As a necessary step in the vampire's destruction, the opened coffin is a part of the hunt for the vampire's daytime hiding place. The vampire's open eyes portend an enemy consciousness, a presence that haunts even the vampire's supposed absence. But the law enforcers' destructive intent crosses the grounds of the forbidden, requiring a return to threatening and denied repressed material that accuses and indicts them for their return to the moment of castration. If they succeed, as they do in some films, in staking the vampire immediately, this second intimation of castration and loss is vengefully repaired by a re-repressing reassertion of phallic order. If the vampire continues, as he does in *Nosferatu*, the moment is unrelieved except by covering the vampire up again.

The eyes thus signify an ulterior consciousness; this suggests the gaze in yet another way. Ever present but invisible, the gaze is again literalized by our unexpected coming upon it in our search for something else. Instead of the supine and vulnerable body, we get the eyes, conscious, alert, and threatening. Although we expect this trope, it shocks; it is uncanny not only because it represents the animation of the presumably inanimate, but because it registers again that vision of prohibition the vampire embodied earlier in the narrative. One cannot come upon a vampire; the vampire always comes upon one because the vampire is already the forbidden who forbids, the phantom father whose power invests in vision instead of the word, the creature of a system that flows in one direction.

164

The corpsical return glance does not, like the vampire's sudden appearance, play with the cinematic apparatus or the rules of its sustenance of a continuous time and space. Rather, it reveals the apparatus's potential, its always-present gaze, which like the gaze, is normally occulted. But looking into the eyes of vampiric death means looking back at the present absence the cinema normally represents. The eyes of the vampire are not only the eyes of death, but also the spectre of the apparatus that we imagine sees.

This is why the return glance is a particularly apt symptom of the vampire's nest of anxieties. The visual and the gaze register prohibition in a cinematic return of the repressed of the image of prohibition itself. The vampire catches us in the act, even while we catch him in the act of being conscious while alone and encoffined. The particularly visual aspect of this uncanny gaze is aligned with reversals in the order of the visible as that incarnates the order of the Word and the Law. As Jean-Louis Comolli reminds us, "the second half of the nineteenth century lives in a sort of frenzy of the visible."[27] "Thanks," he continues, "to the . . . principles of mechanical reproduction, the movements of men and animals become in some sort more visible than they had been. The mechanical opens out and multiplies the visible and between them is established a *complicity* all the stronger in that the codes of analogical figuration slip irresistibly from painting to photography and then from the latter to cinema" (123).

While the analogical figurations Comolli mentions refer to representations rather than to their underlying mode of reproduction, the complicity between the mechanical and the visible results in a visible that is doubly alluring. The visible seems total and omnipresent as it floods the field; in combination with the machines of reproduction that center the viewer and privilege the view, the visible seems to reflect the viewer's omnipotence. Both of these attractions reify an order where the visible serves as the mode of control between subject and object, between state and citizen. The direction of this order—from gazer to object—inscribes a symbolic hierarchy that aligns vision, power, and invisibility with the gazer and ignorance, subjection, and to-be-seenness on the side of the object. In the realm of the cultural imaginary, the line of the gaze is traced by the visible order of mechanical reproduction. The machine can be viewed and can be viewed viewing us. When reversed, the look of looking, the omnipresent visibility, produces a somewhat uncanny sense of being the object of the look, as when one accidentally catches sight of oneself in a surveillance video.

But the difference between the gaze and the linear relation assumed by machines of the visible is that mechanical reproduction is supposed to be seen seeing; hence the fascination with everything from special effects to home video. This machine version domesticates the imaginary gaze, reducing it from a relation to a traceable cause-effect trajectory in the production of image. At the same time, the cinematic apparatus actually reverses the order of the gaze. While we are the gaze's to-be-seen, we are the cinematic apparatus's gazers, except when the system suddenly reverses itself to expose the fiction of our gaze and our always subjectivization, even in the apparatus's imaginary image of our own control. The apparatus gives way—parts on an imaginary level—to provide an intimation of the real the imaginary suddenly reverses. "In our relation to things," observes Lacan, "in so far as this relation is constituted by the way of vision, and ordered in the figures of representation, something slips, passes, is transmitted, from stage to stage, and is always to some degree eluded in it—that is what we call the gaze" (73).

The vampire's return glance, then, is one step further then the accidental sighting of oneself in a video monitor. It is a mask of the gaze itself that breaks for a moment the imaginary process of image production and consumption to suggest—flash—both an image of the gaze from outside individual imagination and a profound disturbance in the order of the visible. The return glance is a paradox—life where death should be—that parallels the paradox of the machine of looking looking back. But the real problem with the return glance is the fleeting appearance of the Real, represented not only by the break in the fabric of visible order, but by the juxtaposition of death as life—of death itself

165

as a living presence linked to the gaze hiding under the mask of Dracula's sudden, unexpected look. The glimpse at the gaze is the glimpse at death, the real of existence, a glimpse that rapidly fades back into the imaginary the glimpse instantly reveals itself to be. In retrospect, this Real becomes only eyes that open too suddenly, taking us by surprise, but in the order of vision and narrative, they still provide the glimpse of a glimpse that breaks open the orders by which the image of that glimpse is produced in the first place, bringing visible relations into question, unsettling hierarchy and control, suggesting the unreliability of our control over vision—and through vision death.

So the vampire's second symptom is our unwitting and fleeting image of death, the prohibition of prohibition and the ultimate end of the gaze. But in revealing death through the production of an uncanny moment, cinematic vampire texts both reverse order and reify it. If seeing death requires a short-circuit—the clash of metaphor and metonymy—in the field of vision, our release from that momentary encounter comes from the imaginary and narrative disposition of the vampire himself. Destroyed, humanized, documented, historicized, the vampire is made safe for patriarchy in a patriarchy already made safe by the vampire whose spectacular performance of metonymical reproduction aligns metonymy with death, forcing our choice of tradition and the safe haven of the metaphorical stake. Representations of the vampire present the uncanny so that the drama of paternal prohibition can replay itself all over again, resecuring anxieties about order that the vampire imports. The vampire's uncanniness is a pretext for and reminder of prohibition and Law through which the vampire began to take a more metonymical form.

BLOOD AND SYMPATHY

If a psychoanalytic reading of the cinematic vampires' symptoms bears out the threat and investments of the vampire's larger narrative, then the contemporaneous trend towards sympathetic vampires endorses, from the other side, the symbolic shift the vampire threatens. The late 1970s witnesses the emergence of a somewhat radically different take on the vampire. George Romero's *Martin* (1977), for example, presents the sympathetic narrative of Martin, a vampire who knows quite well that "there is no magic."[28] Without the vampire's "extraordinary" fictional powers, Martin illustrates that vampirism is a careful compulsion. Using drugs and razor blades, Martin carefully stalks and subdues his victims. He makes their deaths look like suicides. Imaging vampirism from Martin's point-of-view, Romero translates the vampire into human terms. Seeing from the perspective of the vampire relieves the image of the vampire seeing, reducing all threat to cause-effect psychology.

A son of a family traditionally cursed with vampire offspring (the vampire reduced to genetics), Martin visits his Great-uncle, a devoutly religious man who lives in a small Pennsylvania town. His uncle vows to exorcise the devil and then destroy Martin. He dictates rules that Martin must observe: don't talk to your cousin, don't attack anyone in the town. And Martin complies. The shy, quiet vampire befriends a lonely housewife and has his first sexual liaison; he attacks only people in Pittsburgh or other towns. He spends the rest of his time explaining what a vampire's life is really like to the host of a phone-in radio talk show. Keeping his word, Martin's uncle, the old-world patriarch, arranges for an old priest to come and exorcise Martin; Martin leaves in the middle of the droning, low-key rote exercise. Unfortunately for Martin, his housewife paramour, who has been depressed, commits suicide. Martin's uncle blames him, awakening him one morning and staking him in the heart. The sympathetic vampire is destroyed by a Law that hasn't recognized the change—that hasn't noticed that vampires are now human.

Romero's depiction of Martin not only demystifies the vampire's metonymical powers, it also removes the vampire from the realm of repro-duction (Martin produces no revenants) to the sphere of compulsion. Reducing the vampire to a set of pragmatic considerations, Romero elimi-nates his threat, replacing it with the mechanics of serial killers and other nor-mative sociopaths. But Martin is better than a sociopath; he knows his illness and controls it, minimizing cruelty, having pity, retaining only his cunning will to survive. The psychologizing of and empathy for the vampire also reveal something else. If we are invited into the vampire's consciousness, the vampire logic that might represent difference is translated into a human logic that rep-resents mere variation, difficulty, or neurosis. The vampire is no longer a threat; he is one of us. That the vampire could be one of us is linked to the extent to which the metonymic order represented by the vampire is already a function-ing cultural order. The vampire's magical metonymy is reduced to fact when metonymy is a fact of life. The compulsion to explain and articulate every cause-effect relation—even the pragmatics of *untertöt* existence—is the effect of a larger cultural belief in the power of metonymy to account for all. The vampire's threatening reproductive metonymy is thus reduced to the matter-of-fact details of nourishment—to another kind of consumption, an odd diet.

167

The number of sympathetic vampire films increases from the 1970s on. These include *The Bloodsuckers* (1969), where vampirism "is treated as real, but a psychological condition," *Blood for Dracula* (*Andy Warhol's Dracula*) (1974), *Halloween with the Addams Family* (1977), *Fade to Black* (1980), *Mom* (1980), *My Best Friend Is a Vampire* (1987), *A Polish Vampire in Burbank* (1985), *Sundown: The Vampire in Retreat* (1989), *Teen Vamp* (1989), and *Rockula* (1990). These are accompanied by an increasing number of sympathetic vampire novels ranging from Anne Rice's *Interview with the Vampire* (1976) to the *Saint-Germain*, nov-els by Chelsea Quinn Yarbro, which began in 1978, to a series of 1980s nov-els with discreet vampire protagonists. These novels share, according to Joan Gordon, themes about "the nature of power, the nature of love, connection between the two; male and female approaches to the archetype of the vampire; and cross-species responsibility with its implications about ecology and human relations."[29] This final theme represents the anxiety that links vampire narratives to narratives of alien invasion, figuring the vampire's gradually tamed and rationalized reproductive threat.

The coexistence of Martin, Ann Rice's *Interview With a Vampire*, and other sympathetic vampire tales—including Coppola's—with Badham's altered tale of paternal failure represents a transition in the function of the vampire figure, which had operated as the uncanny correlative to mechanical reproduction's threatening metonymy. Just as Badham's *Dracula* dramatizes the extent to which the father is already ineffectual, so the sympathetic vampire reveals the extent to which the vampire's metonymy has already taken hold. Performing its own recuperation, the vampire narrative oddly configures normative modern existence, becoming a figure for consumption, contagion, and alienation, and configuring exactly the temporal-spatial immediacies of the digital. Just as the computer screen can effect sudden appearances, transect space, and appear to telescope time, so the vampire's metonymical transport and uncanny appearances seem like inventions of a computer logic.

If the vampire's fictional rise accompanied mechanical reproduction, its fictional reparation accompanies the emergence of the digital, whose capabilities match the vampire's. The vampire comes to figure not breaches in the apparatus, but its operation. The uncanny specter of the return of a repressed moment of desire and prohibition has become the phantom in a order where the combination of desire and prohibition circles constantly, grounding the commodity market. The vampire's instantaneous appearance is no longer uncanny in a digital apparatus where instantaneity is the norm and time-space continuity has shifted its representation and its meaning. Computers can do what vampires do.

Repatriation/Liquidation

If the terms of the vampire's cultural ascendancy are not quite clear, other 1960s and 1970s phenomena confirm its installation as the figure of changing order. On the one hand, the vampire is domesticated, not only in comedy versions such as *Love at First Bite*, but also in television shows like *The Munsters* with its vampire Grandpa. Frankenstein's monster is not inappropriately transformed into the paterfamilias Herman Munster. That the vampire is an eccentric Grandpa in *The Munsters* demonstrates not only its displacement from functional father to dusty forebear, but also the displacement of its specifically reproductive and regulatory threat. The vampire is cycled out of the reproductive chain just as Frankenstein is implanted as a continuing part.

In the 1960s, this familialization seems defensive. Just as ghoulish comedies like *The Addams Family* work on the absurd incongruities between the macabre and everyday life, so grandfathering the vampire reproduces the vampire as an absurd but acceptable incongruity in a family full of incongruities. But the vampire's domestication accompanies its dilution as vampire signifiers are appropriated or sold. In 1964, Andy Warhol made *Batman Dracula*. The comic-book Batman's television appearance in the 1960s popularized the vampire's bat image as a harbinger of good; the show's campy take on super-heroics makes the bat idiosyncratic. Dracula himself became a Dell Comics superhero in 1962 in a move that countered the 1954 Comics Code prohibiting vampires. He became an animated duck, Count Duckula, in the 1980s. Candy stores sold wax teeth. Children uttered, "I want to suck your blood," in mock-Transylvanian accents. Liquidation, sparagmos, the best forms of repatriation and the first indicators of homogenization signal the vampire's unrepression. Its threat—the threat of an invading changing order—moves (like the metonym it always embodies) into other registers of representation, occupying a public imaginary not in the guise of another image of return, but in the very ways we have come to see.

169

DIGITAL DAD

Generation by Code

chapter 5

OEDIPUS RISES

Dr. Frankenstein attempted to piece together a being from discarded body parts; his map of creation was the body, the site of his intervention corporeal. In the 1994 *Mary Shelley's Frankenstein* the monster is still a body quilt, but his relation to the Law has become crudely, nostalgically, melodramatically oedipal. While the 1818's narrative images Frankenstein as a creator who would usurp heavenly prerogative, 1994's reinscription, in the spectacularly evident name of the writer, images Frankenstein as a neglectful father who tragically gets his oedipal due.[1] Attempting to transform production into reproduction brings down the law, creating an oedipal disorder in which the son punishes the father for failing to observe symbolic limitation, justice, or even compassion.

Although Mary Shelley's *Frankenstein* has oedipal overtones, the monster seeks revenge mainly for Victor Frankenstein's unworthy assumption and fearfully sloppy execution of the role of creator. Since Frankenstein has transgressed order once, the monster demands that he do so again and make him a bride as amends for his abandonment. Frankenstein agrees, but does not complete the task when he considers, among other factors, the possibility that the patchwork pair will procreate: "A race of devils would be propagated upon the earth, who might make the very existence of the species of man a condition precarious and full of terror" (163). Frankenstein, who has been seduced by the delusive power of a false science, belatedly returns to an ethical symbolic. In revenge, the monster threatens to haunt Victor's wedding night and on that occasion kills Victor's cousin/wife Elizabeth. At the end, an exhausted Frankenstein dies without the monster's help aboard ship in the Arctic.

In Branagh's film, the monster becomes too literally the son of a father who has defied the law of divine order and generation. The monster literally takes Victor's place on his wedding night, ripping out Elizabeth's heart. Frankenstein tries to reanimate his bride by attaching her head and hands to the bride body he had been fabricating. The monster claims the rebuilt Elizabeth as his own bride, but Elizabeth's displaced remnants refuse to cooperate as she sets fire to herself and the entire Frankenstein mansion. The Law is served. At the end of the film, the monster completes the oedipal pattern by killing Frankenstein himself. This compensatory overoedipalization (like Coppola's *Bram Stoker's Dracula's* defensive heterosexualization) suggests that messing with the corporeal can lead only to the son's chaotic destructiveness. Even if the son's story, as we have seen in Arnold's frantic interventions, might seem to reground the Symbolic, it is really finally no cure for a system that can now only serve as a gloss.

Master Code

In 1953, James Watson and Francis Crick published their findings on DNA, the amino acid chain that answered questions about the nature and transference of genetic material.[2] DNA's double-helix chains comprised of only four amino acids supplied a molecular answer—or the promise of one—to the question of what paternity, parentage, lineage, and generations consist of. DNA's alternating constituents suggested the possibility of a clear map of humanity's origin and mode of reproduction; its genotypic specificity promised a more reliable mode of identification than blood typing's phenotypical groups. If the Name-of-the-Father stood for lineage, DNA technology threatened to define the father as an enumerable series of chained signifiers that account for every fact, aspect, chemical operation, and anatomical morsel of human existence. There might even be a "gay" gene or a gene that determines the profession one chooses.[3]

DNA, it seems, provides the literal end to the problem of a symbolic crisis. The Name is replaced by the comprehensive code; the nothing secured by the name's metaphor is supplanted to the too-much something of an overexten-sive set of signifiers that replace metaphor with fact and Law with a code whose strategically aligned elements simplify life into grains of molecular sense. DNA is one better than a map or recipe since its biochemical compo-nents are themselves the actual sites of replication, which are imagined as working with other strings of molecules (RNA) whose function it is to trans-fer genetic messages to other sites through a logic of molecular complemen-tarity. Stringing binary pairs of elements, DNA's material code works like a computer program—all complexity reduced to presence or absence, the ordering of switches, the discernable, identifiable, locatable, enumerable oper-ations of existence.

ENIAC

One hundred years after the appearance of *Frankenstein* and *The Vampyre*, William Henry Eccles and F. W. Jordan recognized the "trigger" function of a vacuum tube; it could "hold one of two states indefinitely."[4] The constancy of such tubes enabled the construction of counting circuits that could record complex and rapid changes such as those required to record radiation. "The circuits were chained to one another in such a way that for every two firings of the first one, its neighbor would fire once, and so on down the chain" (Aspray 225). The result was "an electronic counterpart of a mechanical regis-ter consisting of toothed wheels with a carry occurring after one full revolu-tion of a given wheel" (Aspray 225). In other words, the vacuum tubes could imitate mechanical, analogue functions that measured the magnitude of phe-nomena in terms of integers.

173

Predigital computers were cleverly contrived combinations of mechanical repeating mechanisms such as those employed in industrial machines, photog-raphy, and cinema combined with primitive forms of programming provided by punch cards, paper tape loops, and plug boards. Their premise was analogy; gears, loops, and wheels could be designed to perform like an abacus but with greater automation and efficiency. The physical and conceptual restrictions of mechanical analogy (the sheer number of components and constraints on their arrangement), however, limited the number and variety of possible calcula-tions as well as potential storage capacity for data. Sequentially chained oper-ations (equations that required a second operation based on the results of the first) were difficult.

In 1937, George R. Stibitz built a relay-based computer that used binary digits. Adopting a binary rather than a decimal system reduced all functions to combinations of off/on, matching the capabilities of faster, more reliable elec-tronic components. As developed by Bell Labs, this became the Complex Number Computer, which used electronic relays and paper tapes to direct cal-culating sequences.

In the 1930s, John Atanasoff also determined that the fastest way to solve linear systems would be "an electronic, digital machine" that took advantage of the two-term simplicity of binary numbers (Aspray 227). Using capacitors instead of vacuum tubes, Atanasoff's machine never became fully functional, but its invention and Atanasoff's ideas inspired John Mauchy of the Moore School of the University of Pennsylvania who, with the help of the army, built an electronic digital device called the Electronic Numerical Integrator and Computer (ENIAC). The ENIAC was completed in 1945; "it was a transitional device that incorporated many of the features of what we now define as computers: high processing speed, flexible (and from 1948, internally stored) programming, and the ability to solve a wide range of problems in practice insoluble by other means" (Aspray 243). But it was also still too analogue, exhibiting many of the features—and the inherent limitations—of mechanical calculators: "a tedious method of setup, internal use of decimal instead of binary numbers, and the use of accumulators that performed the dual functions of storage and arithmetic" (Aspray 243). The decimal system's ten signifiers perpetuate the illusion of a continuum that must be accounted for; mechanical calculators were physical manifestations of analogical philosophy. Binary numbers and electronic circuitry produce a series of discrete combinations instead of a continuum. It is not that binary machines have lost analogy; analogy is no longer necessary.

IBM made the transition from analogue calculators to the fully digital computer "through an intermediate technology, the Card Programmed Calculator," which, in 1948, "wired together into a system an IBM 603 electronic punched card multiplier and an IBM 405 accounting machine" (Aspray 253). Like photography's transition from painting's metaphor to a metonymical mechanical reproduction that assaults tradition, computers' transition from analogue to digital, from the mechanical to the electronic, provokes another assault on order, one that provides the possibility of such a complete record as to seem to replace the Name with a uniform and comprehensive bank of values and facts so purely metonymical that gaining access to it requires metaphorical interfaces. But the digital also replaces the metaphor's continuum with the discrete and separable; if mechanical reproductions substituted the machine for the human, interpolating metonymy into the reproductive system, the digital computer supplants analogy with the delusive appearance of an accountable, saturated but very intangible presence.

The Raster Grid

As a mechanical reproduction, the photograph is both a metonymical and an analogue representation of light and space registered through photosensitive chemicals. Its analogy reproduces a continuity of gradations that, as J. T. Mitchell, author of *The Reconfigured Eye*, describes it, are like "rolling down a

174

ramp in continuous motion" as opposed to the digital's "walking down stairs" in a "sequence of discrete steps"(3).[5] . The photograph's tracking of continuity creates the illusion of a recording of truth, manifested not only in Bazin's claims for photographic art, but in the close-up's revelations of biological truths. As Allan Poe observed in 1840:

> If we examine a work of ordinary art, by means of a powerful microscope, all traces of resemblance to nature will disappear—but the closest scrutiny of photogenic drawing discloses only a more absolute truth, a more perfect identity of aspect with the thing represented. The variations of shade, and the gradations of both linear and aerial perspective, are those of truth itself in the supremeness of its perfection (qtd. in Mitchell 4).

The photographic close-up exposes painting's components as discrete; close-up photography also distinguishes the photograph's "truth" supremacy in its absolute rendition of gradation. The product of mechanical reproduction becomes "truth"; the means of "truth's" discovery and affirmation is mechanical reproduction itself. The circle is complete: analogy leads to the truth of analogy. The metonymies of the mechanical enable the acquisition and preservation of "truth" registered in the field of vision.

Digital images are digitally encoded "by uniformly subdividing the picture plane into a finite Cartesian [raster] grid of cells (known as *pixels*) and specifying the intensity or color of each cell by means of an integer number drawn from some limited range" (Mitchell 4). Each pixel or value gains significance through its juxtaposition with other pixels. Unlike photography, the more closely one examines a digital image, the more apparent the individual cells become, providing not gradations or continuities, but discrete, separable sites of pure meaning. Digital technology translates photographic analogy into the stepped sequence of metonymy not only as a means, but as an end product. We characterize and wield this metonymical raster grid through metaphors of more traditional technologies such as painting, photography, and geometry. Digital imaging programs have their window glaze: Paint Brush, Photoshop. But unlike photography, the digital image does not necessarily rely upon the actual or natural. Where photography is analogous to the Frankensteinian corporeal, digital imaging is like DNA, dependent on and springing directly from a code. The digital image "may be fabricated from found files," Mitchell points out, "disk litter, the detritus of cyberspace. Digital imagers give meaning and value to computational ready-mades by appropriation, transformation, reprocessing, and recombination; we have entered the age of electrobricollage" (7).

While its programming may come from digital scrap heaps and its images depict scenes that have never before existed in time and space, digital images have better reproductive capacities than photographs. In other words, while the photograph may record indistinguishable variations, its matter-based process permits only increasingly degraded copies. The information plotted on the raster grid can be stored indefinitely, reproduced infinitely, and changed at will in any number of ways without a trace. While photography's mechanical reproductions may have threatened art's aura and provided the hope for a proletarian expression, mechanical reproductions were always only copies, quality, "aura," exactitude sacrificed to the inaccuracies of analogue reproductive machines. But digital copies are always perfect copies of one another, since they are stored in and generated by the code itself rather than being preserved in or produced through reliance on material form. As Mitchell points out, "discrete states can be replicated precisely, so a digital image that is a thousand generations away from the original is indistinguishable in quality from one of its progenitors" (6). The technology and its capabilities change, but the conceptual language clings to the vestiges of a paternal Symbolic.

The digital's reproductive prowess and the fact that it is even conceived of as an infinite number of originals suggests its symbolic paternal proxy, its substitution of the grid for the name, identicality for genealogy, originality for lineage. It locates its generative power in the code, whose unerring replicative capacities and controlled manipulations provide more reproductive reliability and a more exact foundation than the Name. When all the parts are there and accounted for, the name bows to the grid whose illusion of complex fulfillment appears to preempt all uncertainty with the comfort of a bit, a pixel, a definable and ever producible state that suggests immortality. Having become a reproducible formula, the manifestation of an ineluctable Law-like code, generation is displaced from a process to the Code/Law itself. There is no longer any primacy; "progenitors" are no different from their children. Father and child, original and copy are equivalent even a "thousand generations away." The raster grid correlates with a set of chained signifiers like the DNA presumed responsible for human replication. Dreams of genetic manipulation come from the digital as DNA becomes the biological version of a raster grid.

The Law of Electrobricollage

Just as Watson and Crick identified DNA, so digital imaging technologies can finally make it visible. DNA is true, witnessed by atomic resolution images. The fullness of truth lies in the visible identity of discrete parts; the lie of continuity is revealed. The close-up has arrived at the code, the field is the atom. Digital imaging technologies translate the indiscernible into the clear through scanning probe microscopes. As the very molecules of the code become visible, that code becomes a law in itself, wieldable and manipulable like digital images whose make up can be untraceably altered by changing its codes.

That DNA codes have challenged the imaginary place of the father is apparent in films ranging from the 1988 *Twins* to 1995's *Judge Dredd* and *Species*.[6]

Using combinations of DNA taken from groups of highly eligible fathers, *Twins* and *Judge Dredd* trace the strangely duplicitous effects of genetic manipulation. While *Twins* envisions the comically mismatched pair of Danny deVito and Arnold Schwarzenegger, *Judge Dredd*'s genetic experiment, the "Janus Project," produces two equally strong, markedly opposite progeny. What is striking in both of these versions of code-generated reproduction is the production of two offspring that represent the morality play positions of good and evil. Why should genetically engineered sons erupt in binary twos? Why does procreative technology—the extenuation of paternity from the Name to the gene—require a return to Cain and Abel?

The sons play out the binary terms of the code that produces them, replicating not their contributing biological fathers, but the binary process by which their genetic messages were spliced together. If their "father" was actually a process, then they are its "splitting" image. Their diametrically opposite relations to law itself, however, represent obvious ambivalence about a gap in the order of generations that still reflects the metaphorical Symbolic. One son (Arnold or Stallone) represents the strong, virtuous, morally upright, principled values of traditional patriarchy. The other son (deVito or Judge Dredd's imprisoned criminal brother) incarnates the lawless immorality and *übermensch* mentality of the genetically engineered, whose release from the law of the father plays out as their release from the Law itself. In both films, of course, the good son wins. In the comedy Arnold convinces the unscrupulous deVito to undertake the straight and narrow and Judge Dredd melodramatically kills his bad brother to save the law itself. In either case, genetically engineered "good" sons return a version of paternal law. The result of a reproduction that defies the Symbolic, the good son provides a simulation patriarchal cover (not unlike the metaphorical interfaces of computer programs) for a very different metonymical Symbolic. In *Twins,* Arnold demonstrates that some version of paternal law rules no matter how the offspring are produced. Not only is there still mother, but the son does the best he can to translate genetic engineering back into literal paternity, searching out his scattered donors.

Judge Dredd represents a more curious case. Patched from an eclectic mix of superhero comics, melodrama, stylistic shades of *Blade Runner* and *Escape from New York, Mad Max*ian apocalyptic visions of postholocaust worlds, and hints of *Rocky* and *Rambo, Judge Dredd*'s pastiche resembles the imputed genetic cocktail of Judge Dredd's fatherly mix. Spawned from the engineered donations of the members of the governing Law Council, Judge Dredd can literally regard law as his father. "I am da Law," he repeats to malefactors and friends alike, as if his very being incarnates something that is otherwise lost. Not only is he the son of the Law, he is the law, acting as a "Judge," a mobile police, court, and sentencing agent who maintains on-the-spot instant order in the riotous high tech, degenerate streets of the megalopolis. His identifica-

177

tion with the law enables him to withstand not only the revelation of his true origin, but also the fact that his arch nemesis is actually his brother.

But Judge Dredd is more truly the law that, like Arnold, covers over the loss of the paternal, returning the genetically engineered being to the simulated patriarchal fold, importing the old metaphors to mediate and order the new. When his evil brother escapes from prison, Judge Dredd is convicted through DNA evidence, of a crime his twin brother commits. Exiled, Dredd discovers that his enemy is his genetic twin (though the two don't look alike), who is in the process of restarting the Janus program to cultivate more supermen. Realizing the dangers of such hyperbolic reproduction, Dredd returns, destroys the amazingly "alien"-like cocooned foetuses and kills the bad part of the genetic equation. Through this purge, the binary's duplicity is eliminated; the law is reduced to a single "one." The more literal law, too, recommences, this time with a woman as head Council Member. Although this might look like a change, it represents a correction and return to a status quo that had been threatened by the Janus Project's paternal finagling. DNA may be the code, but it is overwhelmingly reappropriated by a superheroic specimen of a digitally translated patriarchy. As the film and all of O. J. Simpson's lawyers would suggest, DNA is not reliable proof of anything.

A Species of Law

Both extolling and deposing DNA, *Twins* and *Judge Dredd* wallow in the overtly paternalized anxiety of a DNA Symbolic. Desperately installing neo-paternal superhero figures in the place of DNA's Symbolic incursion, both films make Symbolic shifts look like some sort of generational legacy, the son taking over where the father left off. The familial logic of these compensations, however, never really seals the gaps opened by a newly metonymized reproduction; the gaps—the failure of identity, the search for parents, the potentials of the evil procreative experiment that threatens law itself—never really disappear, but are only outshone by the glowing figure of filial revival. Anxieties about the digital—about the subtle infiltration and reorganization of the Symbolic itself—manifest not only in the compensatory salvations of paternity plots or characterizations of DNA as unreliable, but, as we have seen, also register as a fear of systemic takeover in the field of reproduction itself. Aliens who invade and twist human forms also enact the drama of a Symbolic shift played out with the rise of the digital. While the paternal gloss is strictly the son's affair, the specter of the alien comes with vestiges of feminine threat; this is as true for the 1980s *Aliens* films as it is for the 1995 *Species*.

Like *Twins* and *Judge Dredd*, *Species* begins with a DNA code, this one transmitted by supposedly friendly aliens contacted through radio waves. When their instructions for methane conversion promise to provide infinite amounts of clean energy, the project scientists decide to trust the transmitted DNA code.

Replicating a being from the code, they produce a child who looks human, but who grows at a furious pace. When the adolescent female seems dangerous and they try to destroy her, she escapes, taking a train and metamorphosing her way to L.A. A day later, the adult female emerges from the train and sets out in search of a mate. But, by this time, a team of specialists, including a hit man, a biochemist, and a psychic, have set out in pursuit, the psychic leading the way through his sense of the alien's instinctive drives.

Finding and rejecting (killing) prospective human partners, the alien finally literally settles on one of the team members, and seducing him, instantly becomes impregnated. Giving birth in about ten minutes, the alien flees into L.A.'s sewer system, pursued by the rest of the team. Finding her newborn, who looks about six years old, the team finally destroys both, but not until a piece of her alienlike tentacle has been detached and eaten by rats.

A morphing form, the alien can switch from her human veneer to an amalgam threat that looks like a combination of winged victory and 1951 Packard. Metallic, tentacled, primitive, horrific, the alien combines the amassed graphics of vampires, digital Frankensteins, and unauthorized reproductions in a figure who can finally only be overcome by psychic power. The psychic takes the position of a symbolic superior to the alien's physical strength and encoded prowess. Pitting mysticism against alterity, *Species* solves the problem of a DNA Symbolic by imaging the even more potent, precious, and powerful functions of the still mysterious human mind, functions that evade digitalization and exceed the machine. *Species*, thus, represents an even more nostalgic and desperate return of the ineffable in the face of the all-too-certain.

The more benign view of the implantation of a genetic Symbolic occurs in *Star Trek*. All-purpose projections of contemporary angst, both *Star Trek* series allay the threat of a digital Symbolic with an appeal to unquantifiable human instinct. In *Star Trek*, the computerlike Spock represents one Symbolic, highly functional, but ever bested by Captain Kirk, who incarnates the intuitive power neither the machinelike Spock nor the ship's computer have. In *The Next Generation*, the android Data stands for the digital Symbolic, counteracted not only by the highly instinctive Captain and a gaggle of intuitive crew members, but also by a specifically empathic character, Deanna Troi, and the all-purpose psychic Guinan. The heavily fortified empathic is the only remaining counter to the digital.

While the *Enterprise* crew is well protected against digital inroads, *The Next Generation* also situates the DNA code as a universal Symbolic. In "The Chase" (4/25/93), the crew of the Enterprise, and the Klingons, the Romulans, and the Cardassians trace the path of amino acid "clues" that supposedly comprise part of some valuable secret. Meeting together on the same planet, the different species learn that the amino codes were scattered throughout the galaxy as a kind of "seed" that resulted in a variety of similar life forms, which not only accounts for the weird coincidence that almost all extraterrestrials look amazingly human, but also situates DNA as a sort of universal master code. Tamed, tracked, controlled by humans, DNA provides the fullness of explanation. The *Enterprise* reads space and finds DNA. Oedipus need look no further.

OUR TWO DADS

While mechanical reproduction threatens to produce surrogate humans, digital logic has been found at humanity's coded center, presenting the frightening possibility of the biological going the way of the digital, of the human becoming the machine in the reverse of the fear that the machine will become human.[7] Proliferation's lack of differentiation actually represents an anxiety about a loss of identity. If I contrast the identitarian logic of the paternal metaphor—the Name of the Father locates me uniquely in a historical, temporal lineage—with the replicative logic of the digital—metonymical codes produce ahistorical, atemporal, identical manifestations of the same genotype— what becomes evident is that a metaphor-based Symbolic can, at best, only endeavor to superimpose order on multiple reproductions of the same. In the face of this kind of reproduction, the Law-of-the-Name-of-the-Father falters.

On one level, challenges to the Symbolic have already taken the form of challenges to naming practices, not only in the court case where the single mother sued to prevent the child from having the name of the father, but where radical feminists, for example, have renamed themselves outside of the order of their familial patronymics and in relation to some vestige of a feminist ethic. Deploying the name to undermine the Name directly confronts the specifically paternal functioning of the Name, while it tries to reinstall another nonpaternal form of a metaphorical Symbolic in its place. On a metaphorical level, this naming politic reflects the kind of identity flexibility enacted by a more metonymical DNA engineering and digital image morphing.

As a marker of identity, DNA produces too much sameness and yet is not total enough. It is perceived as fallible both because it provides the matrix for the production of identical copies and because technology has not yet achieved the ability to record and manage a complete, ordered, definitive list of amino acids. That DNA testing currently involves only small chains of genetic code means that it is possible that more than one person will share those selected codes or their combination (even if the likelihood is only one in one million). Without a total match, DNA testing provides only statistical probability. Even if the technology were available to record and match a complete list of genes, DNA typing would still not be quite the right kind of proof, since it shows that someone has a certain combination of genes, rather than identifying the tested genes as a particular person's genes. The court convicts Judge Dredd because he shares an identical DNA code with someone else. Identicality is mistaken for identification.

But it is, perhaps, not fair to say that DNA is fallible even if on a molecular level it is (it can mutate, for example). Our way of trying to read DNA is fallible, for we read it, as did Judge Dredd's highly scientific court, to try to prove the contextual logic of individual identity. Identification transforms quickly into identity—you share these genetic markers; therefore, you are the culprit—so that the code used to identify becomes the code of identity. While DNA is not really synonymous with the Name because it provides codes of generation instead of a unique generational sign, and enables multiples instead of guaranteeing individuality, DNA is easily confused with the Name in its function as a discrete individual marker. Denoting the microscopic site where reproductive codes come together with social identity, DNA's imagined certainty stands in for the Name, effecting a small change in understandings of identity and social ordering. This change had already commenced with the assignment of social security numbers; an opportune entry into number-based information systems, social security numbers, necessitated by the name's lack of singularity, augmented and eventually replaced the name. Instead of perpetuating traditional paternal logic, the incipient alteration of the order of identification/identity enabled by DNA produces an anxiety about a loss of identity that takes the form of the fear of multiples that DNA also potentially represents. This anxiety isn't necessarily produced by a knowledge of DNA's capacities, but by a generalized suspicion about the capabilities of genetic engineering.

Because DNA's digital logic means that any single code could, if the biotechnology existed, be reproduced infinitely, proliferations of identicality mark the hyperbolic capacity of a logic whose fearsome aspect is that it abandons metaphor and history (the singular personality of patriarchal order) in favor of potentially infinite replication. Aldous Huxley's vision of ninety-six identical Epsilon workers testifies not only to our precocious ability to imagine this code-based engineered reproduction, but also images our anxiety about the production of multiples. In his novel *Brave New World*, the specter of proliferated identicals marks a fear of disindividuation. *Brave New World*'s multiples are lower caste, less attractive, and less intelligent than its singular upper caste productions. Proliferation marks the difference between the custom design that produces the individually identified Alphas and Betas and the mass-produced, chemically invaded, embryonically conditioned lower-caste clones. Multiples signal the absence of metaphor, visually replicating the hypertrophic potential of DNA; their individual identities and personal qualities are sacrificed for quantity and functionality. *Brave New World*'s multiples may not have identity in the old-fashioned patriarchal sense of the word, but they have a place, number, and function all the more determined by the conditions of their generation. Marked by a batch number, Delta and Epsilon multiples redefine identity as a relation between genesis and social function instead of as a nominal relation between the individual and a family history.

181

Huxley's "brave new world" matches its proliferative plenitude with a hyperpaternal Law that has substituted the Name of the Father of mass production for the old metaphorical divine father's name. Fordism governs Huxley's culture more totally than God recently has, controlling every aspect of life and consciousness. Fordist paternalism is analogous to our imaginings of DNA: complete, total, managed in every detail, and centered around the details of (re)production. *Brave New World*'s Ford is not, however, a comforting figure, but rather a puppet Name-of-the-Father who tries to mask the totalitarian manipulations of a culture somehow gone wrong. Anticipating the clash of systems to come, Huxley posits a less subtle version of the same repaternalizing solution that has been occurring in various forms since the 1950s; Ford isn't the Name-of-the-Father, because real value lies in the purity of the untouched residues of primitive patriarchal culture represented by John Savage.

Through this vision of the future, Huxley projects an anxiety about mechanical reproduction's ingress into human generation, but the form his projection takes does trace one possible strategy for redefining identity in relation to an altered Symbolic. His projected mass-production system imitates paternalism, and the ability to match genotype and social function suggests a genetic predestination that literalizes Calvinism. But if we envision this genetic predestination as its obverse; that is, if we filter out Huxley's pessimism and see the totality of control as figuring an actual lack of control or the opening of possibility, identity transforms into a malleable, flexible intersection between social form and individual consciousness. Overcontrol means that there are too many ways things can fall apart. This is not to endorse a new brand of bourgeois individualism, but to suggest that identity (at least the social identity fixed by the Name-of-the-Father) in its Symbolic role of locating the individual can shift from a historically defined notion to a site of negotiation between individuals and culture that reflects a rule of deferral and multiplicity instead of substitution, prohibition, and absence. Of course, this negotiation is not marked by some kind of exercise of free will, but rather reveals the greater variety of determining factors at work in the construction of identity—in this case, ways of masking the illusion of individuality. It enables a more performative notion of identity.

While the digital image is not really analogous to the human being or to the metaphorical function of the name, if we imagine the human as analogous to the digital photograph (engineered from genetic bits), the Symbolic payoff is flexibility. Even though a given individual cannot yet change his/her genotype, phenotypes have been altered for years through plastic surgery, make-up, tattooing, hair dying, and implants. The potential for genotypic change is imagined in cancer cures and other proposed genetic remedies. As we have seen, merely imagining a capability is enough to produce an anxiety about that capability and an imaginary rendition of its possibilities. Like the imagined potentials of DNA engineering, digital imaging can "morph" or seamlessly transform from one appearance to another. The transformations are often a fearsome sign of unauthorized reproduction, or are sometimes interpreted as boundary transgressions, but they also compensate for a shift in Symbolic ground.[8]

In films that provide symptomatic moments of reproductive anxiety—the overt threat to paternal order of the *Terminator* series and the unauthorized reproductions of vampires and aliens—one of the most threatening moments is the possibility of transformation. The *Terminator* threatens a larger transformation from human to machine culture. Vampires transform into various shapes; aliens not only undergo a metamorphosis, but they threaten to transform humans from people to incubators. This transformative capability is, as I have discussed, metonymical, moving through contiguous stages away from the singular self-sameness of Symbolic stability. But while most images of transformation in these films are made through editing or progressive dissolves, digital imaging technologies enable a performance of transformation that captures both the terms of transformative change and the digital/DNA technology by which this transformation is accomplished.

Metamorphoses of the alien in *Species* are astoundingly rapid. While we often do not actually see those transformations since they mainly occur offscreen, the imaginary that governs the idea of the alien's easy transition from humanoid to monster is an imaginary linked to advances in computer imaging called "morphing." A "software technique called 'morph'" "allows a very smooth transition between one form and another so that it looks continuous, making it impossible to detect where the boundary of one character finishes and the other begins."[9] A morph program produces the appearance of analogue—of total gradation—in the place of the stepped sequences of digital imaging, making the digital realize the gradation capacities enabled by its stock of pixel values. In other words, digital imaging is capable of masking its own lack of gradation by producing images of seamless transition that could only otherwise be captured on film through animation (a more primitive form of stepped sequence) or by filming an actual metamorphosis. The effect is one of endless comparison, producing what appears to be a series of morphologically different substitutes in the same image space; the transmuting faces in Michael Jackson's video "Black and White" effect an amazing leveling of the differences among faces of different gender, race, and age. The sequence looks something like a dream metaphor with transitions so smooth as to be surreal.[10]

Morphing makes the difference between Cameron's 1986 *Aliens* and his 1991 *Terminator II: Judgement Day* where the T-1000 Terminator takes the form of "polymorphous polyalloy," a strategic shapechanger that can look like anything it touches. Its logic is entirely metonymical, achieving its successive states

183

through literal contact. Imaged through digital technology, it threatens human patriarchy with a post-digital machine order. But the difference between the Alien's threat and the T-1000's menace, apart from their different narrative functions, is that the Alien presents a specifically stepped, metonymical version of reproduction, while the T-1000 (and the alien in *Species*) present that metonymy masked by a metaphor of seamless transition. The digital has covered its tracks, or covered the tracks of the villains through whom its threat is projected. The T-1000 belongs to the order of the liquid.

While morphing can be realized on-screen as a way of hiding a series of contiguous differences, the imaginary transformations enacted by morphing's successive alterations are, in turn, actually performed on a more physical phenotypical level. If man can change to woman in a seamless image morph, then man can change to woman and vice versa through plastic surgery. Piercings, tattoos, hair coloring all "morph" appearance as an overt sign of the individual production of social identity that works against the register of the name, relocating the Symbolic in a logic of material displacement. Even though sex-change operations historically precede the invention of morph software, they are part of the same identity flexibility enabled by a fading Symbolic. Although it might seem as if sex changes challenge this Symbolic, and in terms of their public visibility, they do, they are only surgically effected because the shifting Symbolic that governs concrete and unchangeable genders already enables such flexibility. And sex changes, in particular, confirm and even reinforce a metaphorical Symbolic in so far as that Symbolic underwrites the rule of binary gender. Sex change believes in the Symbolic which is why one must change one's gender instead of the system of genders.[11]

Morphing provides a particular form for gender flexibility by making surface variations accessible and by providing the imaginary logic for their acquisition. In this way the model of morphing begins to deny the social, cultural, and political valences of phenotypical differences as these marks of difference become a part of an individual cosmetic pantheon. Automorphing permits the illusion of a choice of identity within an existing array of superficial indices, suggesting some individual ownership of "type" as opposed to name, though type is entirely bound up with phenotypical stereotypes linked to class, race, gender, age, and social subgroup. At the same time, automorphing tends also to rely upon existing types and categories; for this reason, phenotypical automorphing tends to be a politically conservative way of responding to the production of identity in relation to symbolic shifts. Rendering the phenotypical signifiers of social differences superficial and/or acquirable means denying the social/political specificity of differences such as race and gender. If we cannot yet alter genotypes as a way of fashioning and owning an "identity," then we can alter phenotypes so as to influence social positioning in a culture where the simulation of being is what counts.

If instead of seeing the phenotypical surface as the locus of identity, I under-stand identity as a given genotype—as the sum product of the biological sin-gularity of genetic dispensation—my chances of "owning" my identity are sta-tistically good, if, in fact, it were possible to completely document my genet-ic list. The genotypic identifier could become my identity, if only its informa-tion could be contained on a portable format like a social security number. But numbered identities are exactly what we fear, the loss of metaphor mak-ing them seem "impersonal." The fact that we are already "identified" by superficial phenotypic expressions of our genetic code (blue eyes, brown hair, 5′ 2″) doesn't bother us because phenotypes somehow act as the metaphori-cal equivalent of the name, expressing (inaccurately) a code that exists invisi-bly somewhere else. At this point in time, we employ the two "laws" togeth-er, using phenotypical characterizations and DNA to discern patriarchal iden-tity except where DNA proves incompatible with patriarchy's individuation.

Apart from philosophical issues around the equation of biology and identi-ty, there are two problems with genetic identification as a means to an identi-ty. One is that a DNA code threatens to work in the same fated, determined way as the name, becoming a substitute, formulaic metaphor, especially since to some degree DNA is a generational legacy. DNA does, however, allow for a recognition of both parents instead of only one. The other problem is of the potential identicality of DNA samples. Identical twins, even with the limited DNA information we can utilize, pose identity problems in fingering putative fathers, for example, since either twin could be the father of the same child. The possibility of identicality means that DNA codes cannot deliver the same singular identity as the father's name; even though many people share the same name, many more would have the same genotype. The difference between nominal similarities and replicable genetic codes is history. People with the same name have different histories; the same name is never really the same name. But sharing the same genotype is a sameness that is already recognized as a problem of identicality judging from research on the affinities of identical twins.

The coexistence of the two systems—Name, code—around the issue of identity points to the two orders' curious temporal displacements. The metaphorical Law of the Father is historical, past tense, nostalgic—a disrupt-ed ideation. DNA's coded order, which relies on the delusion of total knowl-edge, is still imaginary, though its capabilities show up in automorphing's sur-face attempts to construct identity along a flexible, phenotypical order. The Law-of-the-Name-of-the-Father always exists in the past as a debt; for this reason it is certain, established in its Symbolic relation. A DNA Symbolic exists in the subjunctive "If it were . . ." A fully metonymical symbolic represented by something like DNA is the Symbolic of a future Symbolic. In fact, DNA threatens to be no Symbolic at all if we understand the Symbolic as necessar-

185

ily functioning as some sort of figuration. The Law-of-the-Name-of-the-Father and digital order currently coexist in a tension that fitfully clears and fogs as a technological imaginary begins to dominate, not only as the subject, but also as the means of imaging. While photography is used to signify a "this once was," digital imagining, morphing, etc., expand the imaginary to a case of "if it were," tracking the shift from Name to Code. But now digital imaging technologies can imitate photography; the appearance of analogy is no longer a reliable record of an existing relation in time and space. The code subsumes, imitates, refigures itself in a form more like metaphor.

At the same time, the emergence of DNA as an identificatory tool is actually a way of resituating the imaginary of biological fact as a substitute Law of the Father. If the order represented by digital codes is distilled to DNA, which, in its link to the paternal function seems to secure paternity, then the digital appears to function as metaphor's objective correlative. DNA would thus prove the truth of the paternal metaphor. And, certainly, much of the renegotiation around anxieties about the paternal (and order) takes the form of attempting to repaternalize an alienating order by making the paternal show up in everything from gothic images of reproductive threat to national masculinities to legislating reproductive technologies. There is a persistent attempt to remetaphorize what seems to be an emerging emphasis on a metonymical code as an ordering principle.

The problem (or the possibility) is, however, that while DNA seems to secure a preexisting paternal truth, its certitude standing in for the paternal's uncertainty, the paternal itself, like the photograph's time-space referent, can be excised. Just as digital technology can image scenes that never existed, DNA can work without reference to the father, and can, in fact, be engineered and recombined so as to reproduce no single paternal donor. Losing their referent means that digital reproductions stand in as originals, what Baudrillard would call a "hyperreal," that alters not our concept of reality, but our concept of the relations among image, history, and existence. The digital defies history by producing what has never been, even though the image, once produced, enters history. Like the DNA-identified individual, the digital image has a post- rather than a pre-historic existence. Its "identity" comes through what it comes to signify instead of, like the paternally named individual, how it continues someone else's signification.

Know Your Symbolic

Symptoms of Symbolic shifts, manifested in figures of unauthorized reproduction and compensatory repaternalization, play out a peculiar dynamic between metaphor and metonymy. If too much metonymy threatens a metaphorical order and if metaphorical order is, at the same time, undermined by the literalization of its paternal center, the cultural response, if read through the insistent reappearance of remetaphorized fathers in representations of reproduction, is to gloss metonymy with a metaphor that imitates the paternal function. This replacement metaphor takes metonymy itself as its basis; *Junior*'s pregnant father exemplifies perfectly how maternal metonymy is redeployed as paternal agency, not through the metaphor of the Name, but through the figure of the over-full male body. Technology and body remoor the Symbolic in the overly literal father.

Pop's deployments of the name, Arnold's prophylactic muscularity, statutory reckoning with previously nonlegislated definitions of paternity, law's spectacle, the vampire's stake and garlic, and Windows interfaces all supply some metaphorical mask to palliate the emergence of a different metonymical order, perpetuating a paternal Symbolic. On the one hand, these metonymy/metaphor sandwiches simply reverse the previous Symbolic emphasis; they play out the inextricable interrelation of these two modes of organization. On the other hand, there is something fearsomely different about a metonymical as opposed to a metaphorical order.

Metaphor's very operation enacts—performs—continuity through the retention, overlap, and comparison of implied terms. The presence of the Name—of the father, of nation, of political cause—preserves large organizing metaphors whose common characteristic is their lack of facticity, their ideation, and their connective leaps. These metaphors work as "legitimating metanarratives," or what previous generations of critics might call myth, organizing sociopolitical relations through consistent and adaptable metaphors whose main feature is to substitute a concept for a vacancy, to constitute and organize ideological systems as the *raisons d'être* of otherwise dispersed social fields. Metaphor's operation—the production of meaning through the transference of concepts from one site to another—drives this organization and its concomitant illusion of permanence. Its something-for-nothing substitutive practice engineers a Law whose nominal control of the ineffable translates into the Ineffable's control of the nominal, a system with divine beginnings and a heavenly end.

187

The loss or transposition of metaphor, however, is not the same as losing the legitimating metanarratives Lyotard links to postmodernism. Metaphor's displacement occurs both before and after a loss of legitimating metanarratives; metanarratives (of consumption, identity, transnational corporatism) continue to be produced in a postmodern or metonymical rather than a modern register. The Symbolic shift to metonymical predominance is characteristic of an even larger scale change coordinated in some respects with the emergence of the postmodern, and accounting for some of the postmodern's characteristics, but neither completely subsumed within the postmodern nor defining the postmodern moment. The postmodern is not coterminous with the larger span of the shift from metaphor to metonymy. In so far as one might associate postmodernism with commodity-cultural forms of hyperreality, the increasing visibility of the terms of Symbolic change would make the postmodern's multiple manifestations especially convincing correlates. The postmodern is enabled by Symbolic change, helps it along, but like other compensatory tactics, will exhaust itself before the Symbolic has completely shifted.

It would be possible, however, to try to account for some of the functional or performative indices of the postmodern as an effect of the insurgency of metonymy. The postmodern "takes the form of self-conscious, self-contradictory, self-undermining statement" (Hutcheon), or postmodern writers "are skeptical of modernist notions of metaphor" (Bertens), or the postmodern consists of decentered, uncertain, confused codes, rupture, discontinuity (Huyssen), or it represents "the breakdown of older unities and the transgression of prohibitions that had been set up by modernism" (Kolb).[12] Any of these characteristics can be read as an effect of the loss of metaphor and/or the increasing intervention of metonymy. If metonymy predominates, there are gaps, decentralizations, and the apparent breakdown of unities; syntagmatic chaining produces a very different landscape from metaphor. In a sense, the emergence of the category postmodern as an organizing philosophy (or description of an organizing philosophy) is another manifestation of a compensatory metaphorical reglossing on the level of a superstructural category. The category itself reglosses the rifts the category represents, making them contribute again to a larger, more metaphorical unity. While the phenomena labeled postmodern may be examples of a metonymical order, the idea of the postmodern that organizes these rifts is another instance of the compensatory bent of a metaphor-based Symbolic's tendency towards renegotiation.

The coexistence of metonymy and metaphor as competing ordering systems produces gaps or catachreses that, on the one hand, produce anxieties and compensatory refigurations of the paternal (or, in the case of postmodernism, the authorial or the critical) and, on the other hand, afford potential sites for cultural intervention. Unlike metaphor, which contrives continuity, metonymy's structure is characterized by gaps produced by contiguity's inevitable seams. For example, numbers in sequence, such as the numbers that tell time on a digital clock, also represent gaps between one moment and the next that are normally elided by the analogue clock face's sweeping hand. Metonymy fills in and specifies within these gaps instead of substituting and covering seams with a larger idea; a digital timepiece retains a number for much longer than the moment it marks or merely inserts a faster series of running numbers to the right of the decimal point.

If metaphor's continuity is the result of the implied retention of a term, metonymy's gaps come from the joints of discontinuous associations, of comparisons that work because of their differences, their relative positions in a chain or sequence that makes each term as important as the next. This egalitarian arrangement pits the necessary importance of each bit against metaphor's intrinsic hierarchies. At the same time, metonymical chains offer multiple options; one can, at any point, follow one of several different but equally contiguous chains, or one can continue to fill in the gaps with more information. The digital itself, as a form of metonymy, is characterized by gaps—the pause, space, discontinuity between one value and the next. The emergence of the digital and metonymy as an order, then, provides multiple possibilities for interruption, digression, mutation, and redirection. But one needs to know where these gaps are, especially as metaphor and metonymy seem so intertwined. How would we know where to look? If we locate gaps how do we intervene?

One option for Symbolic intervention afforded by a metonymical order works, to use a simile, like alternate routes on a road map. In theory any road can be taken; the choice of route need not be governed by a larger idea of destination, but by a sheer logic of highway contiguity. Even if one uses the analogue map to plot a route to a destination (metaphor), one still has multiple choices for getting there. Metonymy means that the map's alternatives are more important than the destination.

While Baudrillard rejects the map's abstraction for images generated without precedent, or "simulacra," metonymy drives to replace the arching generalizations of analogy with the fullness of a complete range of pixellated facts that occupy every gap while producing new gaps, or a kind of counter-simulacra. DNA is the perfect instance of metonymy's fulfillment; not "hyperreal," but the generating instance of the real, DNA exemplifies the site where the code meets the material, where analogy becomes reality. DNA is the model matrix; its example drives the metonymical hyperreal phenomena of contemporary culture where "the real," Baudrillard asserts, "is produced from miniaturized units, from matrices, memory banks and command models—and with these it can be reproduced an indefinite number of times. It no longer has to be rational, since it is no longer measured against some ideal or negative instance" (*Simulations* 3). Baudrillard goes on to hypothesize that this "real" is "no longer a real at all. It is a hyperreal, the product of an irradiating synthesis of combinatory models in a hyperspace without atmosphere" (3). Understanding, however, the Symbolic's metonymical shift means the simultaneous rejection of the real as an ideal and the acceptance of organizing codes as real. Metonymy does not mean the loss of the real any more than metaphor would, but the delusion of its even more alluring presence in the multiplication of facts, laws, and particulate fullness of a universe that is no longer empty space.

Thus, another option for Symbolic intervention is the act of filling in gaps with facts and data. This is the logical extension of enlightenment science, whose drive inward and outward discovers and supplies additional structures,

189

routes, or elements that make the map ever more complete, ever less an analogue, and ever more the terrain itself. On one level, this filling in is compensatory, an attempted erasure of the gaps metonymy provides. Providing more
facts simply creates more gaps, even if they are ever more microscopic (the
gaps between microparticles) or immense (black holes). Filling in, however,
also effects changes in scale. Micro terrain becomes macro as more information is gleaned. Macro becomes increasingly micro with the acquisition of systemic knowledge. Space begins to look like the atom, the atom like a crowded outer space.

If the map could also be seen as a metaphor of narrative itself, its multiple
digressions suggest that a metonymical order might eventually alter our concepts of narrative as they relate to other ideologies, such as the family, gender,
and sexuality, that depend in part on a narrativized structure. Narrative begins
to shift, as postmodern aesthetics has discerned, since the late 1950s. This gradual change in narrative character, which is still much more potential than realized, is the effect of two different, but interrelated phenomena. If narrative is
oedipal in character, as both Roland Barthes and Teresa de Lauretis have suggested, then altering its basic three-term oedipal premise—that is, altering the
myth grounding the metaphorical Symbolic—invites a different narrative
structuration.[13] If the paternal function ceases to moor identity or to provide
the prohibitive alibi for the desire that drives the oedipal narrative, then the
terms of the narrative open up, as they did in *Junior*'s parentage, to four or
more functions. Instead of a paternal function that steps in to prohibit the relation between mother and child, in a narrative organized through metonymy
the one-on-one relation is already interrupted, and there are multiple pro-
hibitors. Narrative as desire works differently, multiply. Four terms means three
rather than two parental terms, which means that gender binaries no longer
fit neatly or are necessarily produced by familial configurations. And four
doesn't just mean four; it means four or more, where gender is also split from
reproductive functioning. Such a narrative would be the story *Junior* would tell
if Arnold refused to marry the scientist and instead shacked up with his
research team.

This leads to the second phenomenon. If gender is detached from reproduction, the gender binaries that constitute narrative's feminine field and
"masculine" protagonist might change, open up, not to mere substitution, but
to a proliferation of possible positions that no longer correlate gender to specific narrative function. In so far as gender organizes narrative, narrative need
no longer reproduce the terms of a gender binary and in so far as narrative
enforces gendered positions, shifts in narrative might effect a gradual shift in
understandings of gender and, in relation to gender, sexuality. If there are more
than two terms or positions, and if those positions aren't gendered in a particular oedipal way, narrative may no longer drive towards conjoinder and ensu-

ing (re)production. If narrative no longer pushes towards some reproductive conclusion, some coming together of opposites, and if those opposites have been multiplied so as to no longer oppose one another, narrative and sexuality cease to be either heterosexual or homosexual (the terms through which we understand such joinder) and become something else. And in so far as sexuality is narrative and vice versa, the dispersion of narrative positions that spells the disappearance of a dominant reproductive narrative form also signals the dispersion of the sex/gender system, since binaries are no longer functionally necessary and heterosexualities no longer define narrative direction.[14]

If the conjoinder of two is not the anticipated end of narrative, then what shape can a story take? Without the impetus provided by conjoinder or production, or if production ceases to be a terminal desire, narrative might organize itself in relation to other patterns that have already structured narrative such as repetition, alternation, perpetual oscillation, or morphing. One doesn't, however, simply begin to tell a different story one day; change will need to be gradual and conscious. In other words, the story can change, and it may be possible to change the story and through narrative's function, affect all of the layers of ideology that adhere to narrative form. But this is a utopian projection. Narrative, like metaphor, quickly—instantly—recoups itself. Just as metaphor will never disappear from language, but may only cease to ground order, metaphor will never disappear from narrative. Narrative's structural reliance on metaphor, on what Peter Brooks calls its deployment of "sameness and difference," could conceivably move from metaphor to a more metonymical arrangement represented by something more like routes on a map or the multiple and layered choices of hypertext.[15] Narrative would then cease to be conceived of as a singular or primary trajectory and organize itself around multiple and equally viable possibilities or trails (to use a metaphor) that may or may not replicate an oedipal story. But that would enable the telling of stories other than the oedipal, providing a possibility for the promulgation of slightly different reproductive ideologies.

The effect of multiplying the number of terms engaged in reproduction is ultimately to lose the idea of narrative as an organizing episteme that gathers multiples within a directional reproductive dynamic, and to gain an idea of narrative as sets of multiple possibilities that produce a dynamic in their choice and reading. While certainly this production of a narrative dynamic will also be the reproduction of a dynamic located elsewhere—in ideology, psychology—a more metonymically premised narrative inevitably shifts the locus of narrative's dynamic from narrative itself to reading and selection, in a process already enabled by hypertext. The organizational locus of narrative is displaced from narrative structure to the structure of reading and selection as performances of narrative rather than the consumption of one. In so far as the human psyche replays the oedipal, this dynamic may simply relocate an oedi-

191

pal trajectory, but in so far as symbolic shifts make the oedipal less and less relevant as an organizing structure, the dynamic may well change.

Of course, all of this happens together; narrative and the Symbolic interrelate and interact, neither one causing or effecting the other, but mutually defining each other. The resistance to change in narrative is tremendous, since narrative is a very conservative structure, a structure designed, in fact, to conserve. Its ability to reform itself into its oedipal dynamic seems to come not only from the habit of human psychology, but from the flexibility, adaptability, and pervasiveness of narrative's dynamic itself. One way we might understand the compensatory strategies outlined in this book is as a renarrativization—as an attempt to reassert a traditional narrative dynamic on phenomena that represent a breach, even as I try to suggest a different story. And, to some extent, this book unwittingly follows and reinscribes that same narrative dynamic in the course of trying to account for symptoms of change that still look oedipal. We are a long way from being out of metaphor.

Performing Metonymy

To rely on what seem to be mere metaphors of rhetoric might be a weak argument for larger ideological and social changes. As they affect our perceptions of everything from time to identity, metonymy's gaps produce an anxiety that comes from the gaps themselves. But anxiety also comes from a clash in systems as both metonymy and metaphor try to occupy certain cultural spaces at the same time, particularly reproduction as both the site of a metaphorical continuity and as the place where that continuity has already been most affected. Recognizing the emblematic moments of systemic collision enables the identification of sites—and more importantly—tactics of intervention that might enable an enlightened manipulation of cultural priorities.

To think this sounds idealistic or naive is to ignore the fact that this already happens on a large scale in advertising and political rhetoric. The emergence of a highly compensatory appeal to the nuclear family is one such intervention, wielded as a way to restructure popular philosophies and government practices of welfare and cultural subsidy. The familial metaphor intervenes not only when the interests of the overly wealthy are adversely affected, but also when the metonymical functioning (the apparent uncoordinated operation) of government agencies begins to show. In this context, the family actually functions as a metaphor of government, system, and hierarchical order, rather than as a basis for social policy or the object of social concern. The appeal to "family values" provides no real logic for government cutbacks (it would seem, in fact, the opposite), but it does paste a vague, but powerful, regressive, nostalgic metaphor of order over all those threatening emergent metonymies such as computer information systems, uncontrollable cultural diversity, environmental protectionism's breaches of capitalism, independent women, homosexualities, transnational corporatism's erasure of the nation, and welfare's Law-of-the-Name-of-the-Father "travesty" of something for nothing.

"Family values," then, represent one already deployed tactic that intervenes to restore patriarchy rather than to disrupt it. Family values elide systemic differences with a metaphorical configuration whose very embodiment of ideological imperatives prevents their confrontation. One either submits to the paradigm—"we are family"—or argues with it. In either case, the result is the same repaternalization, since on the level of public policy the family really means the Law-of-the-Father as demonstrated by the drive against single-mother welfare families, attempts to locate absent fathers, the outcry against "nontraditional" families, and general preferential treatment of father-centered family units.[16] Try, however, as they might, this revival of the paternal is not a revival of the Law-of-the-Name-of-the-Father, but an attempt to revive the literal father and to restore the father's power. Importing the powerful call of dying tradition itself, appeals to "family values" attempt to wrest the metonymical back into metaphor.

The reason family values have such a powerful effect is because to assert them actually performs the terms of Symbolic shift. Interventions into the Symbolic are inevitably performative as opposed to definitive; that is, instead of depending upon the imposition of metaphorical categorizations, they require the enactment of a structural relation. Naming family values performs an attempted reassertion of the Name in the place from which the name has disappeared—from the center of Law. But the efficacy of this Name, which refers to a more literal version of family than does the Law-of-the-Name-of-the-Father, also depends on the systemic gaps produced by the introduction of a metonymical aegis. Hence, the consumer product becomes an offspring in a "family of fine products." This corporate "family" deserves the special treatment reserved for families in an ideological landscape where the familial is a way of retaining the familiar.

But while family values' appeal to metaphor might work on a large scale precisely because they actually have no single referent, the specific operations of reinstituting this appeal to now literal "family values" are no longer metaphorical, but all-too-literally metonymical, as saving the father becomes the pretext for attempts to disenfranchise the poor. Family values operate like the pregnant father, their inconsistent abstraction mustering metonymies within a very literalized paternal image. While evoking a past order, "family values" change value depending upon their environment, enabling them to work within the interstices provided by law's increasing metonymy and to take advantage of discontinuities in governmental functions. In this way, those working in the name of the family can intervene differently in different places without having to account for ideological inconsistencies. Thus, family values can simultaneously justify terminating school lunch programs (of benefit to children), pro-

193

pose orphanages (breaking up families), cut student-loan programs (that bene-fit families), and oppose abortion (which would seem to force a family).

At the same time, "family values" proponents make the very important step of curtailing First Amendment rights around the American flag. What this dis-jointed, contradictory legislative agenda suggests is that the performance value of family values is not about the family at all, but is about the attempted return of metaphorical order itself. The only kind of "family" that benefits from "family values" legislation is a corporate family as the locus of a paternal Symbolic falsely represented by the overly protected flag. Family values, final-ly, are themselves a metonymy; contiguous to the larger paternalism of nation (read, transnational corporation) and establishing the nation as a paternal enti-ty, their dispersed and illogical operations try to return metonymies to the Name-of-the-Father in the guise of a flag that stands for an organization (a metaphor) that has already fallen victim to the larger exigencies of highly metonymical transnational corporations to which the nation has given birth.[17]

Another, more defensive, example of an intervention that tries to renegoti-ate the patriarchal occurs in the tussle around "political correctness." The Symbolic that political correctness disturbs is a Symbolic confused with an Imaginary image of white male primacy; the disturbance occurs in the realm of all too literal nonwhite and/or nonmale variety. In response to demands that other than white males be considered in classrooms, diction, and social policies, certain citizens decide to exercise what they call their "First Amendment" right to free speech. The speech they want to protect is speech that generally denigrates those whom they see political correctness benefiting. But this response actually engages on a literal level the Symbolic they wish to assert. By demanding the right to "name" others, they point to the anxiety that grounds their complaint in the first place—an anxiety about retaining an imaginary vision of the Law as a white paternal prerogative to name. But such literal naming exposes rather than assuages their anxieties while also revealing the lack of substance inherent to the Symbolic they wish to revivify.

Intervening in metonymical order, as the example of narrative demon-strates, requires more than mere assertions that tend to buy inadvertently into whatever system is in place. Because metonymy itself is performative, in so far as the meaning gleaned from metonymy must come from an active retroactive reading, intervention requires the performative. Metonymy's retroactivity pro-duces meaning instead of meaning prospectively informing, as in metaphor, a comparison that appears as an accomplished combination. To say, for instance, "the family of man" is to compare instantaneously a family with a collection of races and types; the comparison is produced by the preexistent meaning of "family" and enabled by the similarity between family and group imported by the double meanings of both nouns. The work of metaphor appears to have been already done. To say, "family man" is to force a retrospective rereading of "family" in syntagmatic relation to what follows it; chaining does not necessarily signify by similarity or preexistent meaning, but in a series of single meanings.[18] The "paradigmatic axis" of substitution depends upon continuing meaning while meaning on the axis of selection depends upon the selection.

Metonymy's meaning is only gained by linking terms on the basis of their grammatical contiguity, while metaphor produces the illusion of a finished process. Metaphor demands definitive ideational arguments—more metaphors—while metonymy requires a performance of structure itself as the locus of meaning. But effective intervention into metonymy would mean not only that one intervene performatively, but that one know where to intervene, and how to perform. Groups such as Act Up or Queer Nation attempted performative intervention in an insightful and instinctive reading of culture, but their tactics sometimes wield the wrong kind of performance at less effective overly metaphorical sites such as family values or sexual practices. Since the problem isn't so much ideology or behavior as it is forms of order, attacking ideology only ratifies order. The trick would be to find ways to challenge order itself performatively.

Performativity itself, however, isn't a single category, but a collection of strategies for being in imitation. On the simplest level, performativity is simile, a mimetic performance that attempts to replicate something somewhere else and, thereby, evoke its presence. On this level, performativity is most closely aligned with metaphor even though it is already a displacement. Performative similes such as acting, instructive imitation (as in language classes), or following directions arrive at a product accomplished by the fact of imitation itself. Combining the act of imitating an object or social category with an imitation of the object's or category's relation to larger structures—a kind of synecdocichal performativity—results in the critique made by comic impersonators, drag, parody, and satire. This performativity effects a social commentary in so far as it performs a form in relation to structure; but its critique of system is necessarily limited by its detached, synecdochical quality as well as by is conventionalization.[19] Drag may perform gender within a gender structure, but in its somewhat conventionalized practice, it at best critiques gender assumptions rather than the order that produces them. The voguing imaged in Jennie Livingston's *Paris Is Burning* may, by performing the intersection of class, race, and gender systems, perform and expose a more systemic critique, but that critique is resisted by relocalizing voguing as a specifically raced, classed practice as well as by its commodification.[20]

Performing structures, a third performativity, is no longer necessarily mimetic, but becomes the revelatory performance of disjunctions. The performativity of avant-garde cinema, theater, art, and fiction resides in their production of disjunctions that play upon and expose systemic relations and inconsistencies. This performativity tends to be metonymical, forcing juxtapositions and clashes, and opening fissures in closed metaphorical systems. Godard's *Masculin/Feminin* (1966) forces such clashes by stringing together fifteen detached scenarios about gender. Denaturalizing narrative and the discussion of gender invites a consciousness of the constructedness of gender. Sandra Bernhard's oft-cited *Without You I'm Nothing*(1990) juxtaposes systems of gender and race in such a way as to show up their interrelation.[21] The writer Kathy Acker's various experiments with convention and form perform what happens when the naturalized relation between form and content is disturbed by the insertion of content not normally associated with form. This exposes the assumptions of form as a way of challenging cultural assumptions about self-hood, art, gender, sexuality, and authority.[22] Even though these performances reveal disjunctions, they may not always expose system. Sometimes conventionalized, sometimes aimed narrowly (as Dada aims at institutional art), they suffer the same fate as voguing or become the celebrated texts of an intellectual elite.

Another way to perform structures is through hyperbole. Hyperbole—the performance of an excessive version—represents a consciousness of an order exaggerated through some performance of exaggeration. For example, grotesquely conspicuous consumption made with a consciousness of the meaning of consumption in consumer culture is a performance that might expose the structure of consumer culture itself. Some vestiges of Pop art performed hyperbole; Claes Oldenburg's giant cloth food, for example, effected a consciousness of a fast-food system. Warhol's multiple reproductions pointed to the hegemony of mass-produced images. Related to de Lauretis's suggestion of "Oedipus with a vengeance," such hyperbolic performance highlights system as system as long as hyperbole is located as a systemic rather than local performance.[23] What is crucial about hyperbole is the consciousness of system it can evoke as long as it is performed with a consciousness of system in the first place.

"Oedipus with a vengeance" proposes an overoedipalization as a way to show up the oedipal system. This hyperbole enables the denaturalization of the oedipal as a construction. Theoretically, any structure could be made visible through this process of hyperbole—gender, sexualities, consumer culture, class systems. The trick is to discern the structure and then to define an efficacious site for its performance. In one sense, desecrations of the flag actually effect this type of hyperbolic performance. If the flag becomes a stand-in for the Name, and if peoples' responses to flag/name desecrations demonstrate the extent to which people are invested in this symbolization, desecrating the flag performs not only a challenge to the Symbolic, but makes visible the desperate attachment to the symbolic. At the same time, desecrating a flag also reinforces the Symbolic by accepting the flag's position as symbol. That Congress would find it necessary to delimit such performances is a sign of the symbol's desperate straits. In one way the desecration performance has worked to reveal a weakness in the system, spurring a more repressive system in response.

To discern how to intervene more in the very terms of a metonymical order, an instructive example is Indiana University's 1994 ruckus over funding a center for gay and lesbian students. Establishing a center for gay and lesbian students is a Symbolic (i.e., metaphorical) act read as university and/or state support for gay and lesbian students, alternative sexualities' life-styles, and diversity. A state legislator, sensing the symbolic capital of opposing such a project, objected to IU's use of state funds to underwrite services for homosexuals. The ensuing arguments about whether or not IU should establish and fund such a center focused on the problem of funding—the site of greatest metaphorical impact. The problem was "resolved" when IU found "private" funding for the center.

In picking up on the symbolic possibilities of IU's rather enlightened project, the legislator intervened by reasserting the overdetermined catchall of family values to retrieve the Symbolic. The response of students fighting for the center was to accept the legislator's terms of battle. The university rejoined in the same Symbolic register. While the legislator's intervention was effective since it performed the structural problem in the very terms of the symbolic structure that was threatened, the responses to his interference could have been more profitably performative of metonymical rather than metaphorical intervention. If a center is symbolic, how would one perform a metonymical intervention in the institutional terms available?

One way would have been to propose multiple sites for gay and lesbian students, funded multiply from multiple sources. Each department would have its gay and lesbian student service, each student service would have its gay and lesbian student presence in a hyperbolic realization of the model that exists institutionally for families. Proliferating sites of gay and lesbian student presence and support would expose the proliferations of contemporary institutional organization, perform the idea that gay and lesbian students are "everywhere," and would also be an appropriate structural counter to the idea of symbolic centrality. While on a practical level this seems like a lot of work, even proposing such an alternative would shift the debate from an overloaded metaphorical Symbolic to the pragmatic and material. If implemented, such a proliferation of sites performs metonymy, providing centers of interest where needed within the institution instead of centralizing them in the delusion of symbolic efficacy. In a metonymical order efficacy comes from proliferations and multiple sites instead of centrality; pervasiveness is more telling than figureheads, even if we are still attached to our symbols.

An as Yet Unrecognizable Order

Finally, a way to intervene in order is to introduce yet another, third, fourth, or fifth order. If the dominance of metaphor comprises one Symbolic and the dominance of metonymy another, and their layered and articulated combination possibly a third, what then might comprise a fourth? By introducing a alternate but completely alien system is it possible to shock culture into an awareness of order? Does awareness mean change?

Both metaphor and metonymy work within the assumption of a two-dimensional representational system; that is, metaphor's comparisons and metonymy's contiguities exist within the flat plane of language and concept. Digital systems are no exceptions, even though they can produce the illusion of three dimensions through the production of virtual reality. This precocious production of the illusion of a third dimension is analogous to early twentieth-century imagings of digital technology. Anticipating a capability that is yet to be realized, order is, nonetheless, modified by the very imagination of an operative third and even fourth dimension (time). While virtual reality and holograph representations are simulations, the capability of reproducing three-dimensional material space is imagined in *Star Trek: The Next Generation*'s holodek and replicator systems as well as in its transporter mechanism.[24]

Star Trek's "Holographic Environment Simulators," or Holodeks, project the imaginary into three instead of two planes. While representations of the holodek's capabilities are always only in the two dimensions currently available in mechanical or digital reproductions, envisioning the possibility of three, rather than two planes anticipates another possible Symbolic transition also anticipated by Einstein's formula $E=MC^2$. If, like matter and energy, matter and image are interchangeable, then the order that separates representation from the real breaks down.[25] Representation can become realized and vice versa within four rather than three dimensions. Once three dimensions coexist as a way of conceiving reproductions (in a model so sophisticated that sculpture looks like bronze casting in relation to it), a fourth dimension of duration—time—must also exist. And if time becomes a part of an equation that has been conceptually spatial, and if time can be conceived of in other than spatial terms (as the digital promises), then Symbolic change to come will dwarf the transition we are now experiencing.

When the Symbolic catches up to reproductive capabilities, when it is able to represent itself in three or four dimensions, when representation and reality are indistinguishable and meaningless terms, the Symbolic will shift again into a form we can only now vaguely anticipate especially since the element that will shift it the most is time.

NOTES

PROLOGUE

1. L. Frank Baum, *The Wizard of Oz* (London: Puffin Books, 1994). The book was made into a film, *The Wizard of Oz* (1939), dir. Victor Fleming, with Judy Garland, Ray Bolger, Jack Haley, and Bert Lahr.
2. "The Mechanics of Fluids" is the title of an essay by Luce Irigaray in which she questions the gendering of physics, claiming that the lack of knowledge about fluids is linked to their connection to femininity. See Irigaray, *This Sex Which Is Not One*, trans. Carolyn Porter (Ithaca: Cornell University Press, 1985), 106–18.
3. Stuart Culver, "What Manikins Want: *The Wonderful Wizard of Oz* and *The Art of Decorating Dry Goods Windows*," *Representations* 21 (Winter 1988): 97–116, at 98.
4. Mario Puzo, *The Godfather* (New York: New American Library, 1969). Future page references to this edition will be given in the text.

5. For one account of the difference between epic and allegory, see Northrup Frye, *Anatomy of Criticism* (Princeton: Princeton University Press, 1971).

6. "The Miracle of Life" (1982), broadcast through the auspices of *Nova*, photographed by Lennart Nilsson.

7. Mario Brothers is a product of Nintendo of America.

8. Frye, *Anatomy of Criticism*, 33.

9. Jean Baudrillard, "Consumer Society," *Jean Baudrillard: Selected Writings*, ed. Mark Poster, trans. Jacques Morrain (Stanford: Stanford University Press, 1988), 29.

10. See William Schneider, "Chance and Social Setting in the Application of the Discovery of Blood Groups," *Bulletin of the History of Medicine* 57.4 (1983): 545–62.

11. "Increasing Number of Paternity tests," *Science News*, 4, Nov. 1981, 317.

12. See "Not so elementary, my dear Holmes," *The Economist*, 24 June 1989, 81; and "Leaving Holmes in the Dust," *Newsweek* 26 Oct. 1987, 81.

INTRODUCTION

1. Ellie Ragland-Sullivan, *Jacques Lacan and the Philosophy of Psychoanalysis* (Urbana and Chicago: University of Illinois Press, 1986), 152. All subsequent citations are from this edition.

2. Jacques Lacan, *Ecrits: A Selection*, trans. Alan Sheridan (New York: Norton, 1977), 301. All subsequent citations are from this edition unless otherwise noted.

3. Freud began his medical career researching nervous systems.

4. James Twitchell, in *The Living Dead: A Study of the Vampire in Romantic Literature* (Durham, N.C.: Duke University Press, 1981); and Raymond T. McNally and Radu Florescu, in *In Search of Dracula* (New York: Houghton Mifflin, 1994), trace the long history of vampires in folklore.

5. See, for example, Michel Foucault's *The History of Sexuality*, vol. 1, trans. Robert Hurley (New York: Vintage, 1990).

6. Jacques Lacan, "Intervention on Transference," *Feminine Sexuality: Jacques Lacan and the école freudienne*, ed. Juliet Mitchell and Jacqueline Rose, trans. Jacqueline Rose (New York: Norton, 1985), 69.

7. Lacan, "Les Formations de l'inconscient," quoted by Jacqueline Rose, in *Sexuality in the Field of Vision* (London: Verso, 1986), 62.

8. Rose, *Sexuality in the Field of Vision*, 62.

9. François Regnault, "The Name-of-the-Father," *reading Seminar XI: Lacan's "Four Fundamental Concepts of Psychoanlysis,"* ed. Richard Feldstein, Bruce Fink, and Maire Jaanus (Albany: State University of New York Press, 1995), 65. All subsequent citations are from this edition.

10. Catherine Clément, *The Lives and Legends of Jacques Lacan*, trans Arthur Goldhammer (New York: Columbia University Press, 1983), 170.

11. Lacan, "Position of the Unconscious," cited by Regnault, "The Name-of-the-Father," 70.

12. Lacan, *Four Fundamental Concepts of Psycho-Analysis*, trans. Alan Sheridan (New York: Norton, 1981), 34.

13. Aristotle, *Poetics* 1457b6–9.

14. Lacan, quoted in Rose, *Sexuality in the Field of Vision*, 62.

15. See Jacques Derrida, "White Mythology," *New Literary History* 6.1 (Autumn 1974): 5–73.

16. Ibid., 37. For extended discussions of metaphor, see also *On Metaphor*, ed. Sheldon Sacks (Chicago: University of Chicago Press, 1979).

17. Paul Ricoeur, *The Rule of Metaphor*, trans. Robert Czerny (Toronto: University of Toronto Press, 1979), 24.

18. Jonathan Culler, "Commentary," *New Literary History*, 6.1 (Autumn 1974): 219.

19. Roman Jakobson and Morris Halle, *Fundamentals of Language* (The Hague: Mouton, 1956), 76.

20. Russell Grigg, "Metaphor and Metonymy," *Newsletter of the Freudian Field* 3.1–2 (Spring–Fall 1989): 60. All subsequent citations from Grigg are from this essay.

21. Roland Barthes, *Elements of Semiology*, trans. Annette Lavers and Colin Smith (New York: Hill and Wang, 1968), 58.

22. Tsvetan Todorov, "On Linguistic Symbolism," *New Literary History*, 6.1 (Autumn 1974): 125.

23. Umberto Eco, *The Roles of the Reader* (Bloomington: Indiana University Press, 1979), 68.

24. Anthony Wilden, *System and Structure: Essays in Communication and Exchange*, 2nd ed. (London: Tavistock, 1980), 155–56.

25. Nicholas Negroponte, *Being Digital* (New York: Knopf, 1995), 6.

26. In the novel the shoes are silver. Perhaps the change to red was to accommodate new color film technology.

CHAPTER 1

1. Mary Shelley, *Frankenstein or the Modern Prometheus*, ed. James Rieger (Chicago: University of Chicago Press, 1982), 47. All subsequent citations are from this edition.

2. Guillaume Apollinaire, *The Breasts of Tiresias*, trans. Louis Simpson, in *Modern French Theatre*, ed. Michel Benedikt and George E. Wellwarth (New York: E. F. Dutton, 1966), 55–91. All subsequent citations are from this edition.

3. See Allan C. Greenberg, *Artists and Revolution: Dada and the Bauhaus, 1917–1925* (Ann Arbor: UMI Research Press, 1979); and Serge Lemoine, *Dada*, trans. Charles Lynn Clark (New York: Universe Books, 1987).

4. See Arturo Schwartz, *The Complete Works of Marcel Duchamp* (New York: H. N. Abrams, 1969).

5. *Junior*, dir. Ivan Reitman, starring Arnold Schwarzenegger, Danny DeVito, and Emma Thompson.

6. Walter Benjamin briefly traces the development of mechanical reproductions in "The Work of Art in the Age of Mechanical Reproduction," *Illuminations*, ed. Hannah Arendt, trans. Harry Zohn (New York: Schocken, 1969), 217–52.

7. See Susan Stewart's analysis of the reproductive anxiety caused by printing and distribution in seventeenth- and eighteenth-century England in *Crimes of Writing: Problems in the Containment of Representation* (New York: Oxford University Press, 1991).

8. In *Art and Photography: Forerunners and Influences* (Chicago: University of Chicago Press, 1985), Heinrich Schwartz says that, in 1839, Daguerre was able "to announce to the world that his long attempts had, at last, been successful, and that he had found a means to fix the transient image in the *camera obscura*" (86). Schwartz goes on to argue that the invention of photography was more than the arrival of a technology, but that it represented the needs of a changing social organization. See also, Aaron Scharf's summary of the camera obscura in *Art and Photography* (London: Penguin, 1974), 19–23.

9. The nineteenth century birth throes of photography spawned other optical "contraptions," including the "camera lucida, the diagraph, the agatograph, the hyalograh, the quarréograph, pronopiograph and the eugragh," according to Scharf (23).

10. Quoting Erwin Panofsky, Schwartz claims that the spirit of photography has been present since "the Renaissance established and unanimously accepted what seems to be the most trivial and actually is the most problematic dogma of aesthetic theory—the dogma that a work of art is the direct and faithful representation of a natural object" (98).

11. André Bazin, *What Is Cinema?* Vol 1, trans. Hugh Gray (Berkeley: University of California Press, 1967), 14. All subsequent citations are from this edition. Scharf also comments that from the 1870s onward, the photographic camera was "accused of telling too much truth" (15).

12. Various claims about who invented cinema when still focus on the late nineteenth century. Various claimants include Thomas Edison's Kinetoscope (1887), William Friese Greene's patent on kinematography (1889), the Lumière brothers (1895), and Max and Emil Skladanowsky (1895). The number and timing of these inventions witnesses a cultural change that had already occurred. See C.W. Ceram, *Archaeology of the Cinema*, trans. Richard Winston (New York: Harcourt, Brace, and World, 1965).

13. Ceram cites Rudolph Thun, for this list, 16.

14. The Phenakistoscope consisted of a slotted disk with phase pictures painted around the circumference. One rotated the disk and looked in a mirror at the images through the disk's slots. See Ceram, *Archaeology of the Cinema,* plates 1 and 77.

15. The Zoetrope, more famous than the Phenakistoscope, is a self-contained system of slots and images arranged on the inside of a revolving drum. One looks at the images on the inside from the outside. See Ibid., plate 78.

16. See Ibid., plates 87–88. The Choreutoscope's mechanism was "almost identical" to the Maltese Cross device. See Ibid., plates 86–88.

17. Magic lanterns were present in the seventeenth century, but became very popular in the eighteenth and nineteenth centuries in various configurations.

18. David Bordwell and Kristin Thompson, *Film Art*, 4th Ed. (New York: McGraw-Hill, 1993), 32–33.

19. Probably no machine is either purely metaphor *or* metonymy. Mechanical devices are generally analogue, that is, their physical form imitates function (a gear is round and rotates), but their operation as a whole machine depends upon a contiguity that moves energy from one part to the next. Machines like levers, which magnify energy in certain directions, might be understood as metaphorical, though energy itself is still moved through the contiguity of machine parts.

203

20. For explanations of persistance of vision see, Bruce Kawin, *How Movies Work* (New York: Macmillan, 1987), 48. In the second edition of *Film Art*, David Bordwell and Kristin Thompson explain various theories for the illusion of movement, including persistence of vision. But, in fact, persistence of vision or "positive after-image" does not account for the illusion of motion at all, but only for the lack of empty (nonimage) space. Bill Nichols and Susan Lederman dispute all accounts of "the perception of movement" in "Flicker and Motion in Film," in *The Cinematic Apparatus*, ed. Teresa de Lauretis and Stephen Heath (New York: St. Martin's, 1980), 96–105.

21. Kawin includes an explanation of the phi phenomenon, in *How Movies Work,* 48.

22. Bordwell and Thompson include a decreasingly detailed explanation of the various physiological mechanisms understood to account for the illusion of motion in still images. By the fourth edition of *Film Art*, no explanation remains. This follows Nichols' and Lederman's rejection of all such theories. This might be a sign that the need to cover metonymy with metaphor has passed.

23. Jean-Louis Baudry in "The Ideological Effects of the Basic Cinematographic Apparatus," trans. Alan Williams, in *Apparatus*, ed. Teresa Hak Kyung Cha

(New York: Tanam Press, 1980), 25–37, outlines the ideological premises of the viewer-centered lens and the machine's effacement of its processes. Jean Comolli traces cinema's ideological reproduction even more critically in "Machines of the Visible," in *The Cinematic Apparatus*, 121–42.

24. Christian Metz cites the cinematic apparatus itself as cinema's fetish in *The Imaginary Signifier*, trans. Celia Britton, Annwyl Williams, Ben Brewster, and Alfred Guzzetti (Bloomington: Indiana University Press, 1982).

25. Jean François Lyotard discusses such metanarratives in *The Postmodern Condition: A Report on Knowledge*, trans. Geoff Bennington and Brian Massumi (Minneapolis: University of Minnesota Press, 1984).

26. The Republican party's vaunted cure-all for America's metonymical ills—single mothers, crime, a loss of family values—is to reassert, via the overt metaphor of the contract, the nexus of business and benevolent patriarchy whose loss is seen as the cause of the country's ills. One of the most symptomatic ideas is the reestablishment of orphanages, whose assertion of government qua pater familias will resolve the truancy, aimlessness, and crime fomented by single-mother welfare families. Of course, the identification of problems in distinctly familial terms already locates the source of the anxiety. For a spectacular performance of this, see Dan Quayle's *Standing Firm* (New York: HarperCollins, 1994).

27. John Polidori, *The Vampyre* (Pasadena: Grant Dahlstrom, 1968); and Bram Stoker, *Dracula* (London: Puffin Books, 1994). All subsequent citations will be from these editions.

28. This is Mario Amaya's 1965 estimation. See *Pop Art . . . and After* (New York: Viking Press, 1966), 43–44.

29. Pop as a specifically American movement occupies the somewhat paradoxical place of being American and representing Americanness to its European practitioners. In this sense, Pop is both American and part of a larger western cultural scene.

30. John Rublowsky, *Pop Art* (New York: Basic Books, 1965), 31.

31. Both Amaya and Rublowsky list these cultural influences as Pop art's inspiration. They are joined by Reyner Banham, who adds science fiction and video to the list in "Who Is This 'Pop'?" in *Design by Choice*, Penny Sparke ed. (New York: Rizzoli, 1981), 94–96. Andy Warhol himself largely credits commercial culture in both *The Philosophy of Andy Warhol* (New York: Harcourt, Brace, Jovanovich, 1975); and Warhol, with Pat Hackett, *Popism: The Warhol Sixties* (New York: Harcourt, Brace, Jovanovich, 1980).

32. Schwartz 97, *Art and Photography*.

33. In his Preface to the play, Apollinaire must negotiate, of all things, photography. While criticizing the "'photographic' naturalism" of Victor Hugo, Apollinaire wants to make an "original" theatrical "effort" "to

come back to nature itself, but without copying it photographically" (56). Photography's interposition even in considerations of dramatic style seems symptomatic of the amount of anxiety it was causing. In combination with the reproductive ideology of the play, the opening nod to photography seems almost too direct an acknowledgment of its threat.

CHAPTER 2

1. Pat O'Donnell's "cultural Paranoia" has to do with the sense of an antagonistic order; the choice of paranoia is telling, since paranoia has to do with a foreclosure of paternal Law. See O'Donnell, "Engendering Paranoia in Contemporary Narrative," *boundary 2* 19.1 (1992): 181–204.

2. Dan Quayle's autobiography, *Standing Firm*, is on one level a case study in anxiety centered around the loss of a literal father.

3. Sitcoms invariably image functional nuclear families, even where there are no nuclear families to be seen. Interrelationships among singles are just as nuclear as they would be if they were in nuclear families. Examples of this would be 1994–95's *Ellen* and *Friends* where single people interact like brothers and sisters.

4. Various readings of Ronald Reagan's constructed persona argue that his calculated paternalism is about calculated image building. See Susan Jeffords, *Hard Bodies: Hollywood Masculinity in the Reagan Era* (New Brunswick, N.J.: Rutgers University Press, 1994).

205

5. Coppola directed three *Godfather* films altogether, *The Godfather*, (1972), with Marlon Brando, Al Pacino; *The Godfather, Part II*, (1974), with Al Pacino and Robert Duvall; and *The Godfather, Part III*, (1990), with Al Pacino and Andy Garcia.

6. *Goodfellas*, (1991), dir. Martin Scorsese, with Ray Liotta, Joe Pesci, Robert DeNiro.

7. Jeffords, *Hard Bodies*, 34–40.

8. Alan Klein, *Little Big Men: Bodybuilding Subculture and Gender Construction* (Albany, N.Y.: State University Press of New York, 1993).

9. This is from a paper Michael Budd delivered at the Sager Symposium in 1992.

10. See Sam Fussell's autobiographical exposé of the bodybuilding mentality in *Confessions of an Unlikely Bodybuilder* (New York: Avon, 1991). Also see Klein's analysis of bodybuilding as a means to control in *Little Big Men*, 176–78.

11. George Butler, *Arnold Schwarzenegger: A Portrait* (New York: Simon and Schuster, 1990), 9.

12. Fussell documents the amount of food he needed to eat in order to gain muscle mass.

13. Douglas Kellner, "Film, Politics, and Ideology: Reflections on Hollywood Film in the Age of Reagan," *The Velvet Light Trap* 27 (Spring 1991): 9–24.

14. The film *Pumping Iron* (1977) highlights Arnold as the epitome of the bodybuilder. While the film was not widely popular at its release and Arnold was not yet necessarily a star, in retrospect, his late 1970s amalgamation of body and persona seems to be the originary moment of bodybulding's emergence from its very marginal cultural locus.

15. For an analysis of the figure Arnold in relation to bodybuilding, see Jonathan Goldberg's "Recalling Totalities: The Mirrored Stages of Arnold Schwarzenegger," *differences* 4.1 (1992): 172–204.

16. This was in *Pumping Iron* where he responds to questions about weightlifting as compensation.

17. See Butler, *Arnold Schwarzenegger*, 52, and Klein, *Little Big Men*.

18. This is not unlike what Judith Butler situates as the performance of gender, although here the circle between body and signifier seems unusually tight. See Butler, *Gender Trouble: Feminism and the Subversion of Identity* (New York: Routledge, 1990).

19. See Ragland-Sullivan, *Jacques Lacan and the Philosophy of Psychoanalysis*, 279.

20. Regnault, "The Name-of-the-Father," 69.

21. See, for example, Tony Bennett and Janet Woolacott, *Bond and Beyond* (New York: Methuen, 1987).

22. Sigmund Freud, "On Fetishism." The *Standard Edition* of the Complete Psychological Works of Sigmund Freud, Vol. 21 (1927), ed. and trans. James Strachey. London: Hogarth Press, 152–153.

23. See Jean Baudrillard's "Fetishism and Ideology: The Semiological Reduction" *For a Critique of the Political Economy of the Sign*, trans. Charles Levin (Telos Press, 1981), for an analysis of the critical fetishization of the fetish.

24. Laura Mulvey, "Narrative Cinema and Visual Pleasure," Screen 16 (1975), 13–14.

25. See Rose, "The Cinematic Apparatus: Problems in Current Theory," in *The Cinematic Apparatus;* and "*Hamlet*—the 'Mona Lisa' of Literature," in *Sexuality in the Field of Vision*. See also Kaja Silverman, "Lost Objects and Mistaken Subjects," *Wide Angle* 7 (1985): 14–29.

26. Teresa de Lauretis, *Alice Doesn't* (Bloomington: Indiana University Press, 1984), 188.

27. Ken Sprague and Bill Reynolds' *The Gold's Gym Book of Bodybuilding* (Chicago: Contemporary Books, 1983) tries to image both family shots as well as men and women bodybuilders. One caption declares that "family training is 'in' at Gold's" under a picture of Mommy, Daddy, and prepubescent daughter (24). On the next page is a picture captioned "Group

training" with both men and women bodybuilders apparently cooperating.

28. See *Pumping Iron II: The Women* (1985) dir., George Butler, for an intriguing exposé of the relation between anatomy and gender. See also, Christine Holmlund's analysis of the film in "Visible Difference and Flex Appeal: The Body, Sex, Sexuality, and Race in the *Pumping Iron* Films," *Cinema Journal* 28.4 (Summer 1989): 38–51.

29. Mary Ann Doane suggests that distance is necessary for fetishism. The metaphorical distances here between gender and body, between body and muscle, are produced by displacements of what come to be seen as separable (because acquirable) traits. This metaphorical distance, however, still enables a body fetishism, even on (or by means of) one's own body. See Doane's "Film and Masquerade: Theorising the Female Spectator," *Screen* 23 (Sept.–Oct. 1982), 74–88.

30. See *Confessions of an Unlikely Bodybuilder*, Fussell, 193, for the Rives' quote. Serge Oliva shocked the bodybuilding world by appearing nude in pornographic films.

31. For examples of the history of comics and the various origins of superheroes, see Jules Feiffer, *The Great Comic Book Heroes* (New York: Dial Press, 1965); and Mike Benton, *The Comic Book in America* (Dallas: Taylor Publishing, 1993).

32. Comic superheroes' slide into neurosis is noted by Ronald Levitt Lanyi in "Comic Books and Authority: An Interview with "Stainless Steve" Englehart," *Journal of Popular Culture* 18.2 (Fall 1984); 139–148, at 139.

33. Vivian Sobchack, in "Child/Alien/Father: Patriarchal Crisis and Generic Exchange," in *Close Encounters: Film, Feminism, and Science Fiction*, ed. Constance Penley, Elisabeth Lyon, Lynn Spigel, and Janet Bergstrom (Minneapolis: University of Minnesota Press, 1991), 2–30, links this alienation to the family.

34. Jean Baudrillard, *Simulations*, trans. Paul Foss, Paul Patton, and Philip Beitchman (New York: Semiotext[e], 1983).

35. Donna Haraway, *Simians, Cyborgs, and Women: The Reinvention of Nature* (New York: Routledge, 1991).

36. Constance Penley, "Time Travel, Primal Scene, and the Critical Dystopia," *Close Encounters*, 63–80. Goldberg's reading disagrees with Penley, or marks what it calls its "limitation" in the oedipal. Goldberg envisions *The Terminator* as postoedipal.

207

CHAPTER 3

1. Though the entire system of statutory laws in the fifty states of the U.S.A. presents no unified text, hence no sustained metaphorical "unconscious," it is possible to see the law (statutory and judicial) as a system that does,

in fact, contain significant breaks and inconsistencies that are ideological-ly informed. Since I make no claim to read the culture of a particular state in a specific historical period (as a unified legal corpus might permit), my reading of these selected statutes is more in relation to the larger ideolo-gies they reflect, those connected to the register of Law.

2. Lacan, "Subversion of the subject and dialectic of desire," *Ecrits*, 311.

3. Stephen Bates, "United States v. Superman," *National Review* 11 February 1991, 31.

4. L. Gordon Crovitz, "How Law Destroys Order," *ibid.*, 28–33.

5. In his encyclopedic essay "Perry Mason Meets Sonny Crockett: The History of Lawyers and the Police as Television Heroes," *University of Miami Law Review* 42 (1987): 229–83, Steven D. Stark traces the spotty history of public perceptions of the police, noting that throughout the late nineteenth and first half of the twentieth century the police were seen either as bumblers or corrupt. Crovitz's perception seems based on a confusion between a delusive image of the past and wishful thinking in the present.

6. Quayle's autobiography reads like a rondeau with repeating refrains: the press misrepresent me, fathers are good for America. See *Standing Firm*.

7. This is from Rose's translation of Lacan's "Les formations de l'incon-scient," cited on page 62 of *Sexuality in the Field of Vision*.

8. *The Columbus Dispatch*, 11 March 1995, 1.

9. "Position of the Unconscious," quoted in Regnault, "The Name-of-the-Father," 70.

10. One of the effects of 1970s equal rights challenges was statutory reform that tried to remove assumptions of a natural correlation between sex, gender, and ability. This affected, for example, laws about parenting such as the Uniform Parentage Act that delegated to both parents duties that had previously delegated to only one or the other. Equal rights as a ratio-nale for improving women's enfranchisement became simultaneously a way to relegislate the family.

11. For example, in *Weinberger v. Wiesenfeld*, 95 *S. Ct* 1225, the Supreme Court held that "the gender-based distinction mandated by provisions of Social Security Act that grants survivors' benefits based on earnings of deceased husband and father covered by the Act both to his widow and to the cou-ple's minor children in her care but grant benefits based on earnings of a covered deceased wife and mother only to the minor children and not to the widower violates right to equal protection secured by the due process clause of the Fifth Amendment since it unjustifiably discriminates against women wage earners required to pay social security by affording them less protection for their survivors than is provided for men wage earners." As Robin West pointed out in a paper she gave at the Delaware Seminar

in the early 1990s, equal protection tends to come into play mainly when it benefits males.

12. Lacan, "Function and Field of Speech and Language," *Ecrits*, 67.

13. For example, the Uniform Act on Paternity was approved by the National Conference of Commissioners on Uniform State Laws and the American Bar Association in 1960. This act spells out the obligations of fathers, creating obligations that hadn't existed under common law, which included an obligation to illegitimate children. See Uniform Laws Annotated, 9A.

14. Quoted in Ragland—Sullivan, *Jacques Lacan and the Philosophy of Psychoanalysis*, 58.

15. Statutory law responds to perceived gaps in social regulation, something like the way the Internal Revenue Code responds to perceived gaps in sources of taxable income. If university instructors cannot speak English well enough for students to understand them, there ought to be a law. If food labels don't contain enough information to satisfy a rash of suddenly nutrition anxious consumers, there will be a regulation. Such laws are responsive to specific situations rather than representing necessarily principled, coordinated, or ordered rules.

16. Lacan, "Function and Field of Speech and Language," *Ecrits*, 66.

17. *Roe v. Wade* is a 1973 Supreme Court decision that basically held that "life" begins after the first trimester and that, thus, the state cannot interfere until life begins.

18. See Gena Corea's extensive discussion of reproductive technologies in *The Mother Machine: Reproductive Technologies from Artificial Insemination to Artificial Wombs* (New York: Harper and Row, 1985).

19. If challenged it is highly likely that the Delaware statute as it is written would be deemed unconstitutional following *Roe v. Wade*. It is, thus, an example of an abortion statute that does not yet codify the first trimester "delay."

20. This gendered operation of the Law also accounts, in part, for the difficulties encountered in rape legislation and prosecution where, despite reform, rape continues to be notoriously difficult to prosecute. In rape cases, male privilege is transformed into a question of the victim's consent.

21. Quoted in Ragland-Sullivan, *Jacques Lacan and the Philosophy of Psychoanalysis*, 301.

22. An example of a modern paternity law, part of the Uniform Law on Paternity adopted by a number of states, reads: "Obligations of the father—The father of a child which may or may not be born out of lawful wedlock is liable to the same extent as the father of a child born in lawful wedlock, whether or not the child is born alive, for the reasonable expense of the mother's pregnancy and confinement, and the education,

necessary support and maintenance, and medical and funeral expenses of the child and for reasonable counsel fees for the prosecution of paternity proceedings. A child born out of wedlock also includes a child born to a married woman by a man other than her lawful husband (*Rhode Island General Laws* 15-8-1). In line with abortion statutes, this statute clearly situates the child as property and the mother as the medium upon which the father reproduces.

23. The rights of the father are thus contradictory: the father has no duty or connection, but has a complete property right in the child. As noted above (chapter 3, note 11), the "overkill" effect of gender parity also appears in reformations of parenting. While such laws formally inscribe the father, they also reinforce paternal rights beyond tradition and relegate the mother to a less advantageous, almost "objective" status. In the blind zeal of gender equity legal reform, some parentage statutes include provision for an action to declare a mother and child relationship "insofar as practicable." See, for example, the Alabama Uniform Parentage Act, section 26-17-18.

24. Lacan, "Subversion of the Subject and Dialectic of Desire," *Ecrits*, 310.

25. Ragland-Sullivan observes, "The more pressing logical problem that Lacan's epistemology presents is this: if the Name-of-the-Father is an organizing principle of sexual identity and culture, which ensures societal order and psychic 'health,' how can such an effect be changed without dire consequences for the fabric of society itself?" (*Jacques Lacan and the Philosophy of Psychoanalysis*, 300). Perhaps it is the reverse.

26. Christine Overall quotes Donald DeMarco in *Human Reproduction: Principles, Practices, Policies* (Toronto: Oxford University Press, 1993), 143.

27. See Christine Overall's discussion of surrogate maternity in *Human Reproduction*; and Corea, *The Mother Machine*. Corea quotes Sandford Katz, professor at Boston College Law School, "I wouldn't consider this [surrogate motherhood] buying a baby. I'd consider it buying a receptacle" (222).

28. John A. Robertson, "Procreative Liberty and the State's Burden of Proof in Regulating Noncoital Reproduction," *Law, Medicine, and Health Care* 16 (Spring–Summer 1988): 23.

29. David Warren cites this example in "The Law of Human Reproduction: An Overview," *The Journal of Legal Medicine* 3. 1 (1982): 3 n. 11.

30. Culver, "What Manikins Want," discusses the consumerist link between Baum's two works.

31. See Stark, "Perry Mason Meeets Sonny Crockett," 235–240.

32. "Raymond Burr: The Enduring Appeal of Perry Mason," *L.A. Lawyer* II. 3 (May 1988): 9–12. The essay lists the series of Southern Californian scandals from 1928 to 1940 that prompted Erle Stanley Gardner to make a defense lawyer his protagonist.

33. Stark outlines the history of radio law shows, in "Perry Mason Meeets Sonny Crockett," 240–41.
34. This is Stark's account, ibid., 247.
35. Charles Winick and Mariann Pezzella Winick suggest that television's heavy reliance on close-ups "made it uniquely appropriate for presenting trials" (68), in "Courtroom Drama on Television," *Journal of Communication* (Autumn 1974), 67–73.
36. See Gilles Deleuze's discussion of the close-up in *Cinema 1*, trans. Hugh Tomlinson and Barbara Habberjam (Minneapolis: University of Minnesota Press, 1986), 87–101.
37. In "Criminality or Hysteria? Television and the Law," *Discourse* X.2 (Spring–Summer 1988), 48–61, Patrice Petro explains the fascination of law shows as "the attempt to merge theatricality and legality or, more simply, fiction and reality in day-time law" (49).
38. Guy deBord, *Society of the Spectacle,* trans. Donald Nicholson-Smith, (Detroit: Black and Red, 1977), 12.
39. *Hawaii Five-O*'s McGarrett seemed like the complete straight arrow, especially in the late 1960s and early 1970s when the show was first aired. But McGarrett, like Kojak and other dutiful police officers, is often like the defense attorney, working within the system but against the grain, representing ultimately a better law (or a law better for his having participated).
40. See Lyotard's account of the postmodern in *The Postmodern Condition*.
41. Judith Mayne, "*L.A.Law* and Prime-Time Feminism," *Discourse* X.2 (Spring–Summer 1988), 34.

211

CHAPTER 4

1. In his introduction to Polidori's *Vampyre*, Donald K. Adams notes the book's immediate popularity, its translation into French and German, and its adaptation for the stage (xxxiv and xxii).
2. In *The Living Dead,* Twitchell describes the antecedents to Stoker's work. His description of Southey's poem is on pages 35–36. Stoker's guarantee appears on an unnumbered page before the text.
3. Versions of vampire plays appeared throughout the nineteenth century. The first was in 1819, many followed throughout the 1820s, and then more sporadically through the rest of the nineteenth and into the twentieth century. In the 1960s, as the interest in vampires burgeoned, they began to appear more frequently.
4. There are several lists of vampire films in, among others, J. Gordon Melton's *The Vampire Book: The Encyclopedia of the Undead* (Detroit: Visible Ink, 1994), McNally and Florescu, *In Search of Dracula*; Andrew Tudor, *Monsters and Mad Scientists: A Cultural History of the Horror Movie* (New

York: Basil Blackwell, 1989); Gregory A. Waller, *The Living and the Undead: From Stoker's Dracula to Romero's "Dawn of the Dead"* (Urbana: University of Illinois Press, 1986); and Barrie Pattison, *The Seal of Dracula* (New York: Bounty Books, 1975). Information about films is taken from these multiple sources.

5. See Melton, *The Vampire Book;* and Waller, *The Living and the Undead,* for accounts of Hammer Films' importance.

6. See Jeff Rovin, *The Encyclopedia of Superheroes* (New York: Facts on File, 1985) for a complete list of superhero teams.

7. Sheridan LeFanu, "Carmilla," in *In a Glass Darkly* (London: Leonard P. Davies, 1929); and reprinted in *Two Centuries of Great Vampire Stories,* ed. Alan Ryan, (Garden City, N.Y.: Doubleday, 1987), 71-137, Hammer films made a trilogy of Karnstein films in the 1970s—*Vampire Lovers* (1970), *Lust for a Vampire* (1971), and *Twins of Evil* (1971)—based on Lefanu's novel. Carmilla Karnstein is the second most represented vampire character. Elizabeth Bathory, a supposedly vampiric Hungarian countess who lived from 1560–1614, also inspired a number of lesbian vampire films.

8. Warhol produced an almost travesty gothic version called *Blood for Dracula* (1973).

9. In her essay "Evolution and Information, or Eroticism and Everyday Life, in *Dracula* and Late Victorian Aestheticism," in *Sex and Death in Victorian Literature,* ed. Regina Barreca (Bloomington: Indiana University Press, 1990),140–157, Regenia Gagnier links Dracula to a problem of boundaries produced in part by the introduction of machine technology. Gagnier, however, reads Dracula as the scion of a traditional order, comparable to Benjamin's art with aura that is overcome by technology. Seeing Dracula as essentially a nostalgic creature, Gagnier envisions his defeat as the victory of "operations over eros and aesthetics" (155). Although Gagnier's reading is the opposite of the one I wish to make here, the reversability of the elements of technology and eros, past and future, suggests that the vampire intervenes in a highly complex and probably contradictory fashion.

10. *Bram Stoker's Dracula*, dir. Francis Ford Coppola, with Gary Oldman, Winona Ryder, Anthony Hopkins, and Keanu Reeves.

11. See McNally and Florescu's account of Stoker's sources in *In Search of Dracula*, 7–14.

12. Twitchell, among others, documents the vampire's folk forebears in *The Living Dead*, 7–9.

13. These traits are from Manuela Dunn Mascetti's *Vampire: The Complete Guide to the World of the Undead* (New York: Viking, 1992), 21.

14. See ibid., 184–187.

15. See ibid., 68–69.

16. Anne Rice is probably the most famous of those who have contrived sympathetic vampires. See her *Interview with a Vampire* (New York: Knopf, 1976).

17. Georges Bataille, *Erotism: Death and Sensuality*, trans. Mary Dalwood (San Francisco: City Lights Books, 1986).

18. See Freud's *Beyond the Pleasure Principle,* ed. and trans. James Strachey. New York: Norton, 1961.

19. In addition to Hammer Films' three Carmilla entries of the early 1970s', Carmilla graces at least eight other films.

20. For insightful analyses of lesbian vampires, see Andrea Weiss, *Vampires and Violets: Lesbian in Film* (New York: Penguin, 1992); Barbara Creed, *The Monstrous-Feminine: Film, Feminism, Psychoanalysis* (London and New York: Routledge, 1993); and Sue-Ellen Case, "Tracking the Vampire," *differences* 3.2 (1991), 1–20.

21. Michel Foucault, The History of Sexuality, Vol. 1. Trans. Robert Hurley (New York: Vintage, 1990), 106–107.

22. Freud, "The Uncanny," *Standard Edition,* vol. 17 (1919), 219–252 at 241.

23. Joan Copjec, "Vampires, Breast-Feeding, and Anxiety," *October* 58 (1991): 25–43, at 35.

24. Antonio Quinet, "The Gaze as Object," *Reading Seminar XI,* 139–147, at 139.

25. Lacan, *The Four Fundamental Concepts of Psycho-Analysis,* 72.

26. Lacan quotes this episode from Freud's *The Interpretation of Dreams,* in *ibid.,* 70.

27. Comolli, "Machines of the Visible," 122.

28. *Martin,* (1977), dir. George Romero, starring John Amplas.

29. Joan Gordon, "Rehabilitating Revenants, or Sympathetic Vampires in Recent Fiction," *Extrapolation* 29. 3 (1988), 227–34 at 231.

213

CHAPTER 5

1. *Mary Shelley's Frankenstein* (1994), dir. Kenneth Branagh, with Kenneth Branagh, Robert DeNiro, Helena Bonham Carter.

2. James D. Watson and F. H. C. Crick, *The Structure of DNA* (Cold Spring Harbor, N.Y.: Biological Laboratory, 1953).

3. Simon LeVay, for example, locates gay temperaments in the "gay" brain. See LeVay, *The Sexual Brain* (Cambridge, Mass.: MIT Press, 1993).

4. *Computing Before Computers,* ed. William Aspray, (Ames: Iowa State University Press, 1990), 225. Most of the history of the computer retold herein comes from this collection.

5. J. T. Mitchell, *The Reconfigured Eye: Visual Truth in the Post-Photographic Era* (Cambridge, Mass: MIT Press, 1994), 3.

6. *Judge Dredd* (1995), dir, Danny Cannon with Sylvester Stallone and Rob Schneider; *Species,* 1995, dir, Roger Donaldson, with Vandela, Ben Kingsley, Forest Whitaker.

7. Mark Poster, *The Mode of Information: Poststructuralism and Social Context* (Chicago: University of Chicago Press, 1990), 4.

8. See William Sonnega, "Morphing Borders: The Remanence of MTV," *The Drama Review* 39.1 (Spring 1995): 45–61.

9. Robin Baker, "Computer Technology and Special Effects in Contemporary Cinema," in *Future Visions: New Technologies of the Screen*, ed. Philip Hayward and Tana Wollen (London: BFI, 1993), 40.

10. Michael Jackson, "Black or White," *Dangerous: The Short Films of Michael Jackson*. Produced by MJJ Ventures, Inc., dir. John Landis (New York: Epic Music Video, 1993).

11. See Catherine Millot's lacanian analysis of transsexuality in *Horsexe: Essay on Transsexuality*, trans. Kenneth Hylton (New York: Autonomedia, 1990); or Kate Bornstein, *Gender Outlaw* (New York: Routledge, 1994).

12. These brief characterizations of the postmodern come from Linda Hutcheon, *The Politics of Postmodernism* (London: Routledge, 1989), 1; Hans Bertens, "The Postmodern *Weltanschauung* and Its Relation to Modernism: An Introductory Survey," in *A Postmodern Reader*, ed. Joseph Natoli and Linda Hutcheon (Albany: SUNY Press, 1993), 25–70; Andreas Huyssen, "Mapping the Postmodern," in *A Postmodern Reader*, 105–56; and David Kolb, *Postmodern Sophistications: Philosophy, Architecture, and Tradition* (Chicago: The University of Chicago Press, 1990), 5. Bertens quotes Richard Wasson on page 36.

13. In *The Pleasure of the Text*, trans. Richard Miller (New York: Hill and Wang, 1975), Barthes links narrative to the oedipal. In *Alice Doesn't*, Teresa de Lauretis devotes a chapter to the gender ramifications of oedipal narrative.

14. For a more complete analysis of narrative's heterosexual impetus, see my *Come As You Are: Sexuality and Narrative* (New York: Columbia University Press, 1996).

15. Peter Brooks, "Freud's Masterplot," in *Literature and Psychoanalysis*, ed. Shoshana Felman (Baltimore: Johns Hopkins University Press, 1982), 280–300.

16. Commentators for Christian journals have remarked the false character of what they call the "new Paternalism," especially during the 1992 presidential election, as did more cynical mainstream journalists such as Meg Greenfield. See Don Browning, Carol Browning, and Ian Evison, "Family Values and the New Paternalism," *The Christian Century*, 3–10 June 1992, 572–73; Meg Greenfield, "Enough Cant on 'Family Values'," *Newsweek* (14 September 1992, 78).

17. For an analysis of the shape and effect of transnational corporations, see Masao Miyoshi, "A Borderless World? From Colonialism to Transnationalism and the Decline of the Nation-State," *Critical Inquiry* 19 (Summer 1993), 726–51.

18. Although all sentences are series, and hence subject to some process of retroactive signification (the metonymical pole), the difference between metaphor and metonymy as orders exists on the level of organization rather than syntax. The presence of the prepositional phrase in the first example introduces a larger order of organization that presents material as if already grouped.

19. See Butler's estimation of the performative in relation to gender in *Gender Trouble*.

20. *Paris Is Burning* (1992), dir. Jennie Livingston, with Pepper Labeija, Kim Pendavis, and Venus Xtravaganza.

21. *Without You I'm Nothing* (1990), dir. Sandra Bernhard and John Boscovitch. See also, Jean Walton, "Sandra Bernhard: Lesbian Postmodern or Modern Postlesbian," in *The Lesbian Postmodern*, ed. Laura Doan (New York: Columbia University Press, 1994), 244–61.

22. Kathy Acker's novels often take off from and play on convention, from their titles (*Great Expectations*) to their experiments with repetition (*Portrait of an Eye*).

23. For this formulation, see "Oedipus Interruptus," *Wide Angle* 7 (1985): 34–40.

24. For exact details on the functioning of the holodek, see Rick Sternbach and Michael Okuda, *Star Trek: The Next Generation Technical Manual* (New York: Pocket Books, 1991).

25. Stephen Hawking, *A Brief History of Time* (New York: Bantam, 1988).

INDEX

224